English Corpus Linguistics: Looking back, Moving forward

LANGUAGE AND COMPUTERS: STUDIES IN PRACTICAL LINGUISTICS

No 74

edited by
Christian Mair
Charles F. Meyer
Nelleke Oostdijk

English Corpus Linguistics: Looking back, Moving forward

Papers from the 30th International Conference on English Language Research on Computerized Corpora (ICAME 30)

Lancaster, UK, 27-31 May 2009

Edited by

Sebastian Hoffmann, Paul Rayson and Geoffrey Leech

Rodopi

Amsterdam - New York, NY 2012

Cover image: www.morgueFile.com

Cover design: Inge Baeten

The paper on which this book is printed meets the requirements of "ISO 9706:1994, Information and documentation - Paper for documents - Requirements for permanence".

ISBN: 978-90-420-3466-2
E-Book ISBN: 978-94-012-0747-8

Printed in The Netherlands

Table of contents

Introduction: English corpus linguistics – looking back, moving forward

Sebastian Hoffmann, Paul Rayson and Geoffrey Leech

Universities of Trier and Lancaster

1. Introduction

This volume contains a selection of papers from the proceedings of the conference held at the Lancaster House Hotel, Lancaster University, UK, 27-31 May 2009. This was a landmark 30th meeting of the International Computer Archive of Modern and Medieval English (ICAME), and provided an opportunity to look back on the extraordinary growth and progress of corpus linguistics over the past three decades, as well as to look ahead to yet further developments in the future.

Two of the original founding fathers of ICAME, Stig Johansson and Geoffrey Leech, took advantage of this 30th conference to present an event entitled 'The Coming of ICAME', celebrating the foundation of this organization in Oslo in 1977, when corpus linguistics was in its infancy. Even earlier than that, in 1970, Lancaster had seen the founding of CAMET (the Computer Archive of Modern English Texts) which had been the predecessor of ICAME. We informally dedicate this book of proceedings to Stig Johansson, who from 1977 and for many years was the secretary and sole organizer of ICAME, and who played an indispensable role in building it up into the organization we see today. Stig's death, which sadly took place in the year following the Lancaster conference, has been deeply mourned by those who have benefited from his unique contribution to corpus linguistics and English language research.

Part of the title of this book comes from the theme of the 2009 conference – 'Looking back, moving forward' – which reflected ICAME30's thematic emphasis on the history of corpus linguistics as well as on the history of English, while at the same exploring new avenues of research and new interdisciplinary synergies.

The published proceedings of ICAME30 have split conveniently into two separate volumes: the present volume deals with the results or findings of corpus investigations, and a further volume, appearing as an e-publication in the VARIENG series at the University of Helsinki, focuses principally on methodological and historical dimensions of corpus linguistics. The present volume concentrates on Present-Day English, but it does have a backward-looking diachronic component in papers which give attention to the recent history of English, through the growing availability of historical corpora covering the last hundred or so years of the language. These include the Brown family of corpora, the *TIME Corpus* and – for the investigation of very recent changes – the *Corpus of Contemporary American English* (COCA) with its 20 million words per year from 1991 onwards. This field of short-term diachronic change has been developing quickly as new corpus resources enable the researcher to trace recent linguistic history with unprecedented precision and detail.

Further new corpus developments explored in other papers in the book investigate language variation in English in its broadest sense, showing that corpus linguistics has attained a new level of maturity in the inter-corpus and intra-corpus comparisons that can now be made between different genres of the spoken and written language, between regional Englishes across the world, between native-speaking and non-native-speaking varieties, and between English and other languages through parallel translation corpora, not to mention cross-dimensional analyses involving more than one of these comparisons. It is particularly pleasing to see how the resource of *comparable* or *matched corpora*, exemplified on the historical axis by the Brown family already mentioned, is also being increasingly exploited across international English through the ICE (*International Corpus of English*) subcorpora from various countries and regions of the English-speaking world, and by the ICLE (*International Corpus of Learner English*) subcorpora from various countries where English is primarily a foreign language. At the end of this introduction, we list the main corpora which have been used in the research reported in this volume.

The papers are ordered alphabetically by the names of their (first) authors. In the following survey of the contents, numbers in brackets follow the names of authors to indicate the position of a paper in the sequence of contributions to the book. For example, 'Juhani Rudanko (11)' indicates that Rudanko's paper occurs eleventh in the list of contents.

We have already mentioned the recent advances, through newly available corpora or subcorpora, in studying recent diachronic change. **Marcus Callies** (1) uses the *TIME corpus* (consisting of issues of TIME magazine from 1923 to 2006), as well as the BNC, to investigate processes of grammaticalization and pragmaticalization in the recent development of cleft constructions. **Juhani Rudanko** (11) also makes use of the *TIME Corpus*, analysing a developing phenomenon of particular interest to construction grammarians – the [V NP *into* V*ing*] construction, as in *browbeat a girl into marrying him*. A third diachronic paper, by **Marianne Hundt and Stefanie Dose** (5), uses the Brown family of corpora, including new members of the family (BLOB-1931 and B-Brown) to investigate change across the mid-century watershed of the World War II. Hundt and Dose's topic is the increasing frequency of the progressive aspect, a topic taken up from a synchronic rather than diachronic perspective by **Paula Suoniemi** (13), who uses another set of matching corpora, the ICE subcorpora, to compare the frequency of the progressive across a number of regional Englishes, including post-colonial Englishes such as those of the Philippines and Hong Kong. Variation among 'new Englishes' in the use of the English verb is a topic shared also by **Janina Werner and Joybrato Mukherjee** (16), who investigate 'chameleon' verbs like *give* and *take* in Indian and Sri Lankan English, comparing them with the same verbs in British English, seen as the historic input variety. Again, this shows how the now extensive group of ICE subcorpora enables us to study contrasts and similarities across World English.

The same applies to the ICLE corpus and its many learner subcorpora representing the English writing of students who are native speakers of languages other than English. This systematic collection of learner corpora enables both comparisons between ICLE subcorpora and comparisons with a native speaker corpus of student writing, LOCNESS (the *Louvain Corpus of Native English Essays*) to investigate how native-speaker-like the ICLE non-native writers are. Thus **Susan Nacey** (7) studies scare quotes in ICLE's Norwegian incarnation (inevitably called NICLE) in a comparison with LOCNESS. **Svetla Rogatcheva** (9) investigates differences between the use of the English perfect by German and Bulgarian students, comparing the two relevant incarnations of ICLE ('GICLE' and 'BUCLE'). It turns out that the German students are closer to American native speaking students, and the Bulgarian students to British. Other users of NICLE are **Signe Oksefjell Ebeling and Paul Wickens** (2), and **Sylvi Rørvik** (10), whose topics are more discoursal, concerned with how students operate with Halliday's textual function. In Ebeling and Wickens' case, the subject of the chapter is interpersonal themes such as *Of course* and *it is important that* – and here they use, as another valuable comparator, the BAWE (*British Academic Written English*) corpus. In Rørvik's case, the subject is the thematic progression of given-new structures in Norwegian students' writing, as compared with native-speaking students' writing, as well as the expert writing of the Norwegian and English press.

Yet another application of Norway's corpus resources is found in **Thomas Egan's** paper (3) comparing *through* and its translation equivalents in the English-Norwegian Parallel Corpus (ENPC). This has the novel theoretical goal of investigating the hypothesis that senses of a polysemous word in language X (in this case English) that are translated in similar ways into other languages will be seen to be more closely related by users of that language than senses that are translated differently. This is a contrastive topic that extends the theme of corpus comparability one step further, to parallel subcorpora in different languages.

Of course, not all corpus research has to be based on the comparability of corpora or subcorpora. There is another kind of corpus study which stresses the importance of detailed analysis of a given linguistic phenomenon in a given body of data, although comparison between corpora is not excluded. We deal now with a three papers which undertake grammatical (= morphosyntactic + semantic) research involving less studied parts of the English verbal system. **Soili Nokkonen** (8) has made a special study of the fast-emerging semi-modal NEED *to*, and here, using the BNC focuses particularly on spoken business discourse, where she finds that "NEED *to* is useful when addressing subordinates politely". **Sara Gesuato** (4), examining an infrequent verb pattern HAD *been to V*, finds it advisable to search a number of large corpora including the BNC and COCA, supplementing the result with elicited data. **Turo Vartiainen** (14) tackles the age-old debate on the dual (adjectival/verbal) function of the participle, especially in premodifying position, and comes to the conclusion that the key to the distinction lies in telicity.

As corpus linguistics "moves forward", opportunities arise increasingly for new kinds of corpora, representing (for example) popular culture and computer-mediated communication (CMC). **Rolf Kreyer** (6) makes use of an unusual corpus, the *Giessen-Bonn Corpus of Popular Music*, to find that love metaphors in pop lyrics, far from being stereotyped, show true creativity. **Anke Schultz and Elke Teich** (12) explore "the secret life of the negative" in relation to modality using a part of the *Bremen Translation Corpus* (BTC) consisting of CMC newsgroup texts.

Finally, the techniques and resources of corpus linguistics are becoming increasingly recognized as valuable to other disciplines, and the opportunities for interdisciplinary collaboration abound. **Elaine W. Vine and Paul Warren** (15) exemplify this in their paper on ambiguity, which combines the methods of psycholinguistics, the resources and techniques of corpus linguistics, and the value of applying frequency and psycholinguistic data to language teaching materials.

Sebastian Hoffmann, Paul Rayson and Geoffrey Leech

List of corpora referred to

BAWE	*British Academic Written English Corpus*
B-BROWN	(a corpus of American English matched with BLOB-1931; under development)
BLOB-1931	(a million words of British English from 1928-1934; a member of the Brown family)
BNC	*British National Corpus*
Brown family	(the 'family' of comparable corpora modelled on the *Brown Corpus*)
BTC	*Bremen Translation Corpus*
BUCLE	The Bulgarian component of ICLE
COCA	*Corpus of Contemporary American English*
ENPC	*English-Norwegian Parallel Corpus*
GICLE	*The German component of ICE*
GBoP	*Giessen-Bonn Corpus of Popular Music.* (The lyrics of the top 100 albums in the US Album Charts from 2000 to 2010)
ICE	*International Corpus of English*
ICLE	*International Corpus of Learner English*
LOCNESS	*Louvain Corpus of Native English Essays*
NICLE	*The Norwegian component of ICLE*
TIME	The *TIME Corpus* (100 million words of text from *TIME* magazine, 1923-2006)

The grammaticalization and pragmaticalization of cleft constructions in Present-Day English

Marcus Callies

Johannes-Gutenberg Universität Mainz

Abstract

The present paper examines the development of the variation between a marked and an unmarked infinitival complement clause in three types of cleft constructions in 20th century English. Data from corpora of written and spoken British (BrE) and American English (AmE) evidence a significantly divergent development of these clefts types in speaking when compared to writing. The written corpora show a steady increase in the frequency of clefts, and a decrease of the to-*infinitive paired with an increase of the bare infinitive, thus a reversal of preferences in both varieties in all three types of clefts. This erosion of* to *as an (optional) grammatical marker leads to a higher degree of syntactic integration and can be interpreted as the next step in the grammaticalization process of clefts in written English. The spoken corpora also show a significant increase of clefts in spoken BrE in the last quarter of 20th century. While the infinitive marker is still persistent in spoken BrE, especially in* wh- *and* th-*clefts (less so in* all-*clefts), it is virtually absent in spoken AmE. More importantly, though, the majority of* wh-*clefts in the spoken material are difficult to classify in terms of a canonical, bi-clausal structure because they show a lack of syntactic integration to varying degrees, the only link between the* wh-*clause and the focus being their co-reference relation. This suggests a different development of the construction in spoken English.* Wh-*clefts fulfil specific metapragmatic functions in terms of managing temporality in interaction, and have recently been analysed as projector constructions that foreshadow upcoming discourse and are structurally not fixed, but interactively produced, thus emergent and open. Thus, the paper argues that* wh-*clefts in spoken English represent a case of pragmaticalization, i.e. the grammaticalization of discourse functions, in which the initial* wh-*clause develops into a topic marker or discourse-marker-like phrase.*

1. Synchronic and diachronic variation in cleft constructions

Certain types of cleft constructions in English exhibit variation between a marked (*to*) and an unmarked (or bare) infinitival complement clause. Examples (1) - (3) below illustrate the three types that will be investigated in this paper: the *wh*-cleft, the *th*-cleft, and the *all*-cleft, which are often more generally named pseudo-clefts[1] (see Collins 1991: 27ff.).

(1a) Now ideally what I'd like to do is *to* have a chat with somebody [...] (BNC KDJ 88)
(1b) Basically what I like to do is Ø have a conversation about the project and then get the designer to come up with an answer. (BNC KS2 272)
(2a) "I hope you're not getting absurd ideas about her. The best thing you can do is *to* forget her." (BNC EVC 708)
(2b) "The best thing I can do is Ø forget all about him," she told a close friend. (BNC CH1 1878)
(3a) Now all you have to do is *to* take the model up to a safe height, roll it inverted and flip the switch. (BNC CAY 851)
(3b) All you have to do is Ø take a stroll down the high street. (BNC CFS 1334)

Such clefts are focus constructions and involve the splitting of a sentence into two clauses, thereby highlighting a certain sentence constituent, here an infinitival complement clause. Since these three types are functionally equivalent, they can be conceived of as constituting a family of constructions, linked by family resemblance (Hopper 2001: 112).

Sometimes gerund complements are also possible, and these are said to be triggered by a progressive form of *do* in the matrix verb as in (4) (Mair 2008). The examples in (5), however, show that this is not mandatory: *Doing* does not necessarily trigger a gerundial complement as in (5a), and neither does a gerundial complement correspond to a gerund in the matrix verb as in (5b).

(4a) But in essence what we're *doing* is *putting* your business card in front of somebody for two years. (BNC JA3 235)
(4b) Silly, wasn't it, when all I was *doing* was *going* down the road to the Post Office? (BNC H9G 288)
(5a) Basically what we're *doing* is *to count* during training how often a sub-pattern a tuple has a particular state has a particular pattern. (BNC JP6 299)
(5b) All I *did* was *looking* in the windows. (BNC KE6 2992)

Gerund complements are discussed in more detail by Mair (2008, 2009) and will not be dealt with further here.

Patterns of variation and change in such cleft constructions are not well-researched to date. The determinants of the synchronic variation between a *to*- and a bare infinitive in clefts have received some attention in several studies by Rohdenburg (1998, 2000, 2006). He identifies a number of factors that influence this variation, among them regional and stylistic ones. Rohdenburg argues that whether or not the infinitive marker is realised is determined by the overall structural complexity of the cleft construction. He assumes a complexity principle that represents a correlation between two parameters, i.e. processing complexity and grammatical explicitness: in the case of more or less explicit constructional options, the more explicit one(s) will tend to be preferred in cognitively more complex environments. Rohdenburg outlines several properties that determine the relative complexity of an environment, such as i) the form and tense of the verb *do* (simple and present tense forms are more likely to trigger a bare infinitive), ii) intervening elements between the verbs *do* and *be* (the tendency that *to* is used increases with length and complexity of the intervening material), and iii) the form and tense of the verb *be* (simple predicates and present tense forms are again assumed to favour the bare infinitive). For instance, in terms of Rohdenburg's complexity principle the relative structural complexity of the *wh*-cleft in example (6) would be expected to trigger the bare rather than the *to*-infinitive, and that is what we find in this example: there is a complex matrix predicate *wanted me to do*, lengthy intervening material that consists in itself of a complex syntactic structure, and there is a past tense form of the verb *be*.

(6) What Mr. Smith *wanted me to do - and he was of course prepared to pay handsomely, in pounds, dollars, ration books, anything - was* **to** deal him the details, plans and prototypes of the goods being collected. (LOB R04 33-36)

The present study, however, does not focus on the determinants of variation, but rather on the general development of this variation in 20th century English. It has been claimed on occasion that the types of clefts described above represent another "case of the marked infinitive being ousted by the bare infinitive in the second half of the 20th century" (Rohdenburg 2000: 31), suggesting that the variation is not stable but reflects a diachronic change from the full to the bare infinitive (similarly Mair 2008). Moreover, the decrease of the more explicit variant is said to be accelerated in American English (AmE) rather than British English (BrE), AmE being "in the lead of a new drift towards economy while BrE remains more conservative and more explicit" (Rohdenburg and Schlüter 2009: 416). Moreover, Rohdenburg claims that "the infinitive marker, which used to be obligatory in earlier centuries, is less frequent in informal registers than in formal ones", and that "*all*-clefts representing the most informal type, display the smallest proportion of marked infinitives" (Rohdenburg 2000: 194).

While these two last claims largely rely on a paper by Allerton (1991) who does not provide empirical evidence, there are more serious issues with some of the abovementioned previous studies. First, they are mostly limited to either only one type of construction at a time (*all*- or specific types of *th*-clefts), and only one British or American newspaper (*Guardian*, *Times/Sunday Times*, *Washington Post*), hence the results are potentially subject to the influence of in-house styles or copy-editing policies. Moreover, the studies draw on sample corpora consisting of newspapers published in only one specific year or a short time span in the early 1990s, hence corpora that do not enable a detailed diachronic comparison over a longer period of time.

2. Research questions, methodology and data

The present paper uses various spoken and written, synchronic and diachronic corpora of British and American English and investigates the following research questions:

- Are there (recent) historical shifts in the use of the full and the bare infinitive in these cleft constructions? Hence, is there variation or real change?
- Are there any differences between the three structural types?
- If there is change, how can it be explained?
- Are there differences in the development of these clefts in spoken and written English?

Like some earlier studies that looked into the abovementioned variation, I used the so-called Brown family of corpora, consisting of four one-million-word corpora of written English, the *Standard Corpus of Present-Day Edited American English* (Brown, AmE 1960s), the *Lancaster-Oslo/Bergen Corpus of British English* (LOB, BrE 1960s), the *Freiburg-Brown Corpus of American English* (Frown, AmE 1990s), and the *Freiburg-LOB Corpus of British English* (FLOB, BrE 1990s). It has frequently been pointed out that although the Brown family of corpora represents a very carefully compiled, balanced and comparable set of corpora, its disadvantages for a detailed comparison of long-term diachronic developments are for instance the relatively short time span it covers (1960s-1990s), and, depending on the linguistic structure under study, relatively low frequencies of occurrence. To alleviate these shortcomings somewhat, I also made use of the *TIME Magazine Corpus* (TIME) a 100-million-word corpus that consists of the back issues of the *TIME* magazine, representing written AmE from 1923-2006.[2]

While earlier studies have almost exclusively used written corpora, I also take into account corpora of spoken English to see whether there are differences in the development of the three cleft types in spoken and written English. For a diachronic comparison of spoken British English, I used the complete *London-Lund Corpus* (LLC:c) that covers BrE from the early 1960s to the mid-1970s,[3] consisting of 500,000 words, and a subcorpus compiled from the spoken component of the *British National Corpus* (BNC, BrE of the early 1990s) to match LLC:c in size and coverage as shown in Table 1.

Table 1. BNC spoken subcorpus used in the present study

subcorpus	Number of words
S_pub_debate (public debates, discussions, meetings)	283,507
S_interview (job interviews & other types)	123,816
S_sportslive ('live' sports commentaries and discussions)	33,320
S_demonstratn ('live' demonstrations)	31,772
S_lect_nat_science (lectures on the natural sciences)	22,681
Total	495,096

For spoken American English, I used the *Santa Barbara Corpus of Spoken American English* (SBC) which consists of 250,000 words and covers AmE of the 1980s.

From the written corpora, I extracted the targeted cleft constructions by using the lexical anchors *all*, *thing/s* and *what* followed by any form of DO in the range of 5 words (TIME) or 15 words (Brown family) to the right of the node. Due to the sheer size of TIME and the technical impossibility to exclude unwanted *wh*-questions (*What do you think?*), *wh*-clefts were extracted only from three time periods, the earliest one available in the corpus (1923-1929), the 1960s, and the latest time period covered (2000-2006). All hits were then checked and filtered manually. Reverse clefts, exemplified in (7a), questions (7b + c) and instances separated by a colon (7d) were excluded.

(7a) To leave the time bomb lying in the street was one thing I couldn't do. (LOB L12 184-5)
(7b) What could Jones do but return it? (TIME 1929/08/26)
(7c) What do you want to do, crucify us all in November? (TIME 1928/06/25)
(7d) On paper, Roosevelt's new job would seem to be a first-rate launching platform for what he really wants to do: run next year against Nelson Rockefeller for Governor of New York. (TIME 1965/02/21)

The same search strategy was applied to the spoken corpora, from which the relevant clefts were extracted through the keywords *all*, *thing/s* and *what* followed by any form of DO in the range of 9 words (BNC) and 10 words (LLC and SBC) to the right of the node.[4]

3. Corpus studies and results

3.1 Corpus study 1: Brown family

Table 2 gives the frequencies of occurrence of *to*- and bare infinitives in the three types of cleft constructions under discussion. They suggest a decrease of the *to*-infinitive and an increase of the bare infinitive in BrE and AmE, thus a reversal of preferences in both varieties. The diachronic differences within the BrE and the AmE corpora are statistically highly significant.[5] In BrE of the 1930s, there are no unmarked infinitives at all because these start to appear only in the 1960s, first in *all*- and *th*-clefts. By the 1990s, bare infinitives are already the statistical norm in *all*-clefts, and we have a split distribution between *to*- and bare infinitives in the *wh*- and *th*-variants.

Table 2. Three cleft types in the Brown family of corpora

Corpus	*wh*-clefts				*th*-clefts				*all*-clefts			
	total	*to*	∅	% *to*	total	*to*	∅	% *to*	total	*to*	∅	% *to*
1930s BrE (BLOB)[6]	2	2	0	**100**	10	10	0	**100**	9	9	0	**100**
1960s BrE (LOB)	8	8	0	**100**	16	13	3	**81.3**	19	11	8	**57.9**
1990s BrE (FLOB)	6	3	3	**50**	7	4	3	**57.1**	17	3	14	**17.6**
1960s AmE (Brown)	11	6	5	**54.5**	9	4	5	**44.4**	21	8	13	**38.1**
1990s AmE (Frown)	18	2	16	**11.1**	5	1	4	**20**	15	1	14	**6.7**

In AmE of the 1960s, the unmarked infinitive was already established in all three cleft types, with *all*-clefts showing the lowest percentage of *to*-infinitives, and by the 1990s, the bare infinitive is clearly the statistical norm in all variants. The impression that the use of bare infinitives has occurred and does occur more frequently in AmE is confirmed by the statistics.[7] While the findings also seem to suggest differences between the three constructional types in that the reversal of preferences appears to be most 'advanced' in *all*-clefts in both varieties, the relatively low frequencies of occurrence due to the small size of the corpora do not allow statistically valid measures of these differences.[8]

3.2. Corpus study 2: TIME

The results obtained from TIME, which covers the time span from 1923 to 2006, also show a steady increase in the frequency of use of the bare infinitive, and thus a change of preferences in 20th century written AmE in all three types of clefts.[9] Figures 1a + b, 2a + b, and 3 illustrate this diachronic development. In addition, the graphs also nicely show that the observed reversal of preferences in *all*-clefts occurred several decades earlier than in *th*- and *wh*-clefts. We can see in Figure 1a that the TIME corpus does not cover the period in which the reversal must have happened, i.e. the first decade of the 20th century. Figure 2a shows that while the decline of the *to*-infinitive in *th*-clefts already started in the first half of the 20th century, the rise of the bare infinitive was somewhat delayed and took off in the 1970s only, the decade which marks the crossing of the two lines.

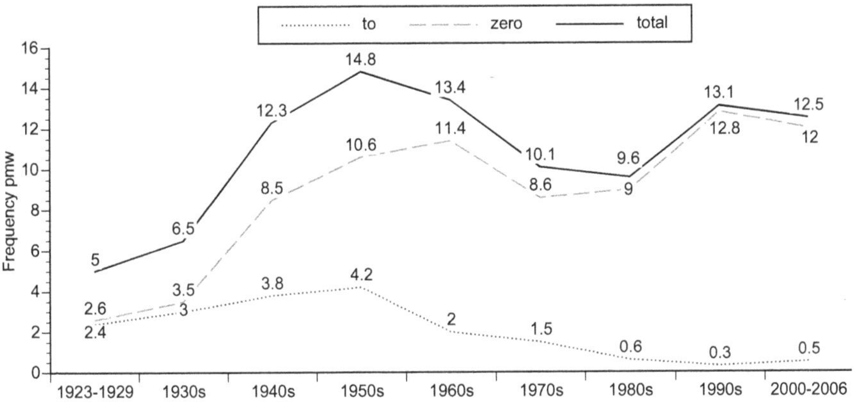

Figure 1a. Development of *all*-cleft variants in TIME (per million words)[10]

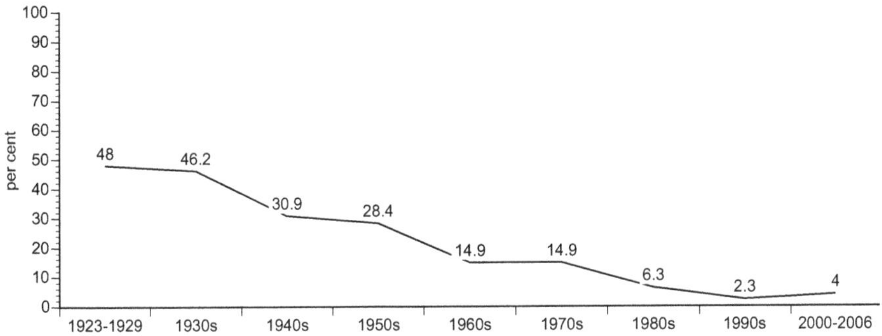

Figure 1b. Percentage of *all*-clefts with *to*-infinitive in TIME

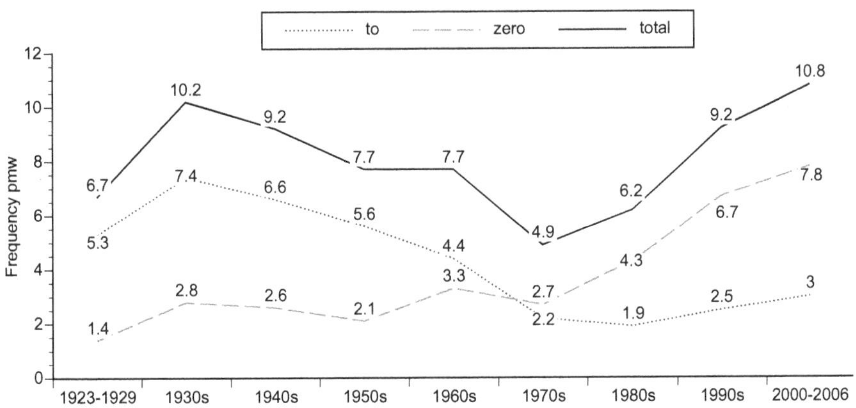

Figure 2a. Development of *th*-cleft variants in TIME (per million words)

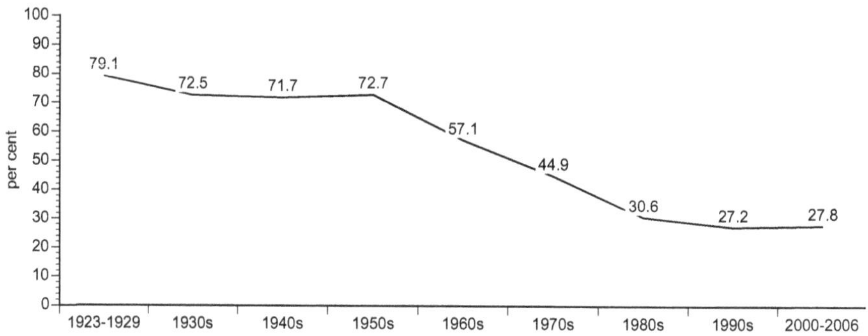

Figure 2b. Percentage of *th*-clefts with *to*-infinitive in TIME

As for the *wh*-clefts, we can see from the three time periods examined that the bare infinitive was virtually non-existent in the 1920s (96.6% *to*-infinitives), but in the 1960s it was already more frequently used than the *to*-infinitive, which dropped to 47.9%. By the 2000s, the bare infinitive had seen a remarkable rise in frequency of use (3.7 to 12.5 per million words) with the *to*-infinitive playing only a minor role (8.8%).

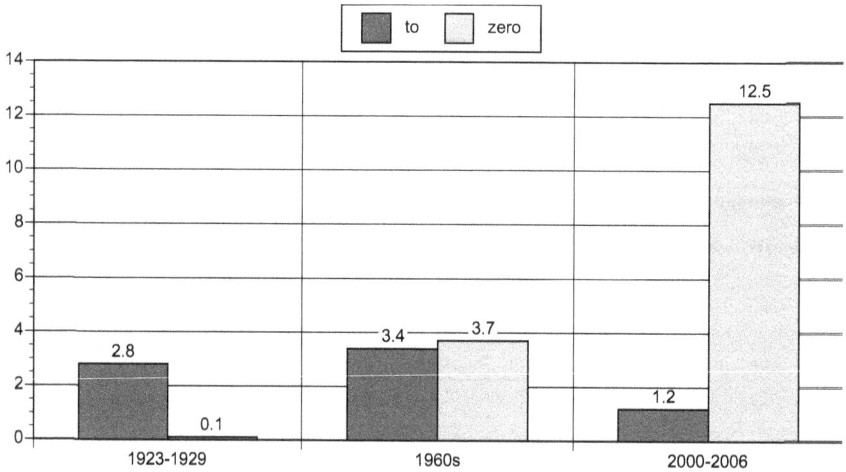

Figure 3. Development of *wh*-cleft variants in TIME (per million words)

3.3. Corpus study 3: LLC, BNC spoken and SBC

The BrE corpora show first of all a significant increase of clefts in spoken BrE in the last quarter of the 20th century: the frequency of occurrence per 100,000 words increases from 3.4 in LLC to 27.8 in the BNC spoken subcorpus for all three cleft types, compare Figures 4 and 5.[11]

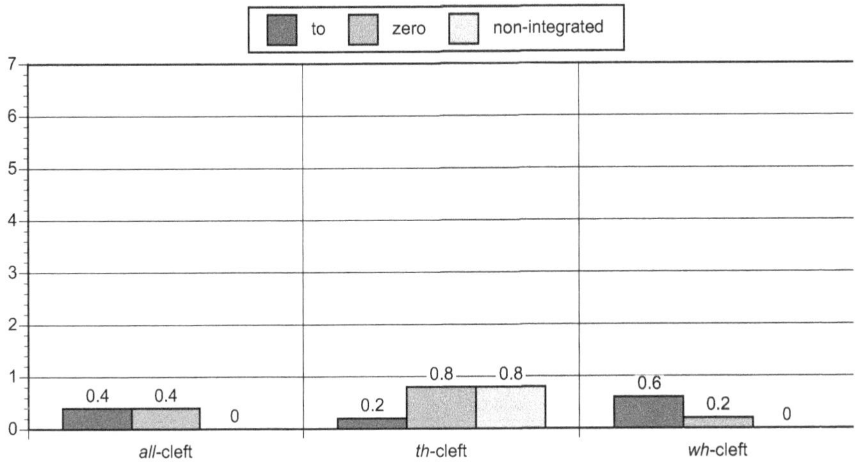

Figure 4. Frequency of occurrence of cleft types in LLC (per 100,000 words)

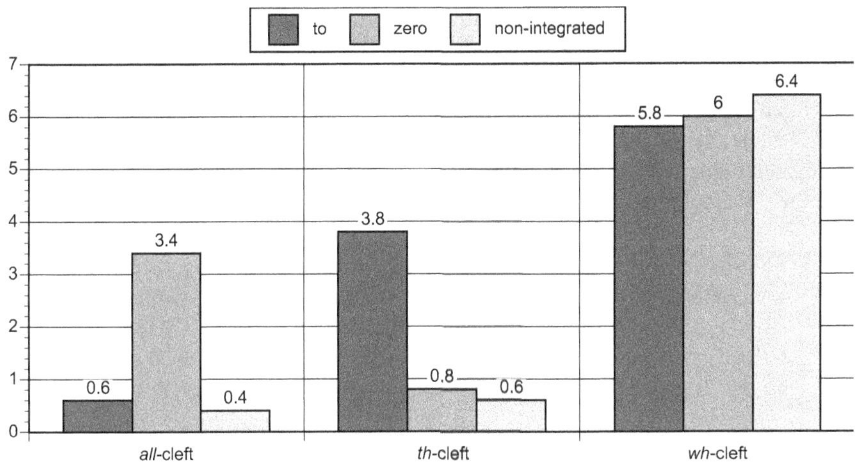

Figure 5. Frequency of occurrence of cleft types in BNC spoken (per 100,000 words)

The increase in *wh*-clefts seems to be most pronounced, but again the low frequencies of occurrence of clefts in LLC do not allow statistically valid measures of the differences between the three types. The BNC findings (see Figure 5) also suggest that the loss of the infinitive marker has progressed furthest in *all*-clefts, but – similar to the findings for written English – that this development is delayed in *wh*- and *th*-clefts. By contrast, the *to*-infinitive is virtually absent in all three cleft types in spoken AmE (see Figure 6).

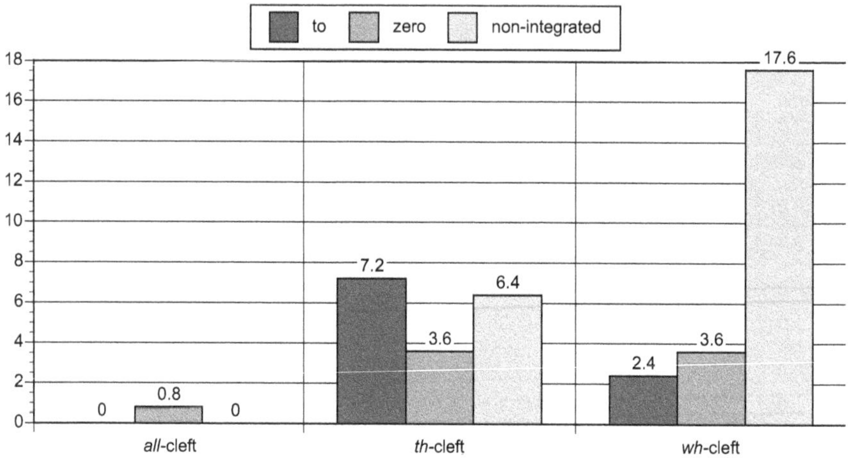

Figure 6. Frequency of occurrence of cleft types in SBC (per 100,000 words)

It needs to be highlighted that the corpora of spoken English exhibit a large number of structural types that are difficult to classify in terms of a 'canonical', bi-clausal cleft-structure because they show a lack of syntactic integration to varying degrees (see also Hopper and Thompson 2008: 102f.). This non-integrated variant is especially frequent in *wh*-clefts (see Figures 5 and 6). In the overall majority of this type, the *wh*-clause subject is either copied into a full finite main clause as shown in (8), or the subject of the full clause is co-referential with the *wh*-clause subject like in (9).

(8a) So what *we*'ve done is *we*'ve applied a simple learning rule which just says remember the sub-patterns. (BNC JP6 52)
(8b) BEN: (..) What *they* did is *they* built four intake towers. (SBC)
(9) KIRST: Okay so it's a gland (..) that (..) stores oil so what *a penguin* will do is *it*'ll go back it'll squeeze the gland. (SBC)

Moreover, there are instances where the *wh*-clause subject is changed as in (10), and also examples where the copula *be* is omitted, see (11).

(10) JIM: And (.) what what what *we* would do is (.) *they* would take care of the account maintainance. (SBC)
(11a) LARRY: Well yeah. (.) What they did Ø
SETH: That's the flue I guess.
LARRY: they they took the stubs and they cleaned em up. (SBC)
(11b) What he did Ø he saw he saw the method and saw well this is quite neat. We can actually implement it very efficiently in hardware. (BNC JP6 93)

Finally, few instances show a lack of agreement in tense/aspect, exemplified in (12).

(12) Basically what I am doing is I want them to reply. (BNC J9X 973)

In all these syntactically non-integrated instances, the link between the *wh*-clause and the focus constituent is reduced to their co-reference relation.

In spoken *wh*-clefts, the non-integrated variant actually represents the most frequent subtype in both BrE and AmE (see Figures 5 and 6), an observation that is supported by previous research (Koops and Ross-Hagebaum 2008; Hopper and Thompson 2008: 102). For example, Koops and Ross-Hagebaum's (2008) study of *wh*-clefts in five conversational corpora, among them SBC and Switchboard, shows that about two thirds of all cases with *do* (N=497) lack syntactic integration. Their high frequency suggests a different development of the construction in spoken compared to written English, providing a strong argument for the inclusion of such types that have been considered exceptional, incomplete, reduced, or deviant from the full, canonical type, caused by processing factors (cf. Collins 1991: 44-48 vs. Hopper 2001: 111 and Hopper and Thompson 2008: 109).

4. Discussion

The data from 20th century written and spoken BrE and AmE corpora evidence a significantly divergent development of these clefts types in spoken and written English that will be discussed in the following in terms of two distinct processes: grammaticalization and pragmaticalization.

4.1. Written English: Grammaticalization

The written corpora show a steady increase in the frequency of clefts, a decrease of the *to*-infinitive paired with an increase of the bare infinitive, thus a reversal of preferences in both varieties in all three types of clefts. These observations for the 20th century have to be seen in the context of the long-term historical development of *wh*-clefts since the late 17th century. On the basis of several diachronic corpora of English, Koops and Hilpert (2009) show that the development of *wh*-clefts has been progressing steadily over the past 300 years, and that there has been a gradual, sustained frequency increase that continues, as we have seen, through the 20th century, suggesting a continued expansion to new contexts of use (Koops and Hilpert 2009: 218f.). They further argue that this is accompanied by a diachronic generalization of the construction as a gradual process, evidenced by three measures of its degree of grammaticalization. First, in the written medium clefts have become more syntactically integrated: cleft types lacking this integration (as e.g. caused by the absence of the copula) are well-attested in 18th century written English, but do not occur in written PDE, except the formulaic *What is more/worse*… Second, there has been a shift from modified *wh*-clauses

(*What is even more important*...) to unmodified ones (*What I mean*...), and third, the *wh*-clause has become lexically constrained and formulaic due to a shift from evaluative predicates (*be* + adjective) to a narrow range of verbs that mark the focused element as either an action or event (*do, happen*) or a paraphrase (*say, mean*).

Grammatical changes that involve the deletion of (optional) elements, like the infinitive marker *to* in the present context, are often explained in terms of grammaticalization. In clefts, the erosion of *to* as an optional grammatical marker leads to a higher degree of syntactic integration and can be interpreted as the next step in the grammaticalization process of cleft constructions in written English. This development appears to be in line with a universal path of grammaticalization (see Haspelmath 1989) in which the preposition *to* lost its semantic meaning (locative goal of motion, purpose) and became a purely grammatical marker. It can also interpreted in line with Hopper and Traugott's (2003: 179) cline of clause-combining and the grammaticalization of clause linkers that suggests a continuum of development from less to more unified clause combining, from less to more bonded: more overt and independent devices for signalling clause linkage (e.g. *that, to*) correlate with minimal-semantic-pragmatic integration, while the least overt (Ø) correlate with maximal semantic-pragmatic integration.

4.2. Spoken English: Pragmaticalization

Many of the clefts in the spoken data (in fact, the majority of *wh*-clefts) are of the non-integrated type, and their high frequency suggests a different development than the one outlined for written English. As reported earlier, clefts that lack syntactic integration are well-attested in 18th century written English (Koops and Hilpert 2009: 221), but, as has been shown in the corpus studies in Section 3 above, are absent from written PDE. Koops and Hilpert (2009: 221) argue that while the integrated type gained in currency, the non-integrated type with its lack of overt syntactic link between *wh*-clause and focus may have come to be perceived as non-standard or too colloquial, hence avoided in writing.

Written English merely features a variant in which the *wh*- and the complement clause are separated by a colon (ignored in the quantitative part of the present study), exemplified in (13). Compared to the two other types of clefts, *wh*-clefts show a higher frequency of such variants, but even among these, they are very rare in the written mode.

(13a) On paper, Roosevelt's new job would seem to be a first-rate launching platform for what he really wants to do: run next year against Nelson Rockefeller for Governor of New York. (TIME 1965/02/21)

(13b) It's been said that Nelly – who scored a chart hit with the punchy title track – is trying to do for St. Louis, Mo., what Master P did for New Orleans: put his hometown on the hip-hop map. (TIME 2000/04/17)

The development of clefts in spoken English is strongly related to their discourse-pragmatic functions. In particular, *wh*-clefts have been shown to fulfil specific interactive, metapragmatic functions in spoken discourse in terms of managing temporality in interaction, e.g. delaying an upcoming utterance, holding the floor, or buying time (Kim 1995; Weinert and Miller 1996; Hopper 2001; Hopper and Thompson 2008). Such clefts have recently been analysed as projector constructions that foreshadow upcoming discourse (e.g. Hopper and Thompson 2008: 105, 114): the *wh*-clause opens a projection span that draws the recipient's attention to the 'missing', i.e. the foregrounded and highlighted, constituent, which can vary in form and may stretch over several turn constructional units. Thus, *wh*-clefts are structurally not fixed, but interactively produced, emergent and open (Hopper 2001; Hopper and Thompson 2008). Similar analyses have been proposed for German *w*-clefts (Günthner 2006, 2008a).

It is clear, then, that the structural properties of clefts in spoken interaction, such as their fragmentary and disintegrated syntax, result from the functions they typically fulfil in the spoken domain.[12] Therefore, it seem plausible to argue that the development of *wh*-clefts in spoken English represents a case of pragmaticalization (see e.g. Aijmer 1997; Günthner and Mutz 2004), a process that can be conceived of as the grammaticalization of discourse functions. Diewald (2011) considers pragmaticalization a subclass of grammaticalization that shows the crucial features of grammaticalization processes, but is distinguished from other such processes by specific characteristics concerning function, domain and syntactic integration. In the present context, there are clear differences as to these three aspects in the way how clefts have developed in spoken and written English. In addition to the general highlighting function of clefts in writing, their special discourse functions of managing temporality only come to the fore in the spoken domain, and while they have become more compact and syntactically integrated in writing, the spoken ones are characterized by disintegration, fragmentation and parataxis. The initial *wh*-clause, which has been shown to be highly formulaic and lexically constrained to a small number of 'metalinguistic' verbs (*do*, *happen*, *say*, *mean*), seems to develop into a topic marker or discourse-marker-like phrase, similar to re-analyses of matrix-clauses like *the thing/fact/point is (that)* as projector phrases (Aijmer 2007; Günthner 2008a, 2008b).

5. Conclusion

In this paper, I have examined the development of *wh*-, *th*-, and *all*-clefts in 20th century British and American English, focusing on the variation between a full and a bare infinitival complement clause. The data retrieved from several spoken and written corpora evidence a significant increase in the frequency of use of all three cleft types in the course of the 20th century. Moreover, the findings suggest a divergent development of these clefts in the spoken and written mode that can be explained in terms of two distinct processes: grammaticalization and pragmaticalization.

The written corpora show a steady decrease of *to* paired with an increase of the bare infinitival complement, i.e. a reversal of preferences in both varieties that leads to a higher degree of syntactic integration and can be interpreted as the next step in the grammaticalization process of clefts in written English. By contrast, the spoken corpora exhibit a large number of syntactically non-integrated variants. In fact, the majority of *wh*-clefts in both spoken BrE and AmE are of this non-integrated type. I have argued that their high frequency and distinct structural features suggest a different development of the construction in spoken compared to written English, a development that is strongly related to its specific metapragmatic functions in spoken interaction, perhaps most importantly managing temporality in interaction (e.g. delaying, floor-holding and time-buying). The development of *wh*-clefts in spoken English may be conceived of as a case of pragmaticalization, distinguished from other grammaticalization processes by specific characteristics concerning function, discourse domain and syntactic integration.

Notes

1 Transformational approaches to cleft sentences focused on the analysis of how clefts and so-called pseudo-clefts were derived. Clefts were merely understood as being derived from pseudo-clefts, a view that neglects the fact that both types actually differ in focus assignment and allow different constituents to be highlighted. In view of its transformational tradition and implications, I avoid using the term pseudo-cleft.

2 This corpus is freely available at http://corpus.byu.edu/time/. The *Corpus of Historical American English* (COHA), covering AmE from 1810-2009, was not yet available at the time the present study was carried out.

3 The majority of texts was recorded between the early 1960s and the mid-1970s. Only few texts were recorded between 1984 and 1988, and even fewer date back to the early 1950s, for full information see http://khnt.hit.uib.no/icame/manuals/londlund/ll.htm.

4 The BNC was searched using the interface provided by Mark Davies at Brigham Young University that can be accessed online at http://corpus.byu.edu. The window span that the interface allows is limited to 9 words to left and right of the node.

5 The log-likelihood ratio (LL) is 32.104 for one degree of freedom (df), $p < 0.001$ for the BrE corpora, and 11.669 (df = 1), $p < 0.001$ for the AmE corpora.

6 B-LOB is short for "before LOB" and refers to a corpus compiled by Geoffrey Leech and Nicholas Smith, covering British English of the 1930s (see Leech, Hundt, Mair and Smith 2009: 10). I would like to thank Christian Mair for giving me limited access to this corpus.

7 The differences between the BrE and AmE corpora are Brown vs. LOB: LL = 8.253 (df = 1), $p < 0.01$, and Frown vs. FLOB: LL = 5.385 (df = 1), $p < 0.05$

8 Many cells have expected frequencies smaller than 5, a fact that renders the chi-square test of independence to examine statistical significance unreliable.

9 *All*-clefts: LL = 137.257 (df = 8), $p < 0.001$; *th*-clefts: LL = 129.422 (df = 8), $p < 0.001$; *wh*-clefts: LL = 76.218 (df = 2), $p < 0.001$.

10 Due to the unequal sizes of the subcorpora for each decade, normalized frequency counts per million words will be reported for this corpus.

11 The differences between LLC and BNC is LL = 12.189 (df = 2), $p < 0.01$.

12 According to the principles of binding and iconicity in syntactic coding, assuming that linguistic distance may be employed to mirror conceptual distance (Givón 1980; Haiman 1985), the delaying function of clefts may actually signal greater conceptual distance, hence the lack of syntactic integration.

References

Aijmer, K. (1997), '*I think* - an English modal particle', in: T. Swan and O.J. Westvik (eds.) *Modality in Germanic Languages: Historical and Comparative Perspectives*. Berlin: Mouton de Gruyter. 1-47.

Aijmer, K. (2007), 'The interface between grammar and discourse: *The fact is that*', in: A. Celle and R. Huart (eds.) *Connectives as Discourse Landmarks*. Amsterdam: Benjamins. 54-72.

Allerton, D. J. (1991), 'The greater precision of spoken language: Four examples from English', *English Studies,* 5: 470-478.

Collins, P. C. (1991), *Cleft and Pseudo-Cleft Constructions in English*. London: Routledge.

Diewald, G. (2008), 'Pragmaticalization (defined) as grammaticalization of discourse functions', *Linguistics*, 49: 365-390.

Givón, T. (1980), 'The binding hierarchy and the typology of complements', *Studies in Language*, 4: 333-377.

Günthner, S. (2006), '"Was ihn trieb, war vor allem Wanderlust". Pseudocleft-Konstruktionen im Deutschen', in: S. Günthner and W. Imo (eds.) *Konstruktionen in der Interaktion*. Berlin: Mouton de Gruyter. 59-90.

Günthner, S. (2008a), 'Projektorkonstruktionen im Gespräch: Pseudoclefts, *die Sache ist*-Konstruktionen und Extrapositionen mit *es*', *Gesprächsforschung*, 9: 86-114.

Günthner, S. (2008b), '"Die Sache ist...": eine Projektorkonstruktion im gesprochenen Deutsch', *Zeitschrift für Sprachwissenschaft*, 27: 39-72.

Günthner, S. and K. Mutz (2004), 'Grammaticalization vs. Pragmaticalization? The development of pragmatic markers in German and Italian', in: W. Bisang, N. Himmelmann and B. Wiemer (eds.) *What Makes Grammaticalization? A Look from its Fringes and its Components*. Berlin: Mouton de Gruyter. 77-107.

Haiman, J. (1985), *Natural Syntax: Iconicity and Erosion*. Cambridge: CUP.

Haspelmath, M. (1989), 'From purposive to infinitive – a universal path of grammaticalization', *Folia Linguistics Historica*, 10: 287-310.

Hopper, P. (2001), 'Grammatical constructions and their discourse origins. Prototype or family resemblance?', in: M. Pütz, S. Niemeier and René Dirven (eds.) *Applied Cognitive Linguistics I: Theory and Language Acquisition*. Berlin: Mouton de Gruyter. 109-130.

Hopper, P. and S. Thompson (2008), 'Projectability and clause combining in interaction', in: R. Laury (ed.) *Crosslinguistic Studies of Clause Combining. The Multifunctionality of Conjunctions*. Amsterdam: Benjamins. 99-123.

Hopper, P. and E. Closs Traugott (2003), *Grammaticalization*. 2nd edition. Cambridge: Cambridge University Press.

Kim, K.-H. (1995), 'WH-clefts and left-dislocation in English conversation: Cases of topicalization', in: P. Downing and M. Noonan (eds.) *Word Order in Discourse*. Amsterdam: Benjamins. 247-296.

Koops, C. and M. Hilpert (2009), 'The co-evolution of syntactic and pragmatic complexity: diachronic and cross-linguistic aspects of pseudoclefts', in: T. Givón and M. Shibatani (eds.) *Syntactic Complexity: Diachrony, Acqusition, Cognition and Neurology*. Amsterdam: Benjamins. 215-238.

Koops, C. and S. Ross-Hagebaum (2008), 'From sentence topic to discourse topic: the information structure of amalgam clefts'. Paper presented at the *34th Annual Meeting of the Berkeley Linguistics Society*, University of California at Berkeley, 8-10 February 2008.

Leech, G., M. Hundt, C. Mair and N. Smith (2009), *Change in Contemporary English. A Grammatical Study*. Cambridge: CUP.

Mair, C. (2008), 'Right in the middle of the s-shaped curve: on the spread of specificational clefts in 20th century English'. Paper presented at the *First Triennial Conference of the International Society for the Linguistics of English* (ISLE 1), University of Freiburg, 8-11 October 2008.

Mair, C. (2009), 'Specificational clefts in LModE: corpus based studies of diachronic trends'. Paper presented at the *30th conference of the International Computer Archive of Modern and Medieval English* (ICAME 30), Lancaster University, 27-31 May 2009.

Rohdenburg, G. (1998), 'Clarifying structural relationships in cases of increased complexity in English', in: R. Schulze (ed.) *Making Meaningful Choices in English*. Tübingen: Narr. 189-205.

Rohdenburg, G. (2000), 'The complexity principle as a factor determining grammatical variation and change in English', in: I. Plag and K. P. Schneider (eds.) *Language Use, Language Acquisition and Language History: (Mostly) Empirical Studies in Honour of Rüdiger Zimmermann*. Trier: Wissenschaftlicher Verlag Trier. 25-44.

Rohdenburg, G. (2006), 'Processing complexity and competing sentential variants in present-day English', in: W. Kürschner and R. Rapp (eds.) *Linguistik international: Festschrift für Heinrich Weber*. Lengerich: Pabst. 51-67.

Rohdenburg, G. and J. Schlüter (2009), 'New departures', in: G. Rohdenburg and J. Schlüter (eds.) *One Language, Two Grammars? Differences between British and American English*. Cambridge: CUP. 364-423.

Weinert, R. and J. Miller (1996), 'Cleft constructions in spoken language', *Journal of Pragmatics*, 25: 173-206.

Interpersonal themes and author stance in student writing

Signe Oksefjell Ebeling and Paul Wickens

University of Oslo and Oxford Brookes University

Abstract

This paper focuses on interpersonal themes and how these can shed light on how students of different disciplines "intrude to stamp their personal authority onto their arguments or step back and disguise their involvement" (Hyland 2005), mirroring their emergent attempts to engage with the values and beliefs of their respective disciplines.

We report on a study focusing on thematic choices in UK undergraduate writing from four disciplines, viz. English Studies, Engineering, Health and Social Care, and Anthropology. In this material, taken from the British Academic Written English Corpus, *disciplinary differences emerge, particularly in terms of interpersonal projection, reflecting the different ways in which students from different disciplines engage with the literature and the object of study.*

In the paper, we also expand the empirical base by looking at one additional discipline from Arts & Humanities (History) and one from Social Sciences (Business). The findings suggest that the difference in use of interpersonal themes in the expression of stance represents variation between individual disciplines rather than variation between broader disciplinary groupings.

1. Introduction

> The literacy practices of a disciplinary community embody different orientations to knowledge constructions [...] The initial constituent of the clause appears to have particular significance in the way it reflects the writer's beliefs and values, and thus provides an indicator of disciplinary difference in professional academic writing. (North 2005a: 435)

As hypothesised in the quotation above there is reason to believe that clause-initial position plays a central role in how writers express stance and that this position may also signal disciplinary differences. Stance, or the "writer's beliefs and values", is here defined as the way in which authors "intrude to stamp their personal authority onto their arguments or step back and disguise their involvement" (Hyland 2005: 176).

Previous studies have shown that, although stance may be "one of the most challenging tasks that faces the apprentice writer" (Charles 2006: 514), writers with different disciplinary backgrounds attempt to highlight their own views and attitudes in accordance with the practices of the discipline they feel part of (Charles 2006; North 2003, 2005a, 2005b).

This paper reports on a study that explores how university students position themselves in their writing across a range of disciplines.[1] The study includes an analysis of thematic choices in undergraduate assessed student writing as such choice is likely to reflect students' emergent attempts to engage with the values and beliefs of their disciplines. Hyland suggests that "we do not simply report findings or express ideas in some neutral context-free way, we employ the rhetorical resources accepted for the purpose of sharing meanings in a particular genre and social community" (Hyland 2002: 1093). According to Charles (2006: 493), "[a] number of studies have shown that academic writers do indeed construct a stance that reflects the ideology and epistemology of their discipline and have indicated the profound extent to which stance is embedded in disciplinarity".

The first part, and main bulk, of the study (Section 4) establishes that there are disciplinary differences in the expression of stance, particularly in terms of interpersonal projection, reflecting perhaps the different ways in which students from different disciplines engage with the literature and the object of study.

In the second part (Section 5), we will further explore the relationship between choice of interpersonal theme and the expression of stance in student writing, by expanding the empirical base of the investigation presented in Section 4 by looking at more disciplines. The findings will suggest whether the difference in use of interpersonal themes in the expression of stance represents a more general tendency of broader disciplinary groupings rather than variation between individual disciplines.

The data used in this study is taken from the *British Academic Written English* (BAWE) corpus of student writing.[2] This is a corpus well suited for the present purposes, since it contains student writing from a number of disciplines. Section 2 gives a fuller account of the material used.

The framework used for the analysis lies within the systemic functional tradition, following Mauranen (1993) and North (2003, 2005a, 2005b) in drawing a distinction between orienting and topical themes (see further Section 3). As pointed out by Mauranen: "From the textual analysis of thematic development it seems that the mutual relevance of two consecutive sentences in a text is largely established by the theme. To see this, it is useful to keep two kinds of sentence themes separate: orienting themes and topical themes" (Mauranen 1993: 112). Of these, we will be mainly concerned with the orienting theme, i.e. the constituent preceding the topical theme, and within the orienting theme, the interpersonal theme. The working hypothesis for this study is that disciplinary variation in the construction of stance in interpersonal themes may point to different epistemologies and literacy practices within given academic disciplines and broader disciplinary groupings.

2. Material

The BAWE corpus contains assessed student writing from four broad disciplinary groupings, viz. Arts & Humanities, Social Sciences, Physical Sciences, and Medical & Life Sciences. The assignments included in the corpus represent proficient student writing at undergraduate and postgraduate level, all being assessed at a II.i or above (> 60%). In total, 2,761 assignments from 34 disciplines were collected and prepared for inclusion in the corpus,[3] amounting to around 6.5 million words. See Nesi et al. (2005) and Heuboeck et al. (2007) for a more detailed account of the corpus.[4]

In Section 4, the investigation focuses on four different disciplines at undergraduate level, one from each of the mentioned groupings. Arts & Humanities is represented by English studies, Social Sciences by Anthropology, Physical Sciences by Engineering, and Medical & Life Sciences by Health and Social Care.

Since the aim was to look at the use of theme throughout whole assignments, typical corpus linguistics methods for data extraction could not be used, and the material had to be manually sampled and restricted in some way. Thus, each of the three UG year groups from each discipline is represented by four assignments, i.e. 12 assignments (mainly essays) from each discipline, or 16 from each year group regardless of discipline, amounting to a total of 48 assignments, approximately 128,000 words. This selection of assignments ensured a fair sample of writing both across and within the chosen disciplines.

In Section 5, 24 assignments from two additional disciplines have been added, one from Arts & Humanities and one from Social Sciences, viz. History and Business, in order to investigate these two broad disciplinary groupings in more detail.

3. Analytical Framework

> Writers are required to establish a stance towards their propositions, to get behind their words and stake out a position. (Hyland 2002: 1094)

In the following we will investigate to what extent students use the theme position in a clause "to establish a stance towards their propositions".

The framework used for the analysis follows North (2005a, 2005b) in drawing a distinction between orienting and topical themes within t-units. By t-unit is meant "an independent clause together with all hypotactically related clauses which are dependent on it" (Fries 1994: 229). A topical theme typically fills a participant role within the clause and is most commonly found to be the grammatical subject or the subject of the main proposition. Other elements that are found as topical themes include predicated themes. Orienting themes are described as the elements preceding the topical theme. The motivation for introduing the notion of an orienting theme is that it serves an important function in signalling semantic relevance between sentences; this is expressed by Mauranen (1993: 96) in the following way:

> ...the ideational theme[5] [...] must bear semantic relevance to the preceding sentence. If this is not the case, either the ideational theme must be preceded by bridging material in the same sentence, which will be called here 'orienting theme', or the preceding sentence must provide the necessary interpretative framework for establishing the connection.

Mauranen elaborates on this and adds that orienting themes can be present also in cases where the topical theme, i.e. the ideational theme, does have relevance to the preceding sentence. The function of the orienting theme in such cases can, for instance, be attitudinal or modal in nature (see Mauranen 1993: 111-112).

An orienting theme may consist of sub-themes: textual, experiential, and interpersonal. Whereas the textual theme typically makes "explicit the way the clause relates to the surrounding discourse" (Halliday 2004: 83), the experiential theme may contain fronted hypotactic clauses and "experiential elements which do not fill participant roles (mainly circumstantial adjuncts)" (North 2005a: 438). It should be noted that North applies the term 'experiential' in a slightly different way than other systemic functionalists. First of all, her experiential element can be seen to deviate from Halliday's in that Halliday does not include adverbial clauses within theme. Further, it should be observed that Thompson's experiential theme would correspond to North's topical theme (cf. Thompson 2004: 159).

Finally, the interpersonal theme is said to typically express the speaker's "own angle on the matter in hand" (Halliday and Matthiessen 2004: 84), and is thus most likely to contain elements expressing stance. Interpersonal themes typically elucidate the writer's stance towards the proposition, as shown in the following examples where the interpersonal theme is realised, in (a), by a modal adjunct and, in (b), by a projecting clause, see Table 1.[6]

Table 1. Interpersonal theme realised by a modal adjunct (a) and a projecting clause (b)

	Orienting theme			Topical theme	Rheme
	Textual	Experiential	Interpersonal		
(a)			Of course	passion, an emotion	cannot be said to physically flow... (BAWE3088c)
(b)	Yet		I think ultimately	it	is powerless... (BAWE3003c)

The correlation between stance and these two interpersonal themes is quite clear. Both the modal adjunct *of course* and the 'mental' projecting clause *I think ulti-*

mately carry stance in that they both express the writer's attitude towards the following proposition. The fact that projecting clauses can be used in this way is substantiated by Forey's findings where "the writer exploits locutionary projection in thematic position in order to establish a particular stance on the topic discussed and to summarise/present previous decisions and statements" (Forey 2002: 199). Or, as Halliday puts it: "if the speaker, or writer, is [...] projecting his or her own angle on the value of what the clause is saying (interpersonal), it is natural to set up such expressions as the point of departure" (Halliday and Matthiessen 2004: 83). We also include interpersonal metaphors of projection within the broader category of 'projection'.[7] These items are "thematic by default".

As the following analysis will show, the disciplinary differences are particularly apparent in the interpersonal sub-group of projecting clauses, thus a more detailed breakdown of projecting clauses is needed in order to describe disciplinary variation. Inspired by previous research (Hunston 1993 and Wickens 2001) the following breakdown of projecting clauses was set up.

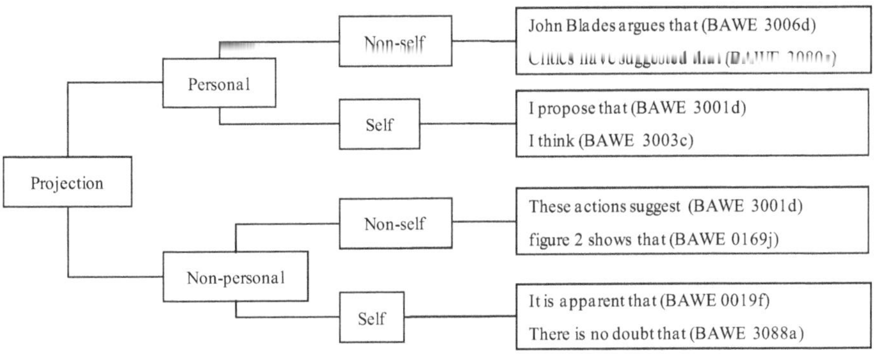

Figure 1. Projection framework

Further sub-classification of this framework is also possible, e.g. attributed vs. non-attributed distinction (in the non-personal category), external vs. internal distinction (in the non-personal/non-self category). However, for the purpose of the present study, the distinctions made in Figure 1 are seen as the most relevant for the analysis undertaken here. It should be mentioned, though, that, although stance is present, some of the personal projecting clauses may be said to lack author/personal stance (e.g. personal/non-self). As pointed out by Biber (2006: 91): "Although such structures [stance expressions that are attributed to the addressee (2nd person) or to a third person] express some kind of attitude or evaluation, they do not necessarily reflect the personal stance of the speaker/writer".

4. Thematic choices in four disciplines

Although interpersonal themes will be the main focus of this paper, the first step in the analysis was to identify orienting themes.

4.1 Orienting themes

The 48 student assignments were first divided into t-units, followed by a classification into orienting theme, topical theme and rheme. We then began focusing on the orienting themes and a further breakdown of the orienting themes into textual, experiential and interpersonal was then performed. Table 2 gives an overview of the distribution of these per 100 t-units.

Table 2. Orienting themes across disciplines per 100 t-units (figures rounded up)

	Orienting theme		
Discipline	Textual	Experiential	Interpersonal
English Studies (1,190 t-units)	22	21	10
Engineering (1,405 t-units)	19	23	10
Health and Social Care (1,306 t-units)	24	20	23
Anthropology (1,536 t-units)	24	23	18

If we look at textual and experiential themes across the disciplines we find little variation; not only do these two types of theme appear to vary little from discipline to discipline, but textual and experiential themes seem to spread evenly within disciplines as well. More interesting, then, is the apparent difference in the use of interpersonal themes across the disciplines. In English Studies and Engineering, textual and experiential themes are twice as frequent as interpersonal themes. In Health and Social Care and Anthropology, on the other hand, interpersonal themes are used to the same extent as textual and experiential themes, and compared to English Studies and Engineering, interpersonal themes are twice as popular.

Although a direct comparison with North's findings is tempting, it would not be a fair one. First of all, North (2005a) finds a discrepancy in the use of orienting themes between students with an Arts background vs. students with a Science background where both groups attended a course in the history of science. Second, her conclusion is that the use of more orienting themes in the 'Arts' students' assignments is connected to the fact that these students received a higher mark than the 'Science' students. In our material, however, all assignments have been awarded a 2.1 or above and have been assessed within their respective disciplines.

As we have seen above, orienting themes can be classified into textual, interpersonal, and experiential themes. Following North (2003: 134), "[t]he first two correspond in principle to the categories of textual and interpersonal theme in Halliday (1994), though with some variation in what is included. The third category comprises experiential elements which are not inherently involved in the process". North provides a breakdown of the categories, repeated here as Table 3.

Table 3. Classification of thematic elements (North 2003: 135)

Orienting Theme			Topical Theme
Textual	Interpersonal	Experiential	
conjunction	modal adjunct	circumstantial adjunct	subject
conjunctive adjunct	impersonal clause eg *It seems that*	adverbial clause	complement
impersonal clause eg *It follows that*	projecting clause eg *I believe that*	preposed attributive	finite
	interrogative finite or wh-element		existential *there*
			impersonal clause eg *It was easy to...*

4.2 Interpersonal themes across the four disciplines

This section provides an overview of the distribution of interpersonal themes in the data from the four disciplines. The classification mainly follows North as described in Table 3. However, some modifications and additions have been made. In the BAWE material five types of interpersonal themes were identified and they are listed and exemplified below.

The first category is *modal adjunct* and is exemplified in (1) below, followed by *interrogative/inversion* (2). While North does not include clause-initial *imperatives* in her classification of thematic elements (cf. Table 3), they were included in this study as a clear case of interpersonal theme (3). Like North, we counted projecting clauses and impersonal clauses as interpersonal themes. However, as seen in Figure 1 the terms *personal* (4) and *non-personal projecting clause* (5) were adopted instead.

(1) Modal adjunct:
Clearly force is essential to the complete turn around of rebellious individuals in 1984, (BAWE 3003c)

(2) Interrogative/inversion:
Does this leave the individual with any hope? (BAWE 3003c)

(3) Imperative:
Consider the use of plastic gears for one stage of speed reduction. (BAWE 0023e)

(4) Personal projecting clause:
In both novels, *Orwell suggests that* every system of power will inevitably abuse the use of language as mechanisms of control, (BAWE 3007a)

(5) Non-personal projecting clause:
It is possible that this is more than a criticism of the Bible itself but of the "canonizing process", which Ostriker also argues has "throughout history rested, not accidentally but essentially, in the silencing of women." (BAWE 3006k)

Table 4 shows the distribution of the various types of interpersonal theme across the four disciplines per 100 t-units.

Table 4. Distribution of interpersonal themes in the four disciplines per 100 t-units

	English Studies	Engi-neering	Health and social care	Anthro-pology
personal projecting clause	3.2	0.3	12.1	8.2
non-personal projecting clause	3.5	5.3	9.7	6.5
modal adjunct	2.9	0.3	0.5	2.9
interrogative/ inversion	0.4	0.5	0.2	0.7
imperative		3.4		0.1
Total	10	9.8	22.5	18.4

As can be seen from Table 4, on average, every tenth t-unit contains an interpersonal theme in both English Studies and Engineering. However, the distribution is very different. While English Studies sees a more or less even spread between personal projecting clauses, non-personal projecting clauses and modal adjuncts, Engineering favours non-personal projecting clauses and the imperative.

When we move to Health & Social Care and Anthropology, we saw in Table 2 that students of these disciplines tend to use twice as many interpersonal themes in their writing than was the case in English and Engineering. Table 4 shows that both these disciplines favour projecting clauses, perhaps suggesting that the most interesting area to explore further is precisely that of projecting clauses.

4.3 Projecting clauses and author stance

On the basis of the figures presented in Table 4, projecting clauses were identified as a good measure for disciplinary variation in the expression of stance. Using the framework presented in Figure 1, a more detailed analysis of the disciplines was carried out. Table 5 shows the distribution of types of projecting clauses, and thereby types of stance, across the four disciplines.

To some degree there is a contrast in the figures for personal/non-self between Health and Social Care (HSC) and Anthropology on the one hand and Engineering and English Studies on the other. For HSC and Anthropology students the literature seems to be the point of departure for how they position themselves in relation to the proposition, while it seems to be less so for English Studies students. For Engineering students the literature does not seem to make its way into projecting clauses in the expression of stance at all, with zero occurrences in the material analysed here.

Table 5. Disciplinary differences in the distribution of projecting clauses

	English Studies	Engineering	Health and Social Care	Anthropology
Personal				
Non-self	**2.7**	**0**	**6.7**	**7.7**
	Makdisi suggests that John Beer states that		Muir (2004) states that Smith (1997) believes	Tim Ingold argues that Putman concurs that
Self	**0.5**	**0.3**	**5.1**	**0.3**
	I believe I think ultimately	we can see that you find that	I realise with hindsight that Personally I feel that	I don't think I concur that
Non-personal				
Non-self	**2.3**	**2.6**	**4.9**	**3.2**
	This symbolises that This parody suggests that	The graph shows that the turnover data suggests that	This suggests that Studies have shown that	This quote shows that It has been suggested
Self	**1.3**	**2.7**	**4.7**	**3.2**
	It seems that it is clear	it appears that it is unlikely that	It is also true that it is possible that	it is unlikely It appears that

Projecting clauses expressing the most personal type of stance – personal/self, i.e. explicit subjective interpersonal metaphor of modality (cf. Halliday 1994: 354-355) – are mainly seen in the writing of HSC students.

In the non-personal/self projecting clauses the distribution is more even, although HSC students make more extensive use of this category than the students of the other disciplines. Perhaps the surprise in terms of expectations was the combined low figures for Self in English Studies.

4.4 Summing up

> A detailed analysis of disciplinary discourse [...] can help not only to bring out characteristic cultural features of disciplines but also to highlight various aspects of the knowledge domains to which they relate. It is possible by this means to discern differences in the modes in which arguments are generated, developed, expressed and reported, and to tease out the epistemological implications of the ways in which others' work is evaluated. (Becher and Trowler 2001: 46)

The question that inevitably arises on the basis of the figures presented above is what they really tell us, or more precisely, what do they tell us about how students express stance through projection?

We have chose to see the above findings in relation to what Laurillard (1993) says about undergraduate learning being mediated learning: teaching in higher education is:

> a rhetorical activity, seeking to persuade students to change the way they experience the world (and to) enable students to learn the descriptions of the world devised by others. (…) It is mediated learning, allowing students to acquire knowledge of someone else's way of experiencing the world. (Laurillard 1993: 28-29)

However, what we suggest is that the "mediating" happens in two ways, which are not mutually exclusive:

(a) The student writer approaches the object of study through the literature as suggested by Laurillard. They need to 'stand in the literature' organising it for the reader and bringing to bear their understanding of it.

(b) The student writer approaches the object of study more directly, drawing on personal observation of, or engagement with, e.g. texts, patients, animals.

This is substantiated in the summarised observations of each of the disciplines:

Health and Social Care

- Draws equally on literature (personal + non-personal/non-self) and personal observation (personal + non-personal/self) as point of departure to orientate reader.
- The key epistemology is that of reflective practitioner, particularly evident in the use of personal/self projecting clauses.

Anthropology

- Draws first and foremost on the literature as point of departure (personal + non-personal/non-self)
- Lack of explicit self (personal/self) combined with some use of non-explicit self (non-personal/self).
- The key epistemology is that of mediated learning through explicit mention of literature, or non-explicit mention of self.

English Studies

- Few interpersonal themes overall (twice as many Textual and Experiential)
- Extensive referencing and quotation exists but little projection; reference to literature is integrated into main clause (use of numerical index system)
- The key epistemology is that of reflective reader where the writer's (i.e. student's) perspective on the text is the main proposition.

Engineering

- Relatively little use of projection overall and personal projection is virtually absent
- Few references and citations, but internal reference to primary data or proposition established in the student texts
- Some use of non-personal projection, including internal reference to tables, data, graphs, etc.
- The key epistemology is writer's (i.e. student's), backed by 'eternal truths', perspective on data.

It was stated in the introduction that novice writers may find that the expression of stance is a challenging task. Nevertheless, it seems that students follow their professional counterparts in attempting to express stance in accordance with some disciplinary standard. This is shown in the BAWE material studied here in that projecting clauses are used in distinctly different ways in the four disciplines.

As a continuation of the study reported so far we wanted to shift the focus slightly and concentrate on two broader disciplinary groupings, viz. Arts & Humanities (A & H) and Social Sciences (SS).

5. Projecting clauses and the expression of stance in two disciplinary groupings

The empirical base was expanded with one discipline from A & H and one from SS, again using 12 assignments from each (mainly essays). From A & H we chose History and from SS we chose Business in order to investigate further the discrepancy found between these two broad disciplinary groupings, as represented by English Studies and Anthropology in Section 4.3.[8] The distribution of projecting clauses in the expression of stance might reveal a more general tendency of broader disciplinary groupings rather than just differences between individual disciplines.

In a preliminary classification of interpersonal themes, the two A & H disciplines (English Studies vs. History) showed a discrepancy of 3.1 per 100 t-units, while the two SS disciplines (Anthropology vs. Business) showed a discrepancy of 5.5. These overall figures suggest that A & H and SS students do not follow broader disciplinary writing practices in their choice of interpersonal themes to express stance, corroborated to a large extent also by the breakdown given in Table 6.

Since the present study is mainly concerned with projecting clauses, the other interpersonal themes will be left for future research. However, it is worth noticing that there are interdisciplinary differences not only in the use of projecting clauses, but also in the use of e.g. interrogative/inversion and modal adjuncts.

Table 6. Distribution of interpersonal themes in A & H vs. SS per 100 t-units

	Arts & Humanities		Social Sciences	
	English Studies	History	Anthropology	Business
personal projecting clause	3.2	2.8	8.2	1.9
non-personal projecting clause	3.5	6.4	6.5	8.8
modal adjunct	2.9	1.7	2.9	0.8
interrogative/ inversion	0.4	2.0	0.7	1.0
imperative		0.2	0.1	0.4
Total	10	13.1	18.4	12.9

Table 6 shoes a clear discrepancy in the use of non-personal projecting clauses within A & H, and an even clearer discrepancy in the use of personal projecting clauses within SS. In the following, we will look at projecting clauses in more detail; Table 7 gives an overview.

Table 7. Distribution of projecting clauses in A & H vs. SS per 100 t-units

	Arts & Humanities		**Social Sciences**	
	English Studies	**History**[9]	**Anthropology**[10]	**Business**
Personal				
Non-self	2.7	2.4	7.7	1.5
Self	0.5	0.3	0.3	0.4
Non-personal				
Non-self	2.3	2.6	3.2	6.8
Self	1.3	3.8	3.2	2.0
Total	6.8	9.1	14.4	10.7

To take A & H first, English Studies and History students show similar writing practices in all types of projecting clauses except non-personal/self. History students seem to differ from English Studies students in that they establish stance, and thereby reveal their attitude towards the proposition, by frequently using a non-personal projecting device to hide their 'self' behind, e.g. example (6).

(6) *It is noteworthy that* criticisms of the Church went as far back as to the late 14th Century (the Lollards) … (BAWE 0019f)

The fact that the use of structures similar to the one found in example (6) is so much more frequently used by History students might indicate that we do not have a strong case for talking about A & H as a uniform discipline in the expression of stance.

In the previous section it was concluded that English Studies encourages the qualities of a reflective reader where the student's perspective on the text is the main proposition. History, although similar to English Studies, additionally puts weight on the student's personal attitude towards the proposition, albeit, in Hyland's (2005: 176) words, "disguising their involvement" by using the non-personal/self category.

In the Social Sciences, the picture is slightly different. While there is a great discrepancy in the use of personal projecting clauses overall between Anthropology and Business, it is mainly the difference in the personal/non-self category that is striking. In Section 4.4 it was seen that Anthropology students rely heavily on the literature as their point of departure, as reflected by the use of personal/non-self. This writing practice of making explicit mention of authors seems to be almost absent for the Business students.

Moving on to the non-personal projecting clauses, which in Table 6 did not look too different for the two SS disciplines, with 6.5 instances per 100 t-units for Anthropology and 8.8 for Business. However, with Table 7 we go into more detail and see that while there is an even distribution of non-self vs. self in Anthropology, Business students prefer a non-personal/non-self strategy as their point of departure, not making explicit reference to authors nor 'self', e.g. example (7).

(7) **The lack of integration between departments suggests that** Pluto may be viewed from a differentiation perspective, especially concerning the differences between departments. (BAWE 0169b)

This observation may point to the fact that Business students engage with their object of study in a very different way from the SS discipline it is compared with here. Business students seem to combine the two ways of mediating as suggested in Section 4.4. Either they have direct access to primary data or they approach their object of study through the literature. If anchored in the literature, they seem to build an argument in a different way from Anthropology students; Business students appear to be more of the reflective writer type, where their own perspective is given through a non-personal/non-self strategy. Anthropology students mainly have access to text books that reveal facts or opinions, and it is the expert authors (or other human 'authorities') that in the majority of cases are felt to be best suited as a point of departure to substantiate what follows in the main proposition, often including a quotation, e.g. example (8).

(8) **Radcliffe-Brown believes that** it is "*the affirmation of a bond of social solidarity between those taking part in it*" (Radcliffe-Brown, 1922: 245). (BAWE 3014a)

As was the case with A & H, SS does not appear as one uniform broad discipline in terms of projecting clauses and the expression of stance. More than anything, this study of two disciplines within A & H and SS confirms what was stated in the introduction, namely that although stance may be "one of the most challenging tasks that faces the apprentice writer" (Charles 2006: 514), writers with different disciplinary backgrounds attempt to highlight their own views and attitudes in accordance with the practices of the discipline they feel part of (Charles 2006; North 2003, 2005a, 2005b). Thus, in the material investigated so far, there is little to suggest that individual disciplines fall into broader categories when it comes to the use of projecting clauses to express attitudes.

6. Concluding remarks and further research

Peck MacDonald (1992: 538) states that it is easier for novice writers to make arguments with simple agents, such as "Children are attached to parents", than to make use of so-called 'epistemic' constructions, such as *The evidence suggests that...* . Although Peck MacDonald's classification system is not entirely matched with the category of projecting clauses, the findings presented here to some degree run counter to her statement that "'epistemic' sentence subjects might not be part of the ordinary repertoire of writers even well into the undergraduate years. The move into postgraduate work almost certainly involves new textual practices in some fields" (ibid.). The BAWE material quite clearly shows that undergraduate students are aware of such epistemic means. However, increased awareness in this area may take place during the course of the undergraduate years, and is an issue that may deserve further study.[11]

The material studied here was, with few exceptions, produced by native speakers (NS) of English, and there is nothing to suggest that the few non-native speakers (NNS) in the material studied here skew the results with regard to projecting clauses. However, it should be noticed that in a study of thematic choice and expressions of stance, Hasselgård (2009) found that there are differences in the way in which Norwegian (advanced) learners of English make use of theme position to express stance as compared to native speakers of English. Thus, a systematic comparison of NS vs. NNS in the use of projecting clauses is worth exploring further.

A systematic comparison between the BAWE data and professional writing in the same disciplines would also be an interesting area for future investigation. This would gain more insight into how students, both NS and NNS, are expected to position themselves in a given discipline.

> ... the writer of an academic paper (as of any other text) has a purpose in constructing her text, a purpose which is conveyed both by the choice of information that she presents and by the choice of the manner in which she presents it. To concentrate only on the information given – to take it at face value – would in many cases be to

> miss or misinterpret the purpose. Evaluation in text is the signalling of this purpose. (Thompson and Yiyun 1991: 367)

This investigation of interpersonal themes and the expression of author stance in student writing has shown that projecting clauses and related interpersonal metaphors of projection are very much part of the students' repertoire and that they use this device in different ways, and to varying degrees, depending on which discipline, rather than to which disciplinary grouping, they belong to. In this respect, the study sheds light on how key epistemologies of each discipline are followed by these novice writers.

Whilst English and History are part of the same broad disciplinary grouping of Arts & Humanities (Becher and Trowler 2001) this study indicates that there are key disciplinary differences in the way resources of authorial stance are used to frame the main propositions. English Studies students appear as reflective readers/writers where their own perspective is given in the main proposition (through non-self, both personal and non-personal). History students, on the other hand, are seen to diverge from this in that they in the majority of cases hide behind non-personal expressions, also non-personal self.

As regards the Social Sciences, Anthropology students follow the key epistemology of mediated learning through explicit mention of the literature (or, to some extent, non-explicit mention of self). For the other SS discipline studied here, Business, the picture is slightly different in that Business students rarely mention expert authors. They mediate either through primary data or the literature; if the latter, they build the argument in a different way compared to the Anthropology students. In fact, they appear as reflective writers hiding behind a non-personal/non-self strategy.

This study reveals that there exists no overarching strategy for broader disciplinary groupings in the use of projecting clauses. Rather, in this study students have been shown to make use of projecting clauses in accordance with the ideology of their discipline, either to explicitly take part in the evaluation of a proposition or to hide their involvement.

Notes

1 Originally presented at the BAAHE Conference, Leuven University, Belgium.

2 BAWE was developed at the Universities of Warwick, Reading and Oxford Brookes under the directorship of Hilary Nesi and Sheena Gardner (formerly of the Centre for Applied Linguistics [previously called CELTE], Warwick), Paul Thompson (Department of Applied Linguistics, Reading) and Paul Wickens (Westminster Institute of Education, Oxford Brookes), with funding from the ESRC (RES-000-23-0800), http://www.coventry.ac.uk/bawe

3 See Ebeling and Heuboeck (2007) for information on the encoding of the corpus.

4 The BAWE corpus files are available from the Oxford Text Archive (http://ota.ahds.ac.uk/). Online versions of the corpus available through: Coventry University (http://www.coventry.ac.uk/bawe), Sketch Engine (http://www.sketchengine.co.uk/).

5 The term 'ideational theme' refers to Halliday's topical theme; "we shall refer to this [the ideational element within the Theme] as the topical theme" (Halliday 1985: 54).

6 "Through projection, one clause is set up as a representation of the linguistic 'content' of another – either the content of a 'verbal' clause of saying or the content of a 'mental' clause of sensing" (Halliday and Matthiessen 2004: 443), i.e. the projecting clause projects the following proposition.

7 "The metaphoric strategy is to *upgrade* the interpersonal assessment from group rank to clause rank [...] There is thus a fundamental relationship between modal assessment, including modality, and projection. To bring this out, we can interpret modal assessment as interpersonal projection [...] Interpersonal projection always involves the speaker or addressee as 'projector': *I think*, *I say*, *do you think*, *do you say*. It is always implicit unless it is made explicit through grammatical metaphor" (Halliday and Matthiessen 2004: 626). And, as pointed out by Thompson (2004: 232-233), both explicit subjective modality, e.g. *I think*, and explicit objective modality, e.g. *it seems possible that*, are interpersonal metaphors.

8 In a paper presented at BAAL 2007, Wickens investigated more data within English Studies and Anthropology and found a similar discrepancy in the use of interpersonal themes to that found in section 4.3.

9 The figures for personal projecting clauses for History deviate slightly from the total given in Table 5, due to 0.1 examples per 100 t-units that we were unable to classify as either self or non-self.

10 The figures for projecting clauses for Anthropology deviate slightly from the total given in Table 5, due to 0.3 examples per 100 t-units that we were unable to classify as either self or non-self.

11 A pilot study showed individual differences in the development over the years rather than general tendencies from year 1 through 3 (Ebeling & Wickens 2006). More data, including assignments from more than 4 individual students, is needed to gain more information on this issue.

Corpus

The *British Academic Written English* corpus <http://www2.warwick.ac.uk/fac/soc/al/research/collect/bawe/>, accessed 15 December 2009. <http://www.coventry.ac.uk/bawe>, accessed 7 October 2011.

References

Becher, T. and P. R. Trowler (2001), *Academic Tribes and Territoties*. 2nd edition. Buckingham: Open University Press.

Biber, D. (2006), *University Language. A Corpus-based Study of Spoken and Written Registers*. Amsterdam and Philadelphia: John Benjamins.

Charles, M. (2006), 'The construction of Stance in reporting clauses: A cross-disciplinary study of theses', *Applied Linguistics*, 27(3): 492-518.

Ebeling, S. O. and A. Heuboeck (2007), 'Encoding document information in a corpus of student writing: the *British Academic Written English* corpus', *Corpora,* 2(2): 241-256.

Ebeling, S. O. and P. Wickens (2006), 'Author stance in theme position: variation across disciplines and years in a corpus of assessed student writing'. Paper presented at the *BAAHE Conference*, Leuven University, Belgium.

Forey, G. (2002), *Aspects of Theme and their Role in Workplace Texts*. Ph.D. Dissertation. Department of English Language, Faculty of Arts, University of Glasgow. Retrieved from <http://www.wagsoft.com/Systemics/Archive/ForeyThesis/Front.pdf>, accessed 7 October 2011.

Fries, P.H. (1994), 'On theme, rheme and discourse goals', in: M. Coulthard (ed.) *Advances in Written Text Analysis*. London and New York: Routledge. 229-249.

Halliday, M. A. K. (1985), *An Introduction to Functional Grammar*. London: Edward Arnold.

Halliday, M. A. K. (1994), *An Introduction to Functional Grammar*. 2nd edition. London: Arnold.

Halliday, M. A. K. and C. M. I. M. Matthiessen (2004), *An Introduction to Functional Grammar*. 3rd edition. London: Hodder Arnold.

Hasselgård, H. (2009), 'Thematic choice and expressions of stance in English argumentative texts by Norwegian learners', in: K. Aijmer (ed.) *Corpora and Language Teaching*. Amsterdam and Philadelphia: John Benjamins. 121-140.

Heuboeck, A., J. Holmes and H. Nesi (2007), *The BAWE Corpus Manual*. Available under 'BAWE documentation' at <http://wwwm.coventry.ac.uk/researchnet/BAWE/Documents/BAWEmanual%20v3.pdf>, accessed 7 October 2011.

Hunston, S. (1993). 'Projecting a Sub-Culture: The construction of shared worlds by projecting clauses in two registers', in: D. Graddol, L. Thompson and

M. Byram (eds.) *Language and Culture*. Clevedon: BAAL and Multilingual Matters. 98-112.

Hyland, K. (2002), 'Authority and invisibility: authorial identity in academic writing', *Journal of Pragmatics*, 34: 1091-1112.

Hyland, K. (2005), 'Stance and engagement: a model of interaction in academic discourse', *Discourse Studies*, 7(2): 173-192.

Laurillard, D. (1993). *Rethinking University Teaching - a Framework for the Effective Use of Educational Technology*. London: Routledge.

Mauranen, A. (1993). 'Theme and prospection in written discourse', in: M. Baker, G. Francis and E. Tognini-Bonelli (eds.) *Text and Technology. In Honour of John Sinclair*. Philadelphia and Amsterdam: John Benjamins Publishing Company. 95-114.

Nesi, H., S. Gardner, R. Forsyth, D. Hindle, P. Wickens, S. Ebeling, M. Leedham, P. Thompson and A. Heuboeck (2005), 'Towards the compilation of a corpus of assessed student writing: An account of work in progress', in: P. Danielsson and M. Wagenmakers (eds.) *Proceedings from The Corpus Linguistics Conference Series,* Vol. 1, no. 1, <http://www.birmingham.ac.uk/research/activity/corpus/publications/conference-archives/2005-conf-e-journal.aspx>, accessed 7 October 2011.

North, S. (2003), *Emergent Disciplinarity in an Interdisciplinary Course: Theme Use in Undergraduate Essays in the History of Science*. PhD Dissertation. The Open University.

North, S. (2005a), 'Disciplinary variation in the use of theme in undergraduate essays', *Applied Linguistics*, 26(3): 431-452.

North, S. (2005b), 'Different values, different skills? A comparison of essay writing by students from arts and science backgrounds', *Studies in Higher Education*, 30(5): 517-533.

Peck MacDonald, S. (1992), 'A method for analyzing sentence-level differences in disciplinary knowledge making', *Written Communication*, 9: 533-569.

Thompson, G. (2004) [2nd ed.], *Introducing Functional Grammar*. London: Arnold.

Thompson, G. and Y. Yiyun (1991), 'Evaluation in the reporting verbs used in academic papers', *Applied Linguisitcs*, 12(4): 365-382.

Wickens, P. (2001), *Computer Based Learning and Changing Legal Pedagogic Orders of Discourse in UK Higher Education: A Comparative Critical Discourse Analysis of the TLTP materials for Law*. PhD Dissertation, University of Warwick.

Through seen through the looking glass of translation equivalence: a proposed method for determining closeness of word senses

Thomas Egan

Hedmark University College

Abstract

This paper advances the hypothesis that translation equivalents may be employed to cast light on the semantic network of a lexeme in its original language. The lexeme investigated is through, *which is commonly taken to have the prototypical sense of 'entrance-traversal-exit'. Some recent research, however, has indicated that various instrumental senses are more common in actual usage. The particular question addressed in this paper is how the various senses of* through *are related to each other. The data consist of all 696 tokens of* through *in the English language original texts in the* English-Norwegian Parallel Corpus. *These are first sorted into various semantic classes using normal corpus linguistic methods. The translations into Norwegian of the various senses are then examined with an emphasis on the similarities and differences between them. The basic hypothesis is that the senses that are translated in similar ways in a particular language are felt to be more closely related by users of that language than senses that are translated in very different ways. Restricted as it is to translations into one language, the study does not contain enough data to test this hypothesis, but the evidence presented suggests that it may be worth exploring in greater detail.*

1. Introduction

This paper investigates the polysemous network of English *through*, as this is reflected in the various Norwegian translations of the form in the *English Norwegian Parallel Corpus* (ENPC). Methodologically, it differs from the Wordnet approach of Dyvik (1998, 2004) in that the translation equivalents are not employed in order to pin down the various senses of the English form. Rather these senses are established using normal corpus linguistic methods, with the translations then being used to throw light on the relationships between them. The basic hypothesis is that the senses that are translated in similar ways in a particular language are seen to be more closely related by users of that language than senses that are translated in very different ways. I return to this hypothesis in the next section, having first explained my reasons for choosing *through* as the object of the study. Section 3 maps out an overview of the various senses of *through* in present-day English, and Section 4 shows how these various senses are translated into Norwegian. Section 5 contains an attempt to illustrate a network for the various senses using the data in Section 4. Finally, Section 6 contains a summary and conclusion.

2. Why *through*?

Lee (2001) contains a case study of *through*, in which various senses are described as extensions from the central meaning of a path extending from one side of a container to another. This is referred to as the "basic, core meaning" (p. 49). According to Tyler and Evans (2003: 219) "the relation described by *through* describes a spatial relation in which a bounded LM [landmark] is transected by virtue of an entrance point and an exit point". In the non-technical language employed by Lindstromberg (1998: 31) the central meaning of *through* is said to be "in and out again". In the same vein the *Oxford English Dictionary* (OED) first definition includes the phrase: "From one end, side, or surface to the other or opposite end, side, or surface of (a body or a space) by passing within it; usually implying into, at one end, side, etc. and out of at the other." One might therefore conclude that this is the prototypical meaning of the preposition in present-day English. Neither Lee nor Lindstromberg, however, present any corpus data to support their analyses.

Gilquin and McMichael (2008) consider five different sorts of evidence bearing on the semantic structure of *through*, corpus evidence (from the spoken demographic part of the *British National Corpus* – BNC), evidence from language history (based on the OED), evidence from first language acquisition (from CHILDES), evidence from second language acquisition (from the *International Corpus of Learner English* – ICLE), and from an elicitation experiment. They were particularly interested in the incidence of the supposedly prototypical 'in-and-out again' physical sense compared to other senses. It transpired that it was only in the case of the spontaneous production experiment that the putative prototypical sense accounted for more than 50% of the tokens, 53% to be exact. In the spoken demographic component of the BNC, on the other hand, only 16% of tokens are prototypical, while for the second language learners represented in the ICLE corpora, the prototype only accounts for 10% of all tokens. Gilquin and McMichael conclude that the picture regarding the prototype status of the physical 'in-and-out again' sense is far from clear, with some types of evidence pointing to the 'entrance-traversal-exit' sense as the most salient one, whereas other types of evidence allot pride of place, at least in terms of frequency, to instrumental uses.

In this paper I approach the question of the semantic structure of *through* from another angle, basing my analysis on the translation equivalents of the form found in the *English-Norwegian Parallel Corpus* (ENPC) (see Johansson 2007).[1] Various studies have shown that translation corpora can reveal which lexemes or constructions in two or more languages are felt to correspond most closely to one another. (See, for example, Dyvik 1998, 2004; Noël 2003 and Johansson 2007.)

Such corpora provide us with access to the intuitive semantic judgments of competent speakers of both languages.

The hypothesis which constitutes the theoretical starting point for the present study claims that translation corpora can also offer us clues about the internal structure of the polysemous network of a lexeme.

Hypothesis: If in language E the various senses of lexeme *x*:

[a], [b], [c], [d], [e], [f], [g], [h], [i] ...

are often translated into language N by lexemes

p, p, p, q, p, r, r, s, t...

respectively, the senses usually translated by one and the same lexeme (or construction) are likely to be more closely related within the semantic network of lexeme *x* than those translated by different lexemes.

In this paper I am concerned with just one lexeme and its translation equivalents in just one language. Far more data than are adduced herein would be required to carry out a thorough evaluation of the hypothesis.

3. The various senses of *through*

There are in all 696 tokens of *through* in the English original texts in the *English–Norwegian Parallel Corpus*.[2] All of these tokens were extracted and classified into one of eight main categories. So as to remove the danger of the translations' influencing the classification, the latter were removed from the files before the process of semantic classification got underway.

Kennedy (1991) classifies the tokens of *through* which he extracted from the LOB corpus into six main classes, some of which are defined according to the means of progress along a path, such as "unimpeded motion" and "penetration of a barrier or obstacle", while others are defined according to the ontological domain of the state of affairs encoded ("time") or the semantics of the predication as a whole ("causation"). In my analysis I grouped together predications encoding physical motion in the space domain, irrespective of whether they involve unimpeded motion or penetration and distinguished these from predications involving non-physical domains, which may also encode both these forms of motion.

The eight categories employed in the present study are labeled *Space*, *Perception*, *Time*, *Channel*, *Means*, *Cause*, *Idiom* and *Other*. They will be illustrated in turn, starting with *Space* in (1) – (5). I will employ the standard cognitive grammar terms *trajector* and *landmark* for the item that is doing the traversing and the area traversed respectively (see, for instance, Langacker 2008: 70 for these terms). All tokens are from the *English-Norwegian Parallel Corpus*.

(1) They shot *through* an underpass. (AT1)
(2) I pushed *through* the water to the steps. (RDO1)
(3) She went *through* the house vacuuming clean carpets and dusting spotless tables – these were the testimony to her lost years. (GN1)
(4) Tom opened the front window and lifted him out *through* it. (MM1)
(5) The large black range stood solidly in an alcove in the back wall, a thick dark pipe curving its way upward *through* the ceiling. (MM1)

There are 292 (translated) tokens of the space type in the corpus. In these the space traversed by the trajector varies along various dimensions. It can be one-dimensional, like a point, two-dimensional like the window in (4) and the ceiling in (5) or three-dimensional like the underpass in (1), the water in (2) and the house in (3). Cross-cutting this distinction is the question of whether the space is bounded, and if so, on how many sides. Thus the underpass in (1) is bounded in two of three dimensions, the water in (2) in one of three and the ceiling in (5) in none of two. Then there is the question of whether the motion encoded involves an entrance and exit, which is the case in (1), (4) and (5), or merely movement within a container, as in (2) and (3). Moreover, (2) and (3) differ in that the former encodes linear motion from one side to another, while the latter encodes wandering on a path within a container without necessarily beginning at one side or ending up at the other. In short, space *through* predications may differ along many parameters. By lumping them together in a broad *space* category, one may risk missing out on potentially significant distinctions in terms of translation equivalents. However, if one begins to break them down into sub-classes where is one to stop? All 292 tokens differ in some respect. As Kennedy points out in connection with his own categories: “A more fine-grained analysis would have been possible, at a cost, however, of reduced reliability and probably of usefulness, since each use of a word is modified semantically, however slightly, by its own peculiar environment and the number of possible subcategories is thus potentially very large” (Kennedy 1991: 105). As I was primarily interested in the translation equivalents of the various types of *through* rather than of individual tokens, I chose to group them in rather coarsely defined categories.

The second largest class of *through* predications, with 101 tokens exemplified here by (6) - (9), encodes states of affairs involving perception.

(6) My dad said that it went that way because it got caught in a draught when Uncle Eddie was looking *through* a keyhole. (RDO1)
(7) He could see right *through* the fog. (ABR1)
(8) We roared *through* the gap in the hedge. (RDO1)
(9) His private parts showed *through* his underpants. (BO1)

Perception *through* resembles space *through* in that the landmark is physical and may be three-dimensional, as in (6) and (7) or two-dimensional, as in (8) and (9). It may also be bounded in all dimensions, as in (9), in two of three dimensions as in (6), in one of two as in (8) or be completely unbounded, as in (7). Tokens varying along these parameters have been conflated for the purposes of analysis into a single category, for the reasons advanced above in the case of *space* predications.

There are 46 tokens in which the landmark has temporal extension, as in (10) and (11).

(10) All *through* a wet and overcast afternoon, the French stalked anti-tank gun positions and machine-gunners through the suburban streets. (MH1)

(11) It was afternoon for hours and hours, *through* drinks and lunch and drinks again – all of which he waved away. (AT1)

In (10) and (11) the trajector is the state of affairs predicated in the main clause which is taken to last throughout the period in question. Thus in (10) it is the stalking of the French that lasts throughout the afternoon, while in (11) it is the afternoon that lasts throughout the drinks. Whether the landmark encodes activities such as drinking or eating lunch, as in (11), or the period of time is itself lexicalised, as in the case of 'afternoon' in (10), the sense is always internal to the container period, that is, the state of affairs is not encoded as beginning prior to the period denoted by the landmark, or as continuing after its conclusion. This does not, of course, mean that its continuation is excluded, merely that it is not implied by the temporal *through* construction. Note in this connection the temporal series sense which occurs in American English, as in 'Monday through Friday', which cannot be taken to include either the previous Sunday or the following Saturday.

The next class, which I have labeled 'channel', is represented by 33 tokens and comprises four sub-classes, *channel*, *medium*, *source* and *circumstance*, exemplified by (12) - (15) respectively.

(12) Thus he will say that God speaks to Abraham *through* an angel. (KAR1)

(13) He will see his father *through* his mother's eyes. (ROB1)

(14) He was well aware of Hamish McRory *through* the freemasonry of the rich, which overrides even politics. (RDA1)

(15) Even when British and American parachutists began to pour down *through* the darkness upon Normandy and the Cotentin peninsula, the German response was bewildered and uncertain. (MH1)

(12) and (13) are quite similar in meaning. However, they differ in that the landmark in (12) may be considered a channel pure and simple, in so far as the angel may not be expected to influence the content of the word of God. In (13), on the other hand, which I have labelled 'medium', the landmark exerts an influence on the subject's perception of his father. Whereas (12) is metaphorically extended from the space sense, (13) is a metaphorical extension from the perception sense.

(14) is very similar to (12) and (13). I have, however, chosen to label it 'source' rather than 'channel' or 'medium', since the freemasonry of the rich represents the source of the subject's knowledge of Hamish McRory. (15) is less similar to the other three than they are to one another. It is one of only three tokens encoding physical, rather than metaphorical, circumstance.[3] Tokens encoding metaphorical circumstance were classified as 'other' and one could make a good case for including the three tokens encoding physical circumstance with these. I decided against doing so because of the physical nature of the landmark, which resembles to some extent the channel sense in (12).

The fifth class of *through* predications I have termed 'means' and it includes tokens encoding both *means* as in (16) and *instrument* as in (17).

(16) Where these deficits were financed *through* resort to the central bank and the printing of more money, the inflationary potential was greatest. (CS1)

(17) He would go on now for weeks, working layer on layer, attempting *through* the medium of oils to build and depict the complexity of the human personality. (MW1)

There are 35 tokens of this type in the corpus and there are 38 'cause' tokens, which I have subdivided into *reason* as in (18), *enablement* as in (19) and *causation* as in (20).

(18) In "The Raven" (Grimm brothers) a young girl changes into a raven when her mother objects to her behavior, and remains so enchanted for years; in the "Six Swans," six young boys turn into swans when the father, *through* his cowardice, opens the house to evil, and the boys remain enchanted for years. (ROB1)

(19) *Through* hunting parties, in work that men did together in farms and cottages, and *through* local sports, older men spent much time with younger men and brought knowledge of male spirit and soul to them. (ROB1)

(20) No other city has this particular smell: stone worn smooth *through* contact with people, for centuries on end. (ABR1)

In (18) the father's cowardice is not the cause of his opening the door, but it is the reason why he does so. In (19) the hunting parties and local sports are not the cause of the of the older and younger men's spending time together, nor, strictly speaking, are they the reason for this. They do, however, facilitate their spending this time together and it is for this reason that I have labeled tokens like (19) as 'enablement'. Finally, in (20) the landmark is the cause of the wearing smooth of the stone.

The seventh class, labeled 'idioms', contains 75 tokens in which *through* occurs as part of a lexicalized multi-word verb. Typical examples are (21) and (22).

(21) Before mating takes place male and female birds usually *go through* a period of courtship. (ML1)

(22) The Union shall provide itself with the means necessary to attain its objectives and *carry through* its policies. (MAAS1)

Multi-word verbs containing *through* may be more or less transparent in meaning. At one extreme are prepositional verbs like *go through* in (21) where *through* bears its normal sense in relation to the temporal landmark. Very different is the phrasal verb *carry through* in (22), in which it is the landmark that is actually encoded as passing along an understood and unexpressed path towards the goal of realisation. Despite the differences between them, all lexicalised multi-word verbs were classed as 'idiom'.

Broad as some of them are, these seven categories cannot accommodate all 671 translated tokens. It was therefore necessary to establish a category for residual tokens, 51 in number, which I labeled 'other'. (23) - (26) exemplify this residual category.

(23) In these gloomy surroundings I stumbled *through* my explanation. (CSA1)

(24) With him to initiate me into the joys of rustic pursuits and Monsieur Menicucci in charge of more scientific matters, all I needed now was a navigator to steer me *through* the murky waters of French bureaucracy, which in its manifold subtleties and inconveniences can transform a molehill of activity into a mountain of frustration. (PM1)

(25) They range from simple, single celled animals, *through* more advanced many celled animals, such as sponges, corals and worms to fairly complex animals, such as insects, spiders and molluscs. (ML1)

(26) Briefly, in its headlong flight *through* the ranges of chemical and physical states, it entered a stage favorable for life. (JL1)

(23) contains a non-lexicalised multi-word verb. Unlike the lexicalised 'stumble upon', for instance, it is completely transparent, with *stumble* being metaphorically extended from the domain of walking to that of talking, and *through* contributing the sense of progression along a path. In (24) *through* again encodes movement along a path, and again a metaphorical extension is involved, from the domain of physical motion to that of a sea of red tape. (25) and (26) encode yet another sort of metaphorical extension, this time from the physical domain to the conceptual domain of scales and clines. In (25) the various sorts of creatures and in (26) the various stages of development comprise a cline, which the human perceiver can scan in both directions. (23) - (26) all involve metaphorical extensions of various sorts. This category might therefore have been labeled 'various metaphorical', instead of 'other'. However, metaphor and/or metonymy are involved in many of the other senses, so it would be misleading to privilege this category by employing the term 'metaphorical' in its label. In the next section I examine how the eight categories in the present study are translated into Norwegian.

4. Translations of *through* in the *English-Norwegian Parallel Corpus*

The eight senses of *through* are translated in Norwegian in three main ways, either using the Norwegian preposition *gjennom*, the equivalent given first in all bilingual dictionaries, by using another preposition, or by means of a construction not containing a preposition. There are 25 tokens in which the translator has omitted to translate the whole predication containing *through*. Setting these aside, we are left with 671 tokens, 394 of which are translated by *gjennom* (or the variant *igjennom*), 185 by another preposition and 92 using a divergent construction.

The preposition *gjennom* accounts for more than half of the Norwegian translations of *through*. If one were to ask a Norwegian speaker of English for the Norwegian equivalent of *through*, they would almost certainly reply *gjennom*. The first definition of *gjennom* in *Norsk Ordbok*, the closest Norwegian equivalent to the OED, is: "used about a movement or something perceived as motion which takes place in (within, surrounded by) that which is encoded by the landmark from one end or side all the way to the other, containing the whole landmark from start to finish; (in) from the one side or end and (out) to the other" (Vikør 2002, my translation). This definition is very similar to the standard definitions of *through* referred to in Section 2. It thus comes as no surprise to find that *gjennom* is used to translate tokens belonging to all eight classes of *through*.

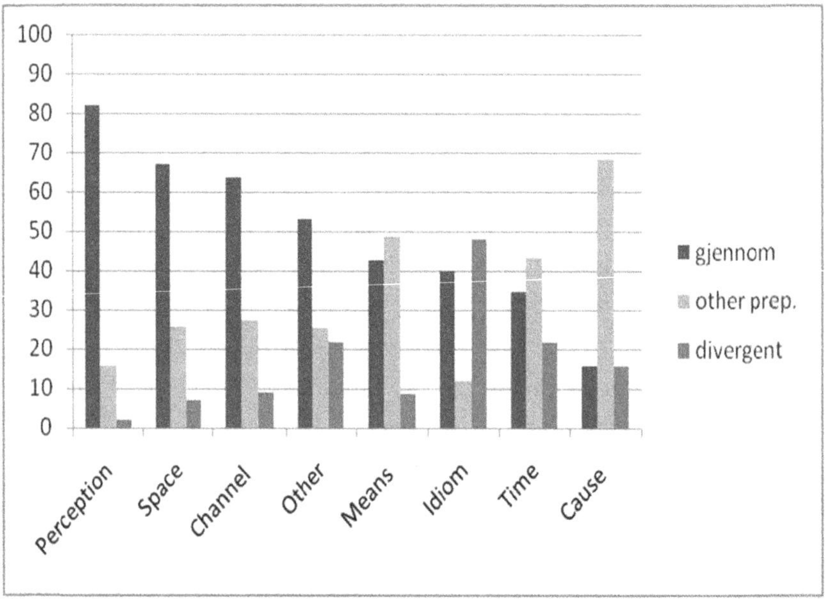

Figure 1. Translation of the various senses of *through* in ENPC by *gjennom*, another preposition, or divergent forms (%)

As shown in Figure 1, *gjennom* is used to translate 80% of the perception tokens. It is somewhat less frequent as a translation of the space sense, accounting for just over 60% of the tokens. The channel and 'other' senses are also translated by *gjennom* more than half the time. *Gjennom* accounted for just over 40% of the means tokens, and almost 40% of the idiom tokens. The time sense is translated by *gjennom* in 30% of all instances. Finally, the cause sense is the least likely to be translated by *gjennom*, with just 15% of tokens represented by that form.

Before moving on to look at other prepositions used to translate *through*, we should consider the possible influence of translation effects on our data, in particular the question of whether *gjennom* is likely to be overrepresented, given its similarity to *through* in so many contexts. If, however, *gjennom* is overused by the translators, there is no reason to suspect that this overuse is peculiar to one particular semantic class. Moreover, if it were to be confined to one particular class, this would in itself constitute a difference that may reflect a difference in the semantic network of *through* as perceived by the translators. As the focus of this paper is on the similarities and differences between the translations of the various classes, the possibility of the overuse of one particular translation equivalent can have no substantive influence on the conclusions reached.

I turn now to other prepositions used to translate *through* in the ENPC. By far the most common of these is *i*, the Norwegian equivalent of *in*, which is used for 52 tokens belonging to six of the eight classes, the exceptions being idiom and channel. If the schematic sense of *through* signals a passage through a container, the trajector must necessarily spend a certain portion of time within that container. The translator who employs *i* foregrounds the fact of this temporary containment, backgrounding the motion aspect. It is possible that in the channel sense the entrance and exit aspects are so salient that they resist this form of backgrounding. (27) - (32) illustrate the six senses that are translated by *i*.

(27) We cut roads *through* the nettles. (RDO1) … *i brenneslene*...

(28) One day I was looking *through* a low-power binocular microscope at … (CSA1) … *i et svakt dobbeltmikroskop*...

(29) All *through* the gloomiest March and April in years, I was cooking for three households ... (JSM1) ... *i hele mars og april*...

(30) It was pretty clear that John Cook had gained, *through* dint of sweat equity, a share in the Davis farm, and when Edith turned sixteen, John, thirty-three by then, married her. (JSM1) ... *i sitt ansikts sved*…

(31) She had been kind *through* inadvertence, *through* absent-mindedness.... (AB1) …*I distraksjon*...

(32) It also circulates widely *through* the animal kingdom. (SJG1) …*i store deler av dyreriket*...

In (27), which exemplifies the space sense, the construction of pathways *through* the nettles obviously involves construction *in* the nettles, and it is this perspective that is taken by the Norwegian translator, and indeed the Norwegian language. In the perception sense illustrated in (28) Norwegian profiles a microscope as a container and focuses on the picture which appears in the lens rather than the fact that this picture travels up the stem of the microscope. The time sense, illustrated in (29), does not involve movement into and out of the period in question. Confined as it is to the period encompassed by the two months, it lends itself readily to being encoded by the Norwegian equivalent of *in*. In (30), which instantiates the means sense, the translator makes use of the Norwegian phrase that corresponds to the English *by the sweat of their brow*. (31) exemplifies the enablement subtype of the cause sense. The Norwegian translator views the inadvertence and absent-mindedness as states in which the subject found herself on the occasion of her displaying kindness. Finally, the 'other' sense in (32) resembles the time sense in (29) insofar as the whole predication is confined to the animal kingdom – there is no hint of entrance and exit. (32) is a metaphorical extension of the 'around about in' space sense of *through*, which we encountered in (3).

No other single preposition approaches *i* in frequency as an alternative to *gjennom*. Two prepositions occur 13 times. These are *mellom*, the Norwegian equivalent of *between*, and *over*, the Norwegian equivalent of *across*. (33) – (35) illustrate tokens translated by *mellom*.

(33) Diana picked her way *through* the women and answered her front door. (ST1) … *mellom kvinnene* …
(34) The skyline is ever changing, though familiar landmarks like St Paul's Cathedral, the Bank of England and the Old Bailey are still distinguishable *through* the cranes. (SUG1) ... *mellom kranene* ...
(35) "Every single car that comes *through* my hands gets the treatment," the father said. (RD1) … *mellom hendene* ...

(33), (34) and (35) instantiate the space, perception and channel senses of *through* respectively. In each case the landmark is a plural countable. While English can profile each of these landmarks as a mass, Norwegian cannot readily do so. Note that one could employ *between* in English in both (33) and (34) with little change in meaning. The women in (33) and the cranes in (34) might appear more individuated if we were to use *between*, but the extent of this perceived change probably depends on the individual language user. (35) differs from (33) and (34), both in the fact that only two entities are involved and insofar as these two are often conceived of as functioning as a unit. *Between* could not replace *through* in English here. In fact both the English form and its Norwegian translation equivalent may be viewed as stock phrases.

The space and perception senses of *through* are also both represented among the tokens that may be translated by *over*, as in (36) and (37). The same preposition is used to translate some idioms, including 'put x through' as in (38).

(36) He said he felt wealthy when he walked *through* the marketplace and took count of all of the things he saw there that he knew he could live without. (JH1) …*over torget*...

(37) The morgue attendant's voice reached us *through* the intercom. (SG1) *...over interkommen...*

(38) "Put him *through*, Jane. (MW1) ... *"Sett ham over...*

The Norwegian preposition *over* overlaps in sense with three English prepositions, *over*, *across* and *above*. In (36) it corresponds to English *across*. For Norwegian speakers marketplaces are two dimensional spaces that one moves across rather than through. In (37) it corresponds to English *over*. In fact it would be perfectly idiomatic to say 'over the intercom' in English.[4] The English idiom in (38) construes the state of affairs as involving an extension from the secretary to her boss, along which the caller moves in order to speak to the latter. In Norwegian the caller is metaphorically lifted up, as it were, from the secretary and deposited with the boss after having traversed the intervening space.

We have now looked at the three most common propositions other than *gjennom* used to translate *through*. Other prepositions utilised by translators, with their closest English counterparts, include, in declining order of frequency, *ved* (by), *til* (to), *fra* (from), *bak* (behind), *forbi* (past), *med* (with), *på* (on), *via* (via) and *under* (under/during). Figure 1 shows that it is the cause, means and temporal senses of *through* that are most likely to be translated by a preposition other than *gjennom*.

The third type of translation option involves the use of a divergent construction, in this case one not containing a preposition or particle. Idiomatic *through* stands out as the sense most likely to be translated using a divergent construction. (39) - (42) are typical examples.

(39) Oh, I did my bit, suggested she *talk it through* with you, suggested she talk it through with a counsellor, but I might have been pissing in the wind for all the good it did. (MW1) *...at hun snakket med deg om det...* (= *she talked to you about it*)

(40) Aunt's kindness *showed through* in the fact that she had not noticed this, or had not objected to it if she had noticed it. (AB1) *...Tante viste sin vennlighet* (= *Aunt showed her kindness*)

(41) I *put a call through* to the Santa Teresa Police Department and asked to be connected to Sergeant Robb. (SG1) *...Jeg ringte ...* (= *I rang*)

(42) The veld had been fired to let the new growth *come through*, the sun burned off the night's frost, vaporized as a cool zest on the smell of ashes. (NG1) *...for å gi plass til det nye gresset...* (= *to leave room for the new grass*)

Although Norwegian does have quite a few multi-word verbs, they are not nearly as common as in English. There are a few cases of multi-word verbs in both languages where both verb and preposition correspond, as in *go through/gå gjennom*, and others where the corresponding verb occurs with a different particle, as in *put through/sett over* in (38). In more than 50% of the cases, however, the translator resorts to a construction without a multi-word verb. One option, chosen by the translators of (39) and (40), is to employ a verb corresponding to the lexical head of the English multi-word verb. In both cases something is lost, or added, in the process of translation. In (39) the Norwegian translation does not convey the element of perfectivity in the English original. If you talk something through you cover the ground in a more comprehensive manner than if you simply talk about it. In (40) the choice in the translation of subject position for the possessor in the trajector and object position for the possessed, lends the former a connotation of agentivity absent from the English original. Less distortion is arguably involved in (41) in which *I rang* makes for a very close paraphrase of *I put a call through*, only differing slightly in register. Finally, in (42) the translator has chosen to encode the English trajector in a prepositional phrase, as in (39), but the verb, too, is changed in this case.

22% of tokens encoding the time sense of *through* are translated by means of divergent constructions. While Norwegian can use *gjennom* to translate temporal *through*, especially when the landmark is a plural countable, it often profiles a period of time as a container for the trajector, rather than a path along which the trajector moves. The only other sense translated by divergent constructions in more than 20% of instances is the 'other' sense.

Figure 1 contains percentages for the three translation options of each of the eight senses of *through*, in descending order of preference for the maximally convergent option, *gjennom*. A quick glance at the figure should suffice to conclude that some senses, such as space and channel, are translated in quite similar fashion, while others, such as perception and cause, differ greatly in this respect. In the next section I will discuss whether we can draw any conclusions about the semantic structure of *through* on the basis of these similarities and differences.

5. A semantic network for *through*

Before embarking on a discussion of whether we can draw any conclusions about *through* from the similarities and differences of the translations of the various senses shown in Figure 1, we must establish which of these differences are statistically significant. Table 1 contains details of chi-squares for all 28 combinations of two of the eight senses. It shows that there are significant differences in mode of translation between the perception sense and the other seven senses. The space and channel senses are most similar to perception, but there is still a significant difference at the p=0.05 (although not the p=0.01) level between the way they are translated and the way perception tokens are translated. The cause and idiom senses resembles the perception sense in having no non-significant counterparts at p=0.05. The space sense is significantly different to all senses other than channel. Translations of the time sense resemble those of 'other' and means, while, the channel, 'other', and means senses all show non-significant differences with three of the other senses.

Table 1. Chi-square values with 2 degrees of freedom for 3 sorts of translation of all 8 subtypes of *through*. Figures in italics are not significant at $p = 0.05$.

	Perception	Space	Channel	Other	Means	Idiom	Time	Cause
Perception		9.0	6.2	20.9	20.1	54.6	35.5	53.4
Space	9.0		*0.2*	11.0	8.8	76.0	20.3	37.8
Channel	6.2	*0.2*		*2.3*	*3.4*	15.5	6.7	17.3
Other	20.9	11.0	*2.3*		*5.6*	10.0	*4.1*	17.6
Means	20.1	8.8	*34*	*5.6*		24.0	*2.6*	6.6
Idiom	54.6	76.0	15.5	10.0	24.0		17.2	37.6
Time	35.5	20.3	6.7	*4.1*	*2.6*	17.2		7.4
Cause	53.4	37.8	17.3	17.6	6.6	37.6	7.4	

Figure 2 is an attempt to convey in a network the resemblance between senses in Table 1.

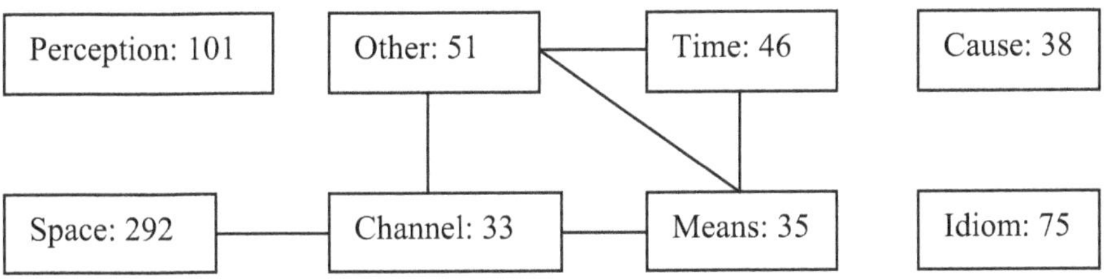

Figure 2. A possible network for *through* as reflected in translations into Norwegian, with the number of tokens of each sense in the ENPC. The solid lines mean 'no significant difference in form of translation at the level of p=0.05'.

Figure 2 illustrates a network of the various senses of English *through* as reflected in Norwegian translations. More accurately, it represents a network of similarities and differences between the way *throughness* is encoded in English and Norwegian. No link is shown between the perception, cause and idiom senses and the other five senses, as they differ from all of these at the level of p=0.05. If we were to apply the more stringent criterion for significance of p=0.01, however, perception would not be significantly different from channel and space, and cause from time and means. These similarities motivate their placement at the two sides of the figure. Idiom would, however, remain significantly different from all other senses.

According to the hypothesis in Section 2, the data in Table 1 should tell us something about the semantic structure of *through* in English. If we take Figure 2 at its face value, what can we conclude about *through*? In the first place we may note that the weightiest of the senses in terms of numbers of tokens, the space sense, does not occupy a central position in the network. Space may be indistinguishable from channel, but the degree of difference between it and the other six senses is in each case statistically significant. Note, in particular, the distance in the diagram between space and time. It is a commonplace for linguists to speak of semantic extensions from the domain of space to the domain of time. Figure 2 indicates that this form of reasoning may be a bit simplistic, at least as far as *through* is concerned. At the very least we can conclude that metaphorical extensions from space to time of schematic *throughness*, while they may conceivably be direct, are more idiosyncratic for the two languages in this study than extensions from space to channel, or from channel to 'other'. Figure 2 appears to indicate that space is first extended to channel, and only to time by way of either means or 'other', or both of these. It would be very interesting in this connection to trace the historical evolution of the various senses. Unfortunately, as is pointed out by Gilquin and McMichael (2008), all the main senses were already to be found in Old English.

6. Summary and conclusion

This paper has dealt with the semantic structure of *through* as this is reflected in Norwegian translation equivalents. A hypothesis about the possibility of using translation equivalents to cast light on the semantic network of a lexeme was presented in Section 2. Restricted as it is to translations into one language, the study did not contain enough data to test the hypothesis, but the evidence of Figure 2 suggests that it may be worth exploring in greater detail.

Figure 2 illustrates a network of the various senses of English *through* as reflected in Norwegian translations. Such semantic networks are generally sketched on the basis of introspection pure and simple or by using a feature matrix. Figure 2 has the advantage of having been generated from the data in Table 1, which in turn are derived from the texts of dozens of translators. It may have the drawback of being influenced in its composition by the semantic network of *thoroughness* in Norwegian. However, the effect of this drawback can be mitigated by incorporating into the model translations of *through* into other languages. Moreover, there is no reason the translations need be of the same texts. One could generate tables like Table 1 and diagrams like Figure 2 using translations of different English texts. The greater the resemblance between the resulting networks, the greater the likelihood that they would reflect the actual semantic network of *through* in English.

Notes

1 The corpus contains both English texts translated into Norwegian and Norwegian texts translated into English. Only the former type were accessed for this study.

2 The total of 696 tokens includes both prepositions and particles. In this paper I use 'preposition' as the default term and do not distinguish between the various syntactic realisations of either prepositions or particles. Thus the study includes all cases where *through* occurs as part of a prepositional or phrasal verb. 25 tokens will not be discussed in this paper as they occur in phrases which are not translated.

3 The other two are both from the same text. "They ran *through* pitch darkness, *through* silence and mists [….]" (BO1).

4 A Google search returned 90 instances of *over the intercom* for every token of *through the intercom*.

Corpus

English-Norwegian Parallel Corpus:
<http://www.hf.uio.no/ilos/english/services/omc/enpc/>

References

Dyvik, H. (1998), 'A translational basis for semantics', in: S. Johansson and S. Oksefjell (eds.) *Corpora and Cross-linguistic Research: Theory, Method, and Case Studies*. Amsterdam: Rodopi. 51-86.

Dyvik, H. (2004), 'Translations as semantic mirrors: from parallel corpus to Wordnet', in: K. Aijmer and B. Altenberg (eds.) *Advances in Corpus Linguistics: Papers from the 23rd International Conference on English Language Research on Computerized Corpora (ICAME 23), Göteborg 22-26 May 2002*. Amsterdam: Rodopi. 313-326.

Gilquin, G., and A. McMichael (2008), 'Measures of prototypicality: convergence or divergence? The case of *through*'. Paper presented at the *Third International Conference of the German Cognitive Linguistics Association*, University of Leipzig, 25-27 September 2008.

Johansson, S. (2007), *Seeing through Multilingual Corpora: On the Use of Corpora in Contrastive Studies*. Amsterdam: John Benjamins.

Kennedy, G. (1991), '*Between* and *through*: The company they keep and the functions they serve', in: K. Aijmer, J. Svartvik & B. Altenberg (eds.) *English Corpus Linguistics: Studies in Honour of Jan Svartvik*. London: Longman. 95-110.

Langacker, R. W. (2008), *Cognitive Grammar: A Basic Introduction*. Oxford: Oxford University Press.
Lee, D. (2001), *Cognitive Linguistics: An Introduction*. Oxford: Oxford University Press.
Lindstromberg, S. (1998), *English Prepositions Explained*. Amsterdam: John Benjamins.
Noël, D. (2003), 'Translations as evidence for semantics: an illustration'. *Linguistics 41*(4), 757-785.
OED. (1994), *The Oxford English Dictionary: On Compact Disc*. Oxford: Oxford University Press.
Tyler, A. and Evans, V. (2003), *The Semantics of English Prepositions: Spatial Scenes, Embodied Meaning and Cognition*. Cambridge: Cambridge University Press.
Vikør, L. S. (ed.) (2002), *Norsk Ordbok, Band IV* (Vol. IV). Oslo: Det Norske Samlaget.

Semantic patterns of *HAVE been to V*: Corpus data and elicited data

Sara Gesuato

University of Padua

Abstract

HAVE been to V *metaphorically represents the performance of a recent past event ('having just V-ed') as round-trip motion to/from a destination (e.g.* she has been to look at the garden*). Data from seven corpora reveals that the construction is used to denote deliberate, goal-oriented, short-duration activities (e.g.* buy a dress, pick up a chap*), that it often expresses the meanings of 'visually perceiving/experiencing (entertaining) events' (e.g.* watch quite a few games*) or 'paying a visit' (e.g.* meet his bankers*), and that it strongly correlates with the verb* see. *Questionnaire data collected from 11 native English speakers shows that the construction typically represents errands (e.g.* look for him; get a hair cut*) – possibly involving exchanges of information or goods/services (e.g.* ask about that trip to Naples; book our seats*) – and generally, but not systematically, prefers the encoding of deliberate telic events (e.g.* say a prayer*). The findings suggest that* HAVE been to V *expresses the general notion of 'coming back from getting something done at a previous location', since it is associated with contexts relevant to the representation of errands. Also, its frequent encoding of the specific notions of 'visiting someone' or 'watching something (for fun)' can be motivated with reference to the errand-like nature of these activities, whose performance requires – by default – a temporary change of location. Therefore, the elicited data hints at the wide semantic scope of the construction, while the corpus data highlights its prototypical meaning.*

1. Introduction

The temporal and aspectual notions involved, or invoked, in the representation of events (e.g. beginning/inception, end/completion/outcome, continuation/duration, interruption, resumption) are fairly abstract concepts. The various stages that a process goes through cannot be directly grasped through the senses, but can only be conceptually abstracted from our experience of phenomena. That is, they can be defined and identified once phenomena have been mentally categorized as instances of given events.

As a result of their relatively abstract nature, the temporal-aspectual properties of "happenings" may need to be understood indirectly, that is, by resorting to the experientially concrete domain of space (cf. Heine et al. 1991). Indeed, verbs that express such notions as concrete motion or location relative to a place may be used for the rendering of metaphorical sources, destinations, locations, goals and causes. The figurative use of such verbs may occur whether these are accompanied by nominal or verbal complementation, and always involves a re-interpretation of the temporal notion of (the unfolding of) an event in the spatial terms of a path or location (McIntyre 2001: 50); e.g.:

(1) This *leads* me *to the conclusion* that (BoE: N0000000788)[1]
(2) if you *get to the stage* where you are panicking (BoE: N2000951216)
(3) They've let the ground *go to ruin* in recent years (BoE: N9119980511)
(4) there isn't any other business can I *bring* the meeting *to a close* (BoE: S0000000015)
(5) I'll never *get to the stage* where that doesn't give me goose bumps (BoE: N0000000571)
(6) I *got to know* him quite well (BoE: N5000950730)
(7) He *was in the process of lodging* a complaint with the ship's master (BoE: N5000950823)
(8) I *am through with the whole thing* now, and glad of it (BoE: B9000001423)
(9) The 1994 dividend *went to fund* important church work (BoE: N5000950325)
(10) I *came to realize* that to get ahead in America, you couldn't depend on others (BoE: B0000001320)
(11) Devotion to their gods *led* them *to build* huge platforms of earth (BoE: N2000960203)
(12) If you could *bring* yourself *to tell* me (BoE: B0000000906)
(13) US and Chinese officials *are to meet* in Beijing (BoE: N5000950118)
(14) I think you have a right to be deeply concerned by what I *am about to tell* you (BoE: E9000000110)
(15) A refreshed ANDREW WEATHERALL *is* just *back from wowing* them in New Zealand (original capitalization; BoE: N0000000710)

The analogical association set up between the spatial domain and the temporal/aspectual domain in examples such as those above may be originally motivated by the need to simultaneously express the temporal and spatial facets characterizing a given event.[2] Later, however, the temporal-spatial ties established may be loosened, so that the verbal constructions involved can freely encode temporal/aspectual notions independently of whether any idea of physical location or motion is involved.[3] That is, a new meaning develops, at the expense of the old one, the former having a direct bearing on the realization of a category in the structure of the language (see, for instance, the historical development of present-day English aspectualizers from original motion verbs; Brinton 1988).

The change whereby words or constructions come to serve or develop grammatical functions is commonly referred to as grammaticalization (Hopper and Traugott 2003: xv, 231). It typically involves a number of related processes such as semantic weakening, category shifting and the loss of autonomous lexical meaning (Meillet 1912: 385; Kuryłowicz 1975 [1965]: 52; Roberts and Roussou 1999).[4] Grammaticalization can be brought about by metaphorical transfer (e.g. Sweetser 1990), metonymic transfer (e.g. Bybee 1988), reanalysis (e.g. Heine et al. 1991), analogy (e.g. Hopper and Traugott 2003), and context-induced, pragmatic inferences such as conversational implicature (e.g. Traugott and König 1991; Traugott 1996; Aijmer 2004: 72). A common cross-linguistic manifestation of grammaticalization is the development of specialized grammatical meanings (e.g. resultativity, futurity) in verbal constructions that literally encode spatial concepts (e.g. location, motion, arrival, departure) as a result of metaphorical re-interpretation (Bourdin 2002: 181). In French, for example, the temporal notions of future and past can be rendered through the constructions *aller à* plus infinitive and *venir de* plus infinitive, respectively. Similarly, in English, the catenative construction *be going to V* is a conventionalized expression of futurity, while the formula *be in the middle of V-ing* expresses the notion of event (currently) in progress, and the catenative construction *come to V* encodes the notion of achievement of an end-result or target state. Finally, in Italian, the catenative construction *essere stato a* (lit. 'have been at') plus infinitive encodes the notion of recent past (or duration of a recent past event),[5] the construction *stare per* (lit. 'to be/stand for') plus infinitive expresses the meaning of imminent inception, *andare a* (lit. 'to go to') plus infinitive may encode either goal-oriented motion or the future projection of an event, while *giungere/arrivare a* (lit. 'to arrive at') plus infinitive encodes the resultative notion of achievement of an outcome or target state.

Grammaticalization is a dynamic phenomenon that takes place in stages, and its evolution is marked by the interplay of various processes (Heine et al. 1991: 15-16, 212-215; Hopper 1991: 22; Lichtenbeck 1991: 76-77; Lehmann 1995 [1982]: 12-14, 25, 164; Diewald 2002: 103-104; Heine 2002: 84-85; Hopper and Traugott 2003: 11-12, 93; van Gelderen 2004: 5, 7). It is a complex, multi-parameter mechanism (Lehmann 1995 [1982]: 121-124), whose causal relationship with the concomitant phenomena of frequency and fusion, as either a motivating or consequential factor, is not clear (Krug 2000: 177; cf. Mair 2004), and whose intricacies need to be explored also by taking into consideration external factors such as language contact and language variety specific uses (Herlin and Kotilainen 2004: 263-264). The degree of grammaticalization of a given linguistic expression (i.e. the extent to which it is integrated into the system of the language) is not predictable (Hopper and Traugott 2003: 31 and 97, 100, 109, 113, 116-117, 120-122 for examples): it varies not only across languages and language varieties (see Krug [2000] on emerging English modals, Miller [2004] on perfect and resultative constructions, Nevalainen [2004] on adverbialization, and van Gelderen [2004] on cross-clausal grammaticalization), but also "depending on which parts of grammar are involved" (Heine et al. 1991: 244).

Some expressions are so well integrated into the grammatical system of a language that their original literal meaning is virtually inaccessible to speakers (e.g. *be going to V*; see Chafe 2002: 409; Mair 2004: 127; contra Miller 2004:

245, note 3).[6] Others, instead, may be used both literally and figuratively, albeit in different contexts, or may be compatible with both a literal and a metaphorical reading in similar contexts (e.g. Hopper's [1991: 22] notion of persistence, Heine et al.'s [1991: 231, 251] notion of persistence, and Hopper and Traugott's [2003: 118-122] notion of divergence; e.g. Miller [2004] on resultative constructions; Gesuato [2009a] on *come to V*; Gesuato [2009b] on *go to V*). Still others may be in the infancy of their grammaticalization process, or their figurative/grammatical use may be limited to specific semantic contexts. This appears to be the case with *HAVE been to V*.

2. *HAVE been to V*

When followed by a noun phrase denoting a place, *HAVE been to* literally expresses the notion of a two-way movement to and from a given location. It can be paraphrased as 'having gone to a place and having now come back from it'. As a case in point, consider example (16):

(16) We expect every child who has been to Kids Campus and leaves for school to be able to read a little, write a bit and do simple arithmetic (BoE: E0000001888)

Here, certain children went to Kids Campus, spent some time there, and have since left that location. Huddleston and Pullum (2002: 114) generically define this use "motional ***be***", saying that it is restricted to "the past participle form after perfect ***have***" (original emphases).

HAVE been to retains its literal meaning also when accompanied by a noun phrase denoting an event, rather than its location, such as *concert, funeral, interview, match, meeting, play, reunion, wedding* or *workshop*; typical examples are shown in (17) to (19):

(17) We'd not been to a concert for a bit (BoE: S9000001375)
(18) Er I've been to a council meeting tonight (BoE: S0000000060)
(19) My friend from work said she'd never been to a happier wedding (BoE: N0000000806)

In such cases, the nominal complementation of *HAVE been to* encodes an event, which stands for the location in which it takes place, and this can be considered a metaphorical destination of the movement expressed by *HAVE been to*. This use is also discussed by Biber et al. (1999: 464), who describe it as "similar to the perfect of *go*" (original emphasis) and as implying "movement to a location followed by return"; see example (20):

(20) We've been to a lot of seminars (Biber et al. 1999: 464)

But in addition, *HAVE been to* can express its motional meaning when followed by a verbal complement that represents an event.[7] In such cases, the overall meaning conveyed by *HAVE been to V* is that of goal-oriented motion, with *HAVE been to* expressing the spatial semantic component (i.e. 'reaching a destination and coming back') and the lexical verb expressing the event-related semantic component (i.e. 'performing an action [while there]'). The overall construction can be paraphrased as 'being back from getting something done', as shown in (21) to (23):

(21) When she *has been to look* at the garden, it seems more beautiful than it was before her visit (BoE: B9000000523)

(22) Not a year had passed since she had explained to me that a young cousin *had* not *been to call* for some months because he'd been on vacation in New Mexico (COCA: Southern Review, vol. 32(4): 697, 1996)

(23) And you knew that after you'*d been to see* him he was perhaps willing to lend you money (ICE-GB:S1B-061)

Although extensive research has been conducted on infinitival clauses and catenative constructions in English (e.g. Eastlack 1967; Stevens 1972; Hoekstra 1988; Tortora 1988; Mair 1990; Fang 1995; Whelpton 2001, 2002; Egan 2008), to the best of my knowledge, no studies have been carried out on the use of *HAVE been to V*. The goals of this paper are to identify and describe the lexico-semantic context in which *HAVE been to V* occurs on the basis of corpus data, and to explore the lexico-semantic scope of applicability of the construction on the basis of elicited data.

3. Corpus findings

To examine the lexico-semantic environments in which *HAVE been to V* occurs, I collected data from two American English corpora, namely the *Michigan Corpus of Academic Spoken English* (MICASE on-line; 2,000,000 words) and the *Contemporary Corpus of American English* (COCA; 385,000,000 words at the time of data gathering), and five British English corpora, namely the Great Britain component of the *International Corpus of English* (ICE-GB; 1,000,000 words), the *British Academic Spoken English Corpus* (BASE; 1,000,000 words), the *British Academic Written Corpus* (BAWE; 8,000,000 words), the Bank of English on-line (BoE; 57,000,000 words) and the *British National Corpus* (BNC; 100,000,000 words).

I searched the above corpora for instances of *been to V* exemplifying the *HAVE been to V* construction in its declarative and interrogative variants (i.e. subject + *have/has/had/having been to V* and *have/has/had/having* + subject + *been to V*).[8] I excluded from the query output concordances including ambiguous or irrelevant examples of *HAVE been to V*, that is, sequences of *HAVE been to V* that could not be unequivocally paraphrased as expressing the notions of 'going somewhere, doing something and coming back'. These included instances of the following:

(i) *the representation of relational processes (both ascriptive and specifying); e.g.:*

(24) She apologised for the mess, wiping her hands on her apron and then shaking my hand while I said *how sorry* I*'d been to hear*. (BNC: FP6; ascriptive)

(25) But general manager Graham Sunderland insists the only serious change *has been to accelerate* the bank's expansion. (ICE-GB:W2C-005; specifying)

(26) "The educational system all their lives *has been to react*" to a teacher (COCA: CSMonitor News, 09-Nov-2005; specifying)

(ii) *the expression of non-finite clauses of purpose (possibly paraphrasable as 'been used/done so as to V' or 'been in such a way so as to V'); e.g.:*

(27) Even though adoption is low overall in rural businesses uptake in arable and livestock sectors *has been to achieve* higher economies of scale and better analysis of individual enterprises (BAWE: 613d)

(28) Most inquiries *have been to explore* the investment potential (BoE: N5000950811)

(29) He thought of his dam that *had been to make* a lake (BNC: ABX)

(30) I feel that my whole life *has been to bring* me here, right now (COCA: English Journal, vol. 86(4): 21, April 1997)

(31) in other words, most of the spacecraft missions that have gone up to orbit recently *have* either *been to service* the International Space Station or *to visit* and *repair* the Hubble Space Telescope (COCA: NPR Saturday, 01-Feb-2003)

(32) The judge took longer than usual for lunch today and that *may* possibly *have been to read* both the papers from the prosecution and from the defense (COCA: CNN News, 25-May-1995, Simpson Trial Analysis, day 79, part 10)

(iii) *the juxtaposition of* HAVE been to *and a verb belonging to a separate syntactic constituent, plausibly interpretable as due to the extraposition or omission of an intervening complement (see also example (24)); e.g.:*

(33) Troops were called in (as they *had been to protect* fueldumps) (BNC: A64; possible interpretations: (a) 'Troops were called in again, as they had already been called in to protect fueldumps' or (b) 'Troops were called in, as they had already come back from protecting the fueldumps')

(34) a far-flung artist's studio *where* he'*d been to purchase* a John Miller watercolour for my birthday (BNC: CA9; extraposition of *where*, which is the complement of *'d been*)

(35) She came in from the kitchen, *whither* she *had been to baste* the roasting pig (COCA: Old Woman Magoun, vol. 20(1): 87, 2006: extraposition of *whither*, which is the complement of *'d been*)

(iv) the occurrence of words of unclear part of speech (i.e. verb or noun, such as sleep, state *and* work*) that could not be disambiguated in context; e.g.:*

(36) It's like it's still night and I [sic] never *been to sleep* at all (BNC: A74; unclear part of speech membership of *sleep*)

(v) the occurrence of HAVE been *with a* to-*infinitive requiring a passive-voice interpretation; e.g.:*

(37) But who *would have been to blame* (BoE: S9000001334; infinitival complement with passive-voice interpretation 'to be blamed')

and (vi) cases of difficult interpretation; e.g.:

(38) The beginning of the process with Egypt in November '77 to the end of what *has been to greet* us is a huge road that we have been going together, all three parties, and otherwise there would have been no agreement (COCA: Newshour, 13-Oct-1991; difficult interpretation)

After thus filtering each query output, I was left with corpus concordances unambiguously exemplifying the construction under analysis here. As the following concordances illustrate, *HAVE been to V* is employed to encode purposeful activities, which thus require agentive subjects. The activities vary in terms of duration or frequency (e.g. recurrent in example (39), extended in (40), instantaneous in (45)), and also in terms of goals (e.g. entertainment in examples (39) and (40); self-imposed or chosen tasks in (41) and (42); official duties in (43) and (44); and errands in (45), (46) and (47)), as illustrated below:

(39) Because Karen and I *have been to see* most of his plays (ICE-GB: S1A-025)
(40) I asked if she *had* ever *been to hear* Billy Graham (BNC: ADK)
(41) the reader is told, at the end of Chapter 29, after the Westons' and Frank and Emma *have been to inspect* the Crown Inn, that, The [sic] party did not break up without Emma's being positively secured for the two first dances by the hero of the evening (BAWE: 0229b)
(42) I *have been to check* on the condition of Father's house (COCA: ReviewContempFic, vol 27(1), 2007)
(43) the police *had been to question* him (BNC: ANF)
(44) the new president *has been to be sworn in* at exactly noon on that day (COCA: CNN_LiveSat, 02-Aug-2003)
(45) after Greg *had been to tell* the referee he couldn't go (BoE: N9119980625)
(46) Mrs Brocklebank *had* not *been to clean* today (BNC: H85)
(47) I don't think they *'ve been to take* the photographs yet (BNC: KB1)

The corpora exemplify motional *HAVE been to V* 362 times. Table 1 shows that the majority of these instances are found in the two largest corpora, COCA and BNC, which account for about 88% of the data. However, a comparison of normalised frequencies shows that the construction is more common in the two large British English corpora, namely BoE and BNC, with 0.719 and 1.910 instances per million words, respectively. On the whole, *HAVE been to V* is more commonly found in oral rather than written sources, but it is not attested in all the corpora: Indeed, the two spoken-only corpora (BASE, MICASE) have no instances of *HAVE been to V*, while BAWE and ICE-GB have only one and three instances, respectively.

Table 1. Frequency and distribution of motional *HAVE been to V* across seven corpora

CORPUS	Tokens in oral texts (pmw)	Tokens in written texts (pmw)	Total (pmw)	% across corpora
MICASE	0 (0.000)	0 (0.000)	0 (0.000)	0
COCA	27 (0.350)	99 (0.321)	126 (0.327)	35
ICE-GB	3 (3.000)	0 (0.000)	3 (3.000)	1
BASE	0 (0.000)	0 (0.000)	0 (0.000)	0
BAWE	0 (0.000)	1 (0.125)	1 (0.125)	0
BoE	12 (1.333)	29 (0.604)	41 (0.719)	11
BNC	50 (5.000)	141 (1.566)	191 (1.910)	53
Total	92 (0.920)	270 (0.593)	362 (0.653)	100

As Table 2 shows, most of the concordances (71%) instantiate the construction with the verb *see*, which encodes both the meaning of ‘looking at, or watching, something or someone’ and that of ‘meeting (and spending time with) someone’. The second most frequent lexeme is *visit* (12%). Only a few verbs occur five or more times (i.e. *look at*, *stay* and *watch*), while many others occur only once (e.g. *buy, call, clean, look for, pay, question, seek, test, weigh*). The total number of different verbs instantiated is 34.

All the events represented in the concordances require the participation of sentient experiencers and volitional agents,[9] and indeed, the subject noun phrases co-occurring with *HAVE been to V* in the concordances examined represent human beings, as the examples throughout the paper illustrate. The temporal nature of the events varies, as these include durative, telic, habitual, and punctual ones,[10] but they are all dynamic, and they all refer to occasions on which something specific has happened; e.g.:

(48) We’d pop in any time, and I *have been to stay* with her (BNC: APT; durative)

(49) ABC’s Jim Wooten *has been to test* the waters in normally Republican territory (COCA: ABC_Jennings, 09-Sept-1992; telic)

(50) I said Well she *has been to tell* them on various occasions (BoE: S9000001172; habitual)
(51) Simon Garrett*'s been to meet* him (BNC: K25; punctual)

Table 2. Frequency of *see*, *visit* and other verbs in the *HAVE been to V* concordances

CORPUS	No. of lexemes	*see* n	*see* %	*visit* n	*visit* %	other verbs n	other verbs %	Total n
MICASE	0	0	*0*	0	*0*	0	*0*	0
COCA	14	87	*69*	25	*20*	14	*11*	126
ICE-GB	1	3	*100*	0	*0*	0	*0*	3
BASE	0	0	*0*	0	*0*	0	*0*	0
BAWE	1	0	*0*	0	*0*	0	*0*	1
BoE	8	31	*76*	3	*7*	7	*17*	41
BNC	23	136	*71*	15	*8*	40	*21*	191
Global	34	257	*71*	43	*12*	62	*17*	362

4. Elicitation findings

In the corpus data, *HAVE been to V* is typically associated with the representation of an agentive human subject engaged in a deliberate action that is part of a round trip. It often co-occurs with the verb *see*, employed in the meanings of 'watching some (entertaining) event' and 'visiting, or getting together with, someone'. However, the construction is also instantiated with various other, much less frequent, verbs. This suggests that it is compatible with a wider range of possibly related meanings. To explore the use of *HAVE been to V* within the latter domain, I elicited data from 11 native speakers.[11] The informants, who comprised seven British, three US American and one Canadian speakers of English, were consulted over e-mail. They were sent a two-part questionnaire requiring them to produce both made-up sentences and acceptability judgements on other sentences.

In the first task, the informants were instructed to make up five sentences illustrating the *HAVE been to V* construction without resorting to the verb *see*. The construction itself was exemplified by means of the following model sentences: *I have been to see Mary*, *Have you been to see your parents?* and *They hadn't been to see me in a long time.*

Of the 31 valid illustrative sentences collected,[12] most are characterized by the occurrence of first-person subjects (18 instances), contracted finite verbs (16), present tenses (28), declarative clauses (27) and affirmative statements (30). From a semantic point of view, 28 of the elicited sentences represent short-duration activities, one represents a possibly open-ended (i.e. temporally unbounded) activity, and two represent presumably punctual acts; e.g.:

(52) I*'ve been to talk* to my son's teachers (errand; Informant-8)
(53) They*'ve been to swim* in the river (durative activity; Informant-3)
(54) I*'ve been to close* the door (punctual act; Informant-3)

The events represented in the made-up sentences can be classified as small jobs, tasks or duties (i.e. errands or other kinds of short-duration activities). More specifically, as summarized in Table 3, they include acts of communication (nine instances), exchanges of goods or services (nine), errands not involving any verbal exchange or transaction (10), and pastime activities (three); e.g.:

(55) She*'s been to complain* to the Mayor (act of communication; Informant-8)
(56) We*'ve been to book* our seats (exchange of goods/services; Informant-3)
(57) I *had* just *been to look for* him, when he walked in the front door (other errand; Informant-11)
(58) He*'s been to watch* the football game (pastime activity; Informant-8)

Table 3. Classification of events represented in 31 made-up sentences

Type of event represented	Sentences	
Acts of communication	A.1	They*'ve been to ask* about that trip to Naples.
	A.2	She*'s been to complain* to the Mayor.
	A.3	When I saw him he *had* just *been to enquire* about a new flat.
	A.4	She *has been to find out* about train times.
	A.5	*Have* you *been to give* your condolences yet?
	A.6	I*'ve been to talk* to his parents.
	A.7	I*'ve been to talk* to my son's teachers.
	A.8	*Have* you *been to talk* to the doctor yet?
	A.9	We*'ve been to talk* to the minister in Rome, not that it will make any difference!
Exchanges of goods or services	B.1	She *has been to ask for* a mortgage.
	B.2	We*'ve been to book* our seats.
	B.3	I *have been to buy* a car.
	B.4	I*'ve been to buy* the vegetables.
	B.5	When we got there, they had just got in; they *had been to do* their weekly shop.
	B.6	He*'s been to get* a hair cut.
	B.7	I *have been to get* that CD you wanted.
	B.8	I *have been to look for* a sweater.
	B.9	- Why don't you nick your neighbours [sic] paper, he always leaves it on the porch. - I*'ve* already *been to steal* it, but someone got there before me![13]

Table 3 (cont.). Classification of events represented in 31 made-up sentences

Other errands	C.1	I*'ve been to close* the door.
	C.2	I*'ve been to eat* at that place.
	C.3	I*'ve been to have* a look at that house.
	C.4	*Have* you *been to have* your hair cut yet?
	C.5	I *haven*'t *been to look for* that book in the library yet.
	C.6	I *had* just *been to look for* him, when he walked in the front door.
	C.7	I *have been to pick* the beans, that's why my hair is such a mess.
	C.8	I*'ve been to take* the dog out for a walk.
	C.9	I*'ve been to visit* my mother-in-law.
	C.10	*Have* you *been to visit* that new Art Gallery?
Pastime activities	D.1	They*'ve been to swim* in the river.
	D.2	I*'ve been to walk* in the park many times.
	D.3	He*'s been to watch* the football game.

In the second part of the questionnaire, the informants were asked to judge on a three-point scale the acceptability of sentences exemplifying the construction *HAVE been to V*. The sentences submitted to the native speakers represent events of varying temporal nature, whose realization requires two different levels of involvement on behalf of their subject arguments. On the one hand, the events include durative dynamic, durative stative, punctual dynamic, and telic dynamic processes. On the other hand, they comprise both deliberate acts and involuntary experiences, requiring the participation of agents and of sentient experiencers, respectively. Table 4 lists the verb phrases from the sample sentences, and shows the temporal-semantic classification of the events represented in them. Items 7, 8 and 9 can be classified as representing errands, that is, short-duration tasks. Items 10 and 12 include reference to a circumstance of place as a result of which the events represented therein can be classified as being spatially delimited. Sentences 11 and 13 count as telic because they include reference to a circumstance of time as a result of which they are effectively temporally bounded. Altogether, the sample sentences represent: (a) 15 deliberate events and five involuntary ones; (b) seven durative events, nine telic ones, and four punctual ones; (c) three events classifiable as errands, two characterized by explicit spatial delimitation and two by explicit temporal delimitation.

I instructed the informants to indicate in writing to what extent each sentence sounded acceptable to them, by choosing an answer from a closed set of options: *Yes*, *No* and *Uncertain*, and I invited them to add comments, if they felt like it.

Table 4. Temporal-semantic characteristics of the verb phrases in the sentences judged by 11 native speakers

Item	Temporal classification	Semantic classification	Other details
I *have been to* …			
1. … *eat.*	durative	deliberate	
2. … *pray.*	durative	deliberate	
3. … *teach.*	durative	deliberate	
4. … *have* dinner.	telic	deliberate	
5. … *say* a prayer.	telic	deliberate	
6. … *give* a lecture.	telic	deliberate	
7. … *have* my fortune told.	telic	deliberate	errand-like
8. … *collect* my papers.	telic	deliberate	errand-like
9. … *inspect* the new plant.	telic	deliberate	errand-like
10. … *pray* at my mother's tomb.	durative	deliberate	spatially delimited
11. … *pray* for ten minutes.	telic	deliberate	temporally delimited
12. … *cry* at my mother's tomb.	durative	involuntary	spatially delimited
13. … *cry* for ten minutes.	telic	involuntary	temporally delimited
14. … *learn* a new song.	telic	involuntary	
15. … *rest* in the garden.	durative	involuntary	
16. … *admire* him.	durative	involuntary	
17. … *grab* his pullover.	punctual	deliberate	
18. … *wake* him *up*.	punctual	deliberate	
19. … *answer* the door.	punctual	deliberate	
20. … *switch* the radio *on*.	punctual	deliberate	

Table 5 summarizes the informants' replies. Overall, the sentences were more often judged unacceptable (55% of the time) than acceptable (42%), and only in a few cases were they classified as uncertain (3%). The sentences that received more positive, rather than negative or uncertain, acceptability ratings were 1, 2, 7, 9, 10, and 12, with sentence 2 receiving the highest number of positive ratings. The sentences that received more negative acceptability ratings were 3, 4, 11, and 13 to 20, with sentences 3, 11, 14 and 15, and especially 13, 16 and 17, receiving markedly negative ratings.[14]

Explicit comments were provided by three informants. The British native speaker who had rated all the sentences as acceptable wrote that for each of them it was possible to think of a suitable context in which they work. Another British speaker commented on the unlikelihood of timing praying and crying sessions (i.e. on the unsuitability of providing an explicit temporal delimitation for temporally unbounded events), and suggested rephrasing the sentences with the verbs *cry* and *pray* as, respectively, "I've been to say 'ten Hail Marys'" and "I've been for a quick cry" (thus turning durative events modified by an explicit temporal delimitation into intrinsically telic events). Another British speaker similarly commented on the strangeness of both timing and deliberately controlling the event of crying. He also pointed out that the sentence with the verb *admire* is acceptable if the event can be considered a willed, rather than spontaneous, action, or if intended ironically (i.e. this informant negatively reacted to the association of involuntary experiences with the notion of deliberate, purposeful motion). Finally, he wrote that the sentence with the verb *teach* sounds more acceptable if followed by a complement such as "that awful group of teenagers" (i.e. if it is reformulated as a telic event). One of the two US American informants who had classified all the sentences as unacceptable stated that, unless the verb *see* is used, the *HAVE been to V* construction is "a British thing". The US American informant who had judged most sentences unacceptable suggested rephrasing them by using the verb *GO* either in the present perfect or, better still, in the past tense.

Table 5. Acceptability ratings of *HAVE been to V* in 20 sentences

Item	Acceptability judgements		
I *have been to* …	Yes	No	Uncertain
2. … *pray*.	7	4	0
1. … *eat*.	6	4	1
9. … *inspect* the new plant.	6	4	1
7. … *have* my fortune told.	6	5	0
10. … *pray* at my mother's tomb.	6	5	0
12. … *cry* at my mother's tomb.	6	5	0
5. … *say* a prayer.	5	5	1
6. … *give* a lecture.	5	5	1
8. … *collect* my papers.	5	5	1
4. … *have* dinner.	5	6	0
18. … *wake* him *up*.	5	6	0
19. … *answer* the door.	5	6	0
20. … *switch* the radio on.	4	6	1
11. … *pray* for ten minutes.	4	7	0
14. … *learn* a new song.	4	7	0
15. … *rest* in the garden.	4	7	0
3. … *teach*.	3	7	1
13. … *cry* for ten minutes.	2	9	0
16. … *admire* him.	2	9	0
17. … *grab* his pullover.	2	9	0
Total	92 (42%)	121 (55%)	7 (3%)

5. Discussion

Motion and location verbs are typically used with adverbials encoding circumstances of place (i.e. source locations, target destinations, current locations). Their use can be semantically and syntactically expanded when they co-occur with adverbials encoding events – rather than the locations in which these take place – or when they are associated with clausal complements, which also encode events. The association of a spatial expression with a clausal complement paves the way for the encoding of temporal and/or aspectual meanings.

The construction *HAVE been to* expresses the literal, motional meaning of 'going [somewhere] and coming back' not only when accompanied by a phrasal adverbial encoding a destination, e.g.:

(59) He*'s been to the library* and comes to us today with some weighty information (BoE: S2000930203)

or an event taking place at a location, e.g.:

(60) it all feels too hopelessly peripheral to make any difference to anyone who*'s* never *been to the Reading Festival* or bought a long-sleeved T-shirt with a long list of towns on the back (BoE: N0000000357)

but also when followed by a non-finite clausal complement encoding an event, e.g.:

(61) It seems that Cumberland *had been to read* a play to the company at Drury Lane (New York Times, January 31, 1915, Section: Society Drama Fashion Music, Page X6).[15]

In this last syntactic context, that is, when followed by a *to*-infinitive, *HAVE been* acquires a temporal overtone, in the sense that it expresses the notion of the (recent) past performance of an action at a previous location. The goal of this paper was to identify the typical context in which *HAVE been to V* occurs and to determine its scope of applicability on the basis of spontaneously produced and specially elicited data.

Corpus data has shown that *HAVE been to V* is an infrequent construction (0.65 pmw), and that it is more commonly attested in spoken than in written texts. Also, its frequency appears to be higher in the British than the American data. Furthermore, the concordances have revealed that the construction mainly encodes the meanings of 'watching something (for entertainment)' and 'paying a visit'. This is due to its very frequent co-occurrence with the verb *see* – which can encode either meaning – and its less frequent co-occurrence with verbs expressing related meanings, such as *look (at), watch, view, meet, visit* and *stay*. In addition, the construction has been found to occur with other verbs in the encoding of three main types of events: exchanges of information (e.g. *hear, question, tell, talk*), exchanges of goods or services (e.g. *buy, collect, get, look for, pay, pick up*), and other kinds of errands (e.g. *check, clean, make, support, take, weigh up*).

The verbs occurring in this construction are events of varying temporal nature – punctual (e.g. *check, take*), durative (e.g. *look (at), stay, view*) and telic (e.g. *watch the Ryder Cup, weigh them up*) – classifiable as dynamic, deliberate acts. The events represented in the concordances all show human agents involved in the volitional realization of specific actions tied to single, or occasionally repeated, contextual circumstances.

Data elicited from native speakers in the form of made-up sentences which excluded the use of the verb *see* has similarly revealed (i) that the construction is perceived as being associated with the encoding of verbal transactions, material transactions and other types of errands, (ii) that it is instantiated with dynamic verbs of varying temporal nature, but especially telic ones, and (iii) that it represents events classifiable as short-duration activities. These specific findings are in line with those from the corpus data. The made-up sentences have also shown that the construction is felt to be acceptable with some of the verbs occurring in the corpus data (i.e. *buy, get, look for, take, talk, visit* and *watch*) and with additional ones (e.g. *ask, ask for, book, complain*). This suggests that *HAVE been to V* expresses a general semantic notion, and is not a-priori restricted to specific sets of verbs. Finally, the comments provided by the three US American speakers consulted – who voiced their dissatisfaction with *HAVE been to V* when not used with *see* – have revealed those informants' lack of awareness of the actual use of the construction in their English variety, as shown in the corpus data. Overall, therefore, the findings from the elicited data mirror in part those from the corpus data.

The native speakers' ratings of sentences exemplifying *HAVE been to V* has revealed three main findings. The construction (i) displays a slight preference for the encoding of deliberate telic events (e.g. *say a prayer*), (ii) is occasionally compatible with other types of processes (i.e. deliberate durative like *eat*, deliberate punctual like *wake up*, involuntary durative like *cry at somebody's tomb*, and involuntary telic like *learn a song*),[16] but especially (iii) manifests a marked dislike for involuntary, punctual and durative events (including durative processes accompanied by explicit temporal delimitation). Thus the informants' made-up sentences and ratings of other sentences shows a convergent preference for the encoding of deliberate telic events.

Altogether, the corpus data shows *HAVE been to V*'s preferential lexical association with the verb *see*, and its consequent preferential semantic associations with the meanings of 'watching something (for entertainment)' or 'visiting someone'. The corpus data and the informants' made-up sentences together reveal that the construction is compatible with a relatively wide range of verbs in the representation of deliberate, short-duration activities, typically errands, requiring a temporary change of location. The informant's ratings of – and occasional comments on – the sample sentences has also shown a slight preference for the encoding of telic events (more easily interpretable as errands), and a marked dislike for the encoding of involuntary, durative or punctual acts (less plausibly classifiable as purposeful, short-duration activities calling for a temporary change of location).

6. Conclusion

HAVE been to V can be said to encode the general meaning of 'coming back from getting something done at a previous, unspecified – but retrievable – location'. It is associated with the encoding of events interpretable as errands requiring transfer to a target destination and return. Its frequent instantiation in the meanings of 'visiting someone' or 'watching something happening' – and thus its co-occurrence with the verb *see* – can be motivated by the semantic compatibility of the meaning conveyed by the construction *per se* and the contextual (i.e. extra-textual) requirements of these two types of events. Paying a visit to someone and watching an entertaining event happen are "classic" errands: short-duration, purposeful activities requiring a human agent's deliberate intervention and temporary transfer to another location. This also accounts for the co-occurrence of *HAVE been to V* with other, less frequent, verbs encoding the same meanings (e.g. *visit, watch*). From a complementary perspective, the instantiation of *HAVE been to V* with other verbs, which contribute to the representation of other volitional, short-duration, goal-oriented acts, indicates that the construction conveys a more general meaning, and is compatible with the encoding of a wider range of telic events.

The distribution of the native speakers' acceptability judgements can be accounted for with reference to how the temporal nature of the events represented in the sample sentences interacts with the motional meaning component conveyed by *HAVE been to*. The informants' more frequent positive ratings of telic events (see items 4 to 9, 11, 13 and 14 in Table 4) can be related to the general preference of *HAVE been to V*, as attested in the corpus data, for the encoding of short-duration activities – possibly interpretable as envisaging an endpoint – and thus calling for a temporary change of location. The speakers' negative judgements of punctual events (see items 17 to 20 in Table 4) can be motivated by the irrelevant duration of these events, which does not justify (the implicit encoding of) transfer to another location. (That is to say, instantaneous events can take place "on the spot".) Finally, the informants' negative ratings of durative events (see items 1 to 3, 10, 15 and 16 in Table 4) can be ascribed to the mismatch between the potentially unbounded nature of those events and the intrinsically bounded nature of the movement expressed through *HAVE been to*, which involves a starting point (i.e. departure from the current/original location) and an endpoint (i.e. return to the current/original location).

In conclusion, the corpus data appears to illustrate an instance of what Mair (2004: 135-136) calls "static grammaticalization", namely the diachronically stable and entrenched, but marginal and experimental, use of suitable lexical items in chiefly grammatical functions. *HAVE been to* can be easily re-analysed as an expression of 'recent past or perfect' in the local context in which round-trip motion occurs with an infinitival complement. The re-analysis is possible because there is an inference of completion (thus, perfect aspect or past tense) from the expression of 'returning from (an event)': if someone returns from an event, that event has already/just happened (cf. Heine and Kuteva 2002: 33). If the event in question is carried out by the subject, this allows one to equate 'returning from an event' with 'having performed it'. The concordances show that that 'paying a visit' and 'watching an event' are the best semantic representatives of the *HAVE been to V* construction. The short duration of these activities, whose past performance typically requires returning to one's original location, perfectly fits the bounded nature of the motional meaning component of *HAVE been to*.

On the other hand, the elicited data, and part of the corpus data, indicates that, even if *HAVE been to V* is strongly associated with the verb *see* and with the meanings of 'going to visit someone and returning' and 'going to watch something and returning', it can co-occur with additional predicates, as long as these represent events whose internal temporal nature does not openly clash with the boundedness of the motional meaning of 'going and returning'. This suggests that the construction has not grammaticalized to the point where it can be freely used independently of a motional meaning component (i.e. so as to only convey the notion of 'having just *V*-ed').[17]

Further insights into the degree of grammaticalization, and general use, of *HAVE been to V* could be gained in at least three ways: (i) by comparing its frequency of occurrence with that of semantically similar constructions (i.e. *HAVE just V-ed; got back from V-ing*) so as to outline the conceptual frequency (Hoffmann 2004: 190) of the meaning 'having just *V*-ed', which *HAVE been to V* encodes; (ii) by examining the specific lexical associations of these alternative expressions; and (iii) by eliciting native speakers' judgements on the compatibility of these expressions with a non-motional meaning. In particular, native speakers' judgements would be necessary to explore whether and to what extent *HAVE been to V* is actually perceived as an expression of recent past: its *HAVE been* component might be considered a temporal modulator of temporal distance, that is, a marker of contraction of the time interval separating the time of the event from reference/speech time (Bourdin 2002: 181-182, 190-191), given that the directional *HAVE been* marks motion in space closer to the speaker's deictic centre, and thus closer to the temporal location of the event being referred to as well.

The study therefore suggests that corpus data and elicitation data can fruitfully complement each other. The former can help highlight the prototypical meaning of a construction (i.e. to explore its depth of application), and the latter to investigate its domain of applicability (i.e. to explore its breadth of application). At the same time, a more accurate picture of the use a construction can be drawn only by examining it in relation to the other phraseologies in the language competing for the same semantic space.

Notes

1 Here and elsewhere: (a) BoE stands for *Collins Cobuild Bank of English On-line*, a 57,000,000-word corpus of present-day English; (b) italicization is added.

2 For example, the sentences "All the money will go to the Schools to buy extra equipment for the children" (BoE: E0000002037)" and "We are going up as [sic] group to try to get tickets from the ground" (BoE: N6000950228) encode goal-oriented motion, that is, both literal motion (*will go* signalling 'transfer of money' and *are going up* 'departure from the present location') and the projected achievement of goals (*to buy extra equipment for the children* encoding 'the funding of an initiative' and *to get tickets from the ground* 'the purchase of tickets').

3 If reference to the physical destination of the transfer or the direction of motion is removed from the examples in note 2 (i.e. "All the money will go [...] to buy extra equipment for the children" and "We are going [...] to try to get tickets from the ground"), the infinitival constructions end up overtly encoding only the orientation of the events towards a specific goal (re-interpretable as an outcome in the first case). In this way, the verbs become available for the generalized encoding of the notions of 'contributing to' and 'having the intention to', respectively (e.g. "and there are too many factors that go to make up a great marathon runner" BoE: S1000900927; "We are going to teach them how to get through the audition process" BoE: N5000950106).

4 For a discussion of the term *grammaticalization* and the concept of grammaticalization, see Lehmann (1995 [1982]: 9-14). On the differences between grammaticalization and lexicalization, see Lehmann (2002) and Brinton and Traugott (2005).

5 Depending on context – i.e. on what the speaker wants to focus on – *essere stato a* plus infinitive may simply identify a recently occurred event (e.g. *Sono stato a sciare questo fine-settimana* 'I went skiing this weekend') or also signal that a given length of time was spent in the performance of a recent act (e.g. *Sono stato a spiegargli tutto in dettaglio* 'I explained [lit. 'I have stayed to explain', i.e. 'I stayed there to explain' or 'I spent time explaining'] everything thoroughly to him').

6 Grammaticalization studies on *be going to* can be found in Hopper and Traugott (2003), Danchev and Kytö (1994), Mair (1997), Nicolle (1998), and Berglund (1999).

7 The generalization from NP complements to infinitival ones is one of the processes responsible for the rise of a lexical verb to modal status (see Krug 2000: 144, 147 on *want to*).

8 The notion of subject is here defined syntactically by the feature of position: a subject is placed before the predicate in declaratives and in *wh*-interrogatives when realized as (a phrase containing) a *wh*-element; it is placed after the finite part of the predicate elsewhere.

9 Even *hear* and *see* are to be interpreted as 'listen to' and 'watch/look at', respectively, in the concordances.

10 Durative events are temporally unbounded and may extend indefinitely (e.g. *draw, read books*), telic events have an in-built endpoint (e.g. *write a letter*), habitual events take place repeatedly over a period of time (e.g. *work on Mondays*), and punctual events are perceived as happening instantaneously (e.g. *arrive*).

11 They included a musician, a remover, an editor, two PhDs in linguistics, and five language teachers.

12 One US informant did not provide any sample sentences, explaining that she only uses *HAVE been to V* with the verb *see*; the Canadian informant gave only two out of the required five sentences; two informants did not follow the instructions, and produced irrelevant examples (i.e. a British informant wrote sentences with the verb *to have* such as "George has the keys in his pocket", while a US informant wrote sentences exemplifying present and past perfect tenses such as "She had run a marathon 6 times"); finally, a British and a US informant produced strings of *HAVE been to V* that could not be unequivocally paraphrased as expressing the notion of 'going somewhere, doing something and coming back' (e.g. "Her aim has been to illustrate some aspect of the English language"; "We were once detained briefly for trespassing there, but I can't imagine where he's been to get into such trouble"; cf. examples (24) to (38) above).

13 B.9 and C.7 are also classifiable as 'other errand' and 'exchange of goods or services', respectively.

14 One British informant judged all the sentences acceptable; two of the US ones judged all of them unacceptable, and another one judged most of them unacceptable (7/11), one acceptable, and the remaining three uncertain.

15 Source: http://query.nytimes.com/gst/abstract.html?res=9E00E3D7113EE733A05752C3A9679C946496D6CF.

16 However, involuntary durative and involuntary telic events may have been reinterpreted as instances of volitional behaviour by some informants.

17 *HAVE been to V* can thus be likened to vector verbs (Hook [1991], quoted in Hopper and Traugott [2003]), intermediate between full verbs and auxiliaries, which add "nuances of aspect, direction, and benefaction to the clause" (Hopper and Traugott 2003: 112).

References

Aijmer, K. (2004), 'The semantic path from modality to aspect. *Be able to* in a cross-linguistic perspective', in: H. Lindquist and C. Mair (eds.) *Corpus Approaches to Grammaticalization in English.* Amsterdam and Philadelphia: Benjamins. 57-78.

Berglund, Y. (1999), 'Exploiting a large spoken corpus: an end-user's way to the BNC', *International Journal of Corpus Linguistics,* 4(1): 29-52.

Biber D., S. Johansson, G. Leech, S. Conrad and E. Finegan (1999), *Longman Grammar of Spoken and Written English*. London: Longman.

Bourdin, P. (2002), 'The grammaticalization of deictic directionals into modulators of temporal distance', in: I. Wischer and G. Diewald (eds.) *New Reflections on Grammaticalization.* Amsterdam and Philadelphia: Benjamins. 181-199.

Brinton, L. J. (1988), *The Development of English Aspectual Systems.* Cambridge: Cambridge University Press.

Brinton L. J. and E. C. Traugott (2005), *Lexicalization and Language Change.* Cambridge: Cambridge University Press.

Bybee, J. L. (1988), 'The diachronic dimension in explanation', in: J. Hawkins (ed.) *Explaining Language Universals.* Oxford: Blackwell. 17-34.

Chafe, W. (2002), 'Putting grammaticalization in its place', in: I. Wischer and G. Diewald (eds.) *New Reflections on Grammaticalization.* Amsterdam and Philadelphia: Benjamins. 395-412.

Danchev A. and M. Kytö (1994), 'The construction *be going to* + infinitive in Early Modern English', in: D. Kastovsky (ed.) *Studies in Early Modern English.* Berlin: Mouton de Gruyter. 59-77.

Diewald, G. (2002), 'A model for relevant types of contexts in grammaticalization', in: I. Wischer and G. Diewald (eds.) *New Reflections on Grammaticalization.* Amsterdam and Philadelphia: Benjamins. 103-120.

Eastlack, C. L. (1967), 'Catenative verbs in Portuguese and English: a contrastive study', *Estudos Lingüísticos*, 2(1-2): 43-56.

Egan, T. (2008), *Non-finite Complementation: A Usage-based Study of Infinitive and* -ing *Clauses in English.* Amsterdam and New York: Rodopi.

Fang, A.C. (1995), 'Distribution of infinitives in contemporary British English: A study based on the British ICE Corpus', *Literary and Linguistic Computing*, 10(4): 247-257.

Gesuato, S. (2009a), 'Encoding of goal-directed motion vs resultative aspect in the *COME* + infinitive construction', in: A. Renouf and A. Kehoe (eds.) *Corpus Linguistics: Refinements and Reassessments*. Amsterdam and New York: Rodopi. 381-414.

Gesuato, S. (2009b), '*GO to V*: Literal meaning and metaphorical extensions', in: A.H. Jucker, D. Schreier and M. Hundt (eds.) *Corpora: Pragmatics and Discourse*, Amsterdam and New York: Rodopi. 343-359.

Heine, B. (2002), 'On the role of context in grammaticalization', in: I. Wischer and G. Diewald (eds.) *New Reflections on Grammaticalization*. Amsterdam and Philadelphia: Benjamins. 83-101.

Heine B., U. Claudi and F. Hünnemeyer (1991), *Grammaticalization: A Conceptual Framework*. Chicago: University of Chicago Press.

Heine B. and T. Kuteva (2002), *World Lexicon of Grammaticalization*. Cambridge: Cambridge University Press.

Herlin I. and L. Kotilainen (2004), 'External factors behind cross-linguistic similarities', in: O. Fischer, M. Norde and H. Parridon (eds.) *Up and Down the Cline: The Nature of Grammaticalization*. Typological Studies in Language, 59. 263-280.

Hoekstra, T. (1988), 'Small clause results', *Lingua*, 74: 101-139.

Hoffmann, S. (2004), 'Are low-frequency complex prepositions grammaticalized? On the limits of corpus data – and the importance of intuition', in: H. Lindquist and C. Mair (eds.) *Corpus Approaches to Grammaticalization in English*. Amsterdam and Philadelphia: Benjamins. 171-210.

Hopper, P. J. (1991), 'On some principles of grammaticalization', in: E. C. Traugott and B. Heine (eds.) *Approaches to Grammaticalization*, Vol. I. Amsterdam and New York: Benjamins. 17-36.

Hopper P. J. and E. C. Traugott (2003), *Grammaticalization*. 2nd ed. Cambridge: Cambridge University Press.

Huddleston R. and G. Pullum (2002), *The Cambridge Grammar of the English Language*. Cambridge: Cambridge University Press.

Krug, M. G. (2000), *Emerging English Modals: A Corpus-based Study of Grammaticalization*. Topics in English Linguistics Series, 32. Berlin and New York: Mouton de Gruyter.

Kuryłowicz, J. (1975 [1965]), 'The evolution of grammatical categories', *Esquisses Linguistiques,* 2: 38-54.

Lehmann, C. (1995 [1982]), *Thoughts on Grammaticalization*. Lincom Studies in Theoretical Linguistics, 1. Munich: Lincom Europa.

Lehmann, C. (2002), 'New reflections on grammaticalization and lexicalization', in: I. Wischer and G. Diewald (eds.) *New Reflections on Grammaticalization*. Amsterdam and Philadelphia: Benjamins. 1-18.

Lichtenbeck, F. (1991), 'On the gradualness of grammaticalization', in: E. C. Traugott and B. Heine (eds.) *Approaches to Grammaticalization*, Vol. I. Amsterdam and New York: Benjamins. 37-80.

Mair, C. (1990), *Infinitival Complement Clauses in English: A Study of Syntax in Discourse*. Cambridge: Cambridge University Press.

Mair, C. (1997), 'The spread of the *going-to* future in written English: a corpus-based investigation into language change in progress', in: R. Hickey and S. Ruppel (eds.) *Language History and Linguistic Modelling: A Festschrift for Jacek Fisiak on his 60th birthday*. Berlin and New York: Mouton de Gruyter. 1537-1543.

Mair, C. (2004), 'Corpus linguistics and grammaticalization theory: statistics, frequencies, and beyond', in: H. Lindquist and C. Mair (eds.) *Corpus Approaches to Grammaticalization in English*. Amsterdam and Philadelphia: Benjamins. 121-150.

McIntyre, A. (2001), 'Argument blockages induced by verb particles in English and German: event modification and secondary predication', in: N. Dehé and A. Wannen (eds.) *Structural Aspects of Semantically Complex Verbs*. Berlin, Frankfurt and New York: Peter Lang. 131-164.

Meillet, A. (1912), 'L'Évolution des formes grammaticales', *Scientia (Rivista di scienza)*, 12(6): 384-400. Reprinted in A. Meillet, *Linguistique historique et linguistique générale*. Paris: Champion. 130-148.

Miller, J. (2004), 'Perfect and resultative constructions in spoken and non-standard varieties', in: O. Fischer, M. Norde and H. Parridon (eds.) *Up and Down the Cline: The Nature of Grammaticalization*. Typological Studies in Language, 59. 229-246.

Nevalainen, T. (2004), 'Three perspectives on grammaticalization: lexico-grammar, corpora and historical linguistics', in: H. Lindquist and C. Mair (eds.) *Corpus Approaches to Grammaticalization in English*. Amsterdam and Philadelphia: Benjamins. 1-31.

Nicolle, S. (1998), '*Be going to* and *will*: a monosemous account', *English Language and Linguistics*, 2(2): 223-243.

Roberts I. and A. Roussou (1999), 'A formal approach to grammaticalization', *Linguistics*, 37(6): 1011-1041.

Stevens, W. J. (1972), 'The catenative auxiliaries in English', *Language Sciences*, 23: 21-25.

Sweetser, E. (1990), *From etymology to pragmatics: metaphorical and cultural aspects of semantic structure*. Cambridge Studies in Linguistics. Cambridge: Cambridge University Press.

Tortora, C. M. (1988), 'Verbs of inherently directed motion are compatible with resultative phrases', *Linguistic Inquiry*, 29(2): 338-345.

Traugott, E. C. (1996), 'Semantic change: an overview', *Glot International* 2: 3-7.

Traugott E. C. and E. König (1991), 'The semantics-pragmatics of grammaticalization revisited', in: E.C. Traugott and B. Heine (eds.) *Approaches to Grammaticalization*, vol. I. Amsterdam and Philadelphia: Benjamins. 189-218.

van Gelderen, E. (2004), *Grammaticalization as Economy*. Linguistik Actuel/ Linguistics Today Series, 71. Amsterdam and Philadelphia: Benjamins.

Whelpton, M. (2001), 'Elucidation of a telic infinitive', *Journal of Linguistics*, 37(2): 313-337.

Whelpton, M. (2002), 'Locality and control with infinitives of result', *Natural Language Semantics*, 10: 167-210.

Differential change in British and American English: Comparing pre- and post-war data

Marianne Hundt and Stefanie Dose

Universities of Zürich and Giessen

Abstract

This chapter uses data from the extended Brown family of corpora (see Hundt and Leech, forthcoming), i.e. material from the 1930s, 1960s and 1990s, to study ongoing linguistic change in British and American English (BrE and AmE) in the twentieth century. Since the prequel to the Brown corpus *(B-Brown) is still being compiled, this study focuses exclusively on material from the academic writing and general fiction sections of the corpora, which represent registers that have previously been shown to display substantial linguistic differences (see e.g. Leech et al. 2009). The present case study looks at quantitative as well as qualitative changes in the use of the progressive. By extending the time frame into the past, we are able to shed light on the fine-grained differential developments in the two varieties: For instance, BrE and AmE converge in their use of the progressive in the second half of the twentieth century in terms of overall frequency. At the same time, qualitative analyses taking into account text type, tense, aspect and voice, paint a more varied picture of change in the two varieties. It turns out that BrE and AmE sometimes develop in tandem and at other times show divergent trends, and that changes in BrE are not necessarily due to an American influence.*

1. Introduction

Ongoing syntactic change in British and American English has been studied quite extensively on the basis of the Brown family of corpora. So far, the focus has mostly been on the second half of the twentieth century (see Leech et al. 2009). Individual studies (e.g. Övergaard 1995 on the mandative subjunctive) hint at the possibility that a comparison of data from before and after the Second World War might be particularly illuminating: influence of American English (AmE) on British English (BrE) is more likely to have occurred during and after the Second World War. The reason why developments in the first half of the twentieth century have not been studied more systematically so far is that the American counterpart of the B-LOB corpus has not been completed yet. Similarly, the *ARCHER* corpus so far only provides evidence on AmE from the second half of the twentieth century. A possible source of information on diachronic developments in AmE is e.g. the *Time Magazine Corpus* (Mark Davies/Brigham Young

University) which, however, is a single-register corpus and thus not directly comparable with the British members of the Brown family.

In the present study, we test the hypothesis of a post-war convergence of British English on the American model on the basis of preliminary data from the 1930s sibling of Brown (B-Brown) and corresponding evidence from the LOB prequel (B-LOB), LOB and Brown as well as F-LOB and Frown. The focus of this case study is on the progressive aspect.

After a brief review of previous studies on differential change and developments of the progressive in the second half of the twentieth century (Section 1.1), the hypotheses and research aims will be outlined (Section 1.2). Section 2 describes the methodological preliminaries of the study, such as the corpora used and the retrieval of the progressives. Section 3 summarizes the findings on the overall frequency developments (3.1) and presents three close-ups, i.e. co-occurrence patterns with tense and aspect (3.2.1), progressives in fictional dialogue (3.2.2) as well as the use of the progressive passive (3.2.3).

1.1 Previous research on the progressive in BrE and AmE

Longitudinal data from ARCHER show that, overall, the progressive has been increasing in both varieties without apparent regional differences in late Modern English (see Figure 1).

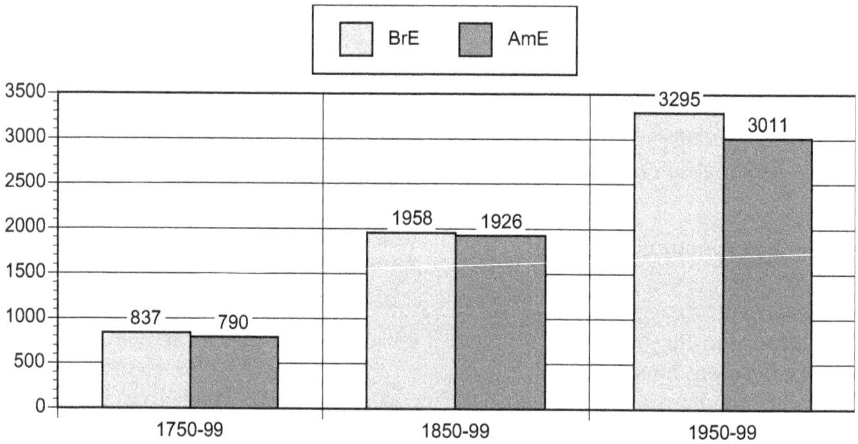

Figure 1. Progressives per million words (pmw) in BrE vs. AmE (ARCHER, based on Hundt 2004a: 69)[1]

This is corroborated by data from the Brown family of corpora, which do not provide evidence of statistically significant regional differences in the overall spread of the progressive during the second half of the twentieth century (see Figure 2).[2]

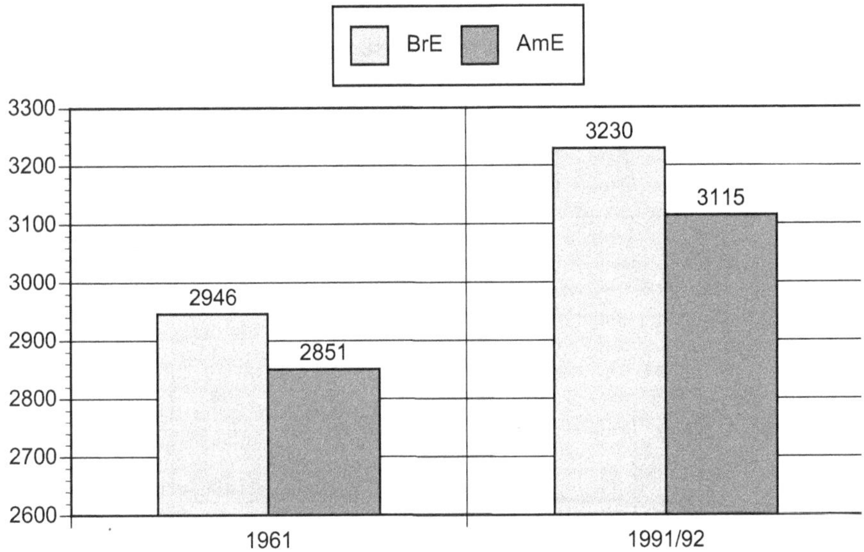

Figure 2. Progressives (absolute frequencies) in the Brown family of corpora (based on Leech et al. 2009: 288)

However, a more fine-grained analysis of individual registers shows that in BrE, the progressive increases modestly in academic writing while it has apparently reached a saturation point in fictional writing (see Figure 3.1)

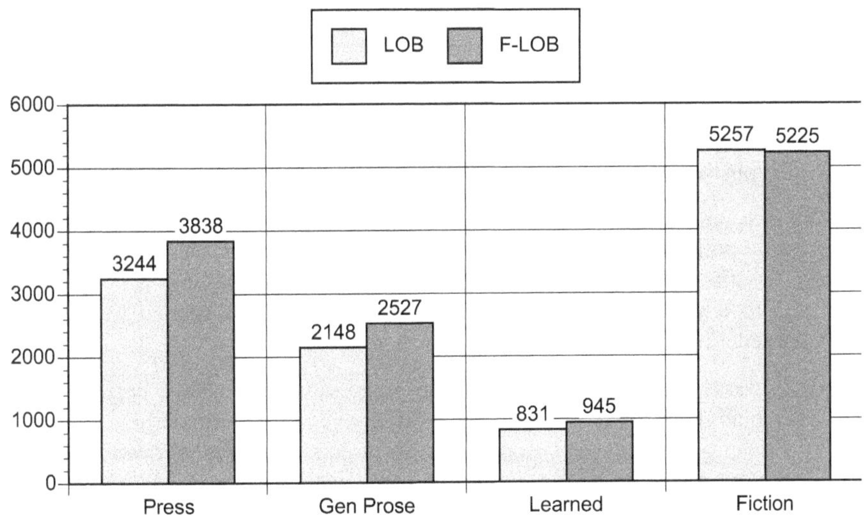

Figure 3.1. Progressives by subcorpora in LOB and F-LOB (1961-1991): frequencies pmw (from Leech et al. 2009: 123)

In AmE, on the other hand, progressives are decreasing in learned prose whereas there is a further increase in fictional writing (see Figure 3.2).

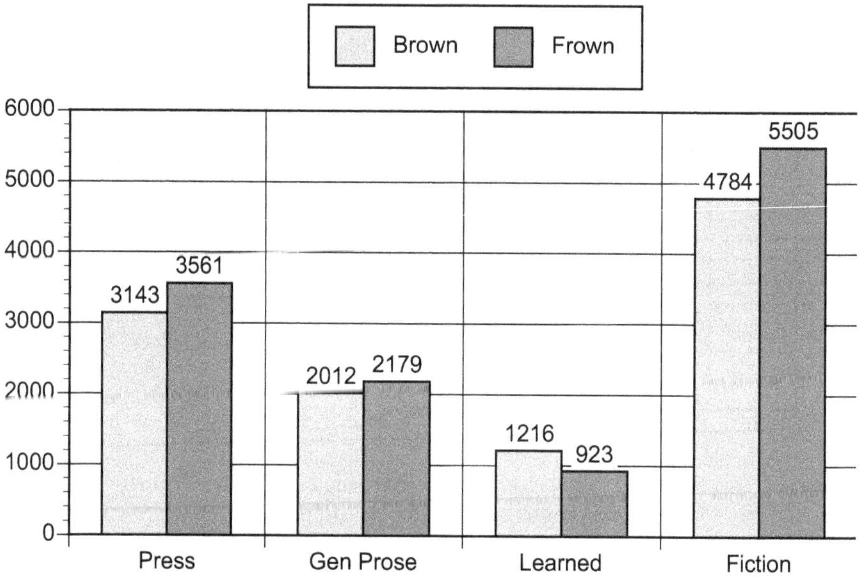

Figure 3.2. Progressives by subcorpora in Brown and Frown (1961-1992): frequencies pmw (from Leech et al. 2009: 123)

Interestingly, the overall effect of these register-specific regional developments is a convergence of the two varieties, because in AmE, the progressive was used more frequently in academic prose but less frequently in fictional writing in the 1960s than in the corresponding BrE subcorpora.

1.2 Hypotheses

On the basis of these findings, we expect that frequency data on the use of the progressive will also reveal regional differences in academic and fictional writing during the first half of the twentieth century. If anything, pre-war data are expected to amplify the differences that we observe in the second half of the twentieth century. Our hypotheses are thus as follows:

- In American academic writing, the progressive might have been used as frequently in the 1930s as in the 1960s or even more frequently;
- The progressive was used even less frequently in American fictional writing of the 1930s than in the 1960s.

With respect to some qualitative aspects of variation, we expect

- no regional differences in the co-occurrence with tense and aspect in the 1930s data; to be precise, we expect a preference for present tense in academic writing and for past tense in general fiction (see Leech et al. 2009: 288);
- that the increase of progressives is more likely to occur in present tense VPs than in past tense VPs (see Leech et al. 2009: 127);
- that additional evidence from the 1930s will confirm that the progressive passive is more widely used in BrE than in AmE in the first half of the twentieth century (see Hundt 2004b and Smith and Rayson 2007).

2. Data

The data used for this study come from the prequels to the Brown and LOB corpora. B-LOB, a sample of 1930s BrE, was compiled at the University of Lancaster (see Leech and Smith 2005).[3] Work on the corresponding sample of 1930s AmE (B-Brown) was begun in Heidelberg in 2006 and is still under way at the University of Zurich. Due to limited resources, so far, only the sub-corpora of academic writing (category J) and general fiction (category K) have been completed.[4] The sampling frame for B-Brown uses the original categories established for the Brown corpus but allows for a somewhat wider temporal margin: while the actual target year was 1931, we allowed for a leeway of three years on either side, i.e. we sampled texts from 1928-1934 (see Leech and Smith 2005: 87 on the same procedure for B-LOB). Table 1 gives an overview of the number of words thus available for the two categories across the two varieties in the twentieth century.

Table 1. Samples of academic writing and general fiction (Brown family of corpora)

	B-Brown (1930s)	B-LOB	Brown (1960s)	LOB	Frown (1990s)	F-LOB
Category J	161,408	161,679	162,109	161,241	160,411	160,969
Category K	58,410	58,556	58,421	58,477	58,344	58,309
Total	219,818	220,235	220,530	219,718	218,755	219,278

We extracted the progressives from the 1930s prequels with WordSmith 4.0, searching for all forms of the auxiliary followed by V*ing* (allowing for up to five elements[5] to occur between the auxiliary and the participle). The resulting concordances were manually post-edited. As in previous studies, we excluded the following patterns:

- ambiguous cases

(1) The family field has, it is true, increasingly been interested in the social relationships expressed through the institution of the family but in this it is

> not distinguished from other forms of case work, most of which treat some aspects of family relationships, nor does it sufficiently distinguish an area to say that the family field treats more family relationships. A quantitative distinction *will not be clarifying*; nevertheless, linking the family consideration with the economic consideration we can see a tendency within the family field, public and private, to define an area and an approach for itself. (B-Brown, J27)[6]

- instances of BE *going to* + infinitive with future reference

(2) "Who is going to stop me"? (Brown K08)

- constructions where the participle has adjectival rather than verbal function

(3) It was very interesting. (LOB K26)

- constructions with BE + gerund

(4) We are above being jealous. (Brown K18)

- examples with participles that function as an apposition

(5) Then the boards were nailed together, holding the cross section of the model river channel securely between them. (B-Brown J80)

In cases where two participles were coordinated (e.g. *All the time the children were singing and praying to their God*, B-Brown K22), only one progressive was counted. In general, as in previous studies (e.g. Leech et al. 2009: 122, footnote 12), only complete verb phrases were included in the count, which excludes instances such as *Annie is all hysterical and yelling her head off* (B-Brown K18). Results for academic writing (J) from the post-war corpora are taken from a previous study (Leech et al. 2009).

3. Results

3.1 Quantitative findings

The results for the academic subcorpora of the Brown family in Figure 4.1 show that the development in the second half of the twentieth century is not simply a continuation of a previous trend.

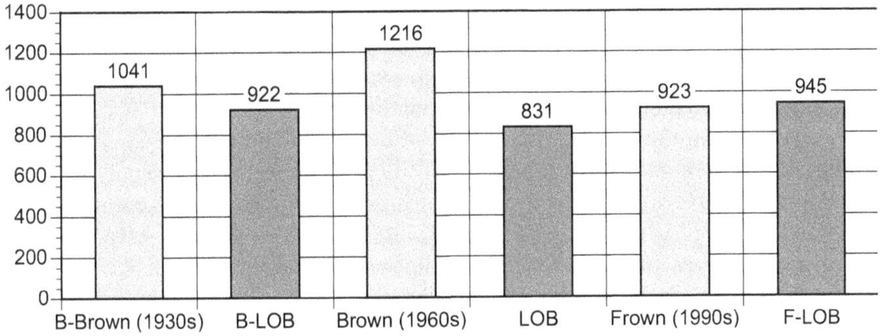

Figure 4.1. Progressives in academic writing: frequencies pmw in the extended Brown family of corpora[7]

In American academic writing, we first see an increase and then a decrease towards the end of the century. The development in British academic writing is the reverse: first a decrease and then an increase again between the 1960s and 1990s. In other words, our initial hypothesis regarding the development of American academic writing (i.e. that in the 1930s the progressive was used as frequently, or even more frequently than in the 1960s) cannot be corroborated on the basis of our data. In terms of differential change in the two varieties, these developments result in a divergent development in the first half of the century and then a re-convergence in the second half of the century, at least in academic writing. (Note that the difference between the prequels to Brown and LOB does not prove statistically significant in a log-likelihood test.)[8] Let us now look at the general fiction part of our corpora.

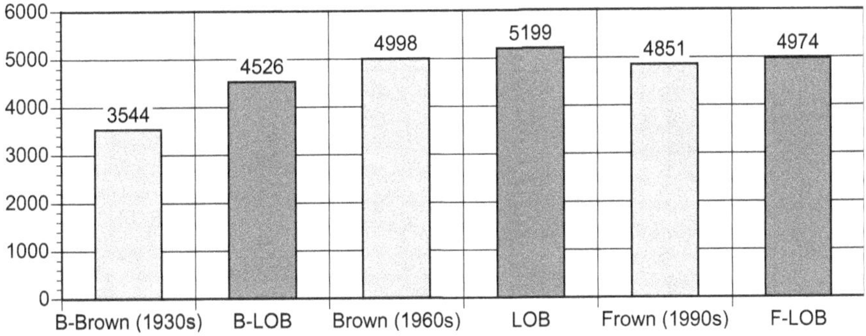

Figure 4.2. Progressives in general fiction: frequencies pmw in the extended Brown family of corpora

The data from the extended Brown family confirm our hypothesis: the progressive is used even less frequently in American fictional writing in the 1930s than in the 1960s (see Figure 4.2). This results in a statistically significant difference in the general fiction section of the 1930s prequels to Brown and LOB.[9] Overall, we see a long-term convergence of the development in fictional texts of the two national varieties, with AmE general fiction starting out as a significantly more conservative text category than the corresponding BrE texts in the 1930s.[10]

To sum up the quantitative results of our study and what it contributes to studies on differential change in the use of the progressive: the evidence from the two sub-corpora is quite heterogeneous because AmE in the 1930s comes out as the more advanced variety in academic writing and as the more conservative in its use of progressives in general fiction when we compare it with BrE. The long-term development in both genres across the century, however, is one of convergence.

Let us now turn to the qualitative aspects of variation. We will start by looking at the co-occurrence of progressives with certain tense and aspect forms.

3.2 Qualitative findings

3.2.1 Tense and aspect

The overall results on the co-occurrence of the progressive with certain tense and aspect forms in academic writing confirms our hypothesis in that the present tense progressive is by far the most frequent pattern in both prequels. The past progressive is another quite frequent pattern, more so in B-LOB than in B-Brown, whereas combinations of the progressive with a modal auxiliary or future progressives (here subsumed under 'Other') are a lot less common in both varieties.

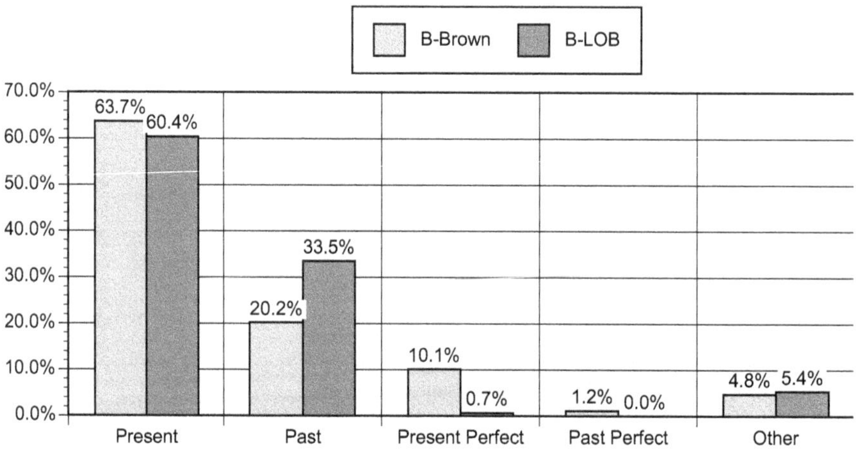

Figure 5.1. Distribution of progressives (proportions) according to tense/aspect in the academic writing section of the Brown and LOB prequels[11]

A look at Figure 5.1 also reveals some surprising results, most notably the fact that the progressive co-occurs more often with the perfect (present and past) in our 1930s American data, despite the fact that the present perfect, overall, tends to be used more frequently in British than in American English (see Hundt and Smith 2009 for evidence on this case of relatively stable regional variation in the second half of the twentieth century).

The findings from the general fiction section of our prequels are more homogeneous: as can be seen in Figure 5.2, in both varieties the past progressive is by far the preferred pattern, with the present progressive as the second most frequent pattern. The preference for the past over the present progressive in narrative writing is not surprising and has been noted before (Leech et al. 2009: 123). They comment on tense in fiction as follows: "Fiction attains a high level because it has frequent recourse to the progressive both in narrative (typically the past progressive) and in dialogue (typically the present progressive)."

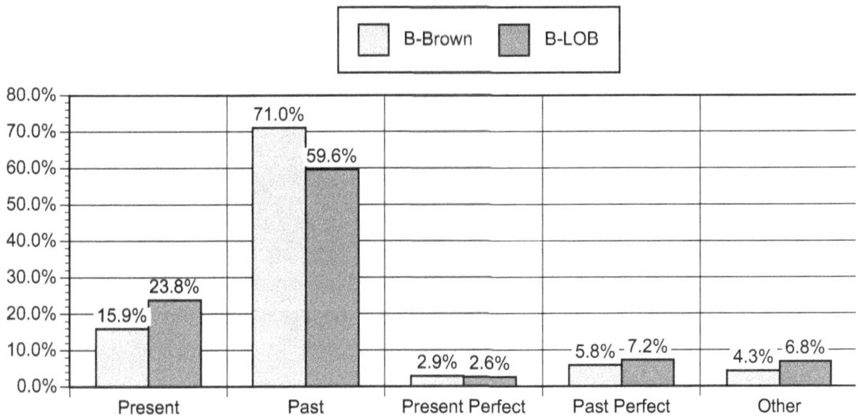

Figure 5.2. Distribution of progressives (proportions) according to tense/aspect in the general fiction section of the Brown and LOB prequels

All other combinations of the progressive are much less frequently used in both varieties. In this context the diachronic tense/aspect developments in category K of the Brown family are of interest. We therefore compared the normalized frequencies pmw of tense-aspect combinations in category K of the prequels against the results from the other members of the Brown family. The results are given in Figure 5.3. In this case, our data from the first half of the century provide interesting additional information: Contrary to our initial hypothesis, the present progressive does not increase throughout the century. Instead, we first see an increase of past progressives at the beginning of the century. This is more marked in the American than in the British data. In the second half of the century, it is the present progressives that increase whereas past progressives decrease, and again, American is ahead of British English in this trend.

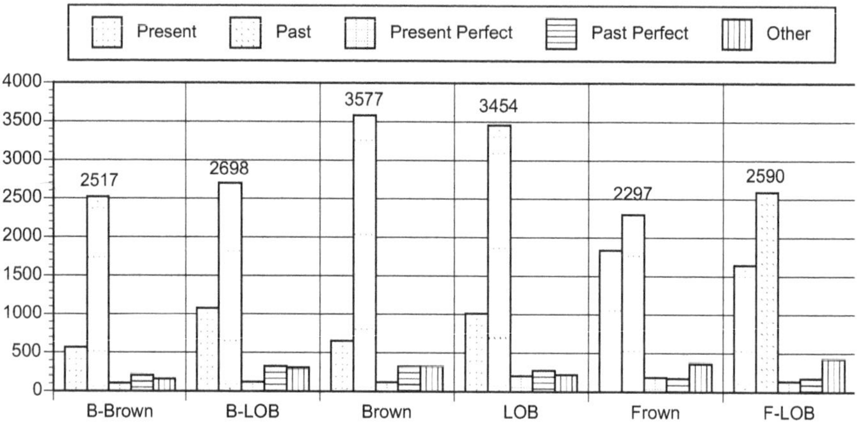

Figure 5.3. Distribution of progressives (frequencies pmw) according to tense/aspect in the Brown family of corpora (category K, general fiction)[12]

The decrease of the past progressive and the increase in present progressives in this genre are likely to be linked to an increase in direct speech over time. In other words, if the present tense is particularly dominant in dialogue, i.e. fictional representations of direct speech (Leech et al. 2009: 128), and dialogue sections have generally increased over time in fictional texts (as compared to narrative sections), then an increase in present progressives in the second half of the twentieth century appears to be a logical by-product, even if the increase in direct speech only accounts for part of the increase of progressives in the Brown family of corpora.

3.2.2 Progressives in fictional dialogue: tense, direct speech and style

In order to investigate the exact relation between tense, the progressive aspect and direct speech, it would be best to determine for each corpus the total number of words in dialogue on the one hand, and the total number of words in narrative passages on the other hand. Subsequently, it would be possible to see whether a general increase in direct speech over time brought along an increase in present progressives, or whether the progressives increased despite a relatively stable number of words in direct speech.[13] Unfortunately, however, this procedure was impracticable, as the only way to determine the total number of words in direct speech would have been to go through every corpus sample and count the words in direct speech manually.

What we could do was classify the progressives we had retrieved from the corpora according to whether they occurred in direct speech or not. The results were expected to at least provide further clues as to whether an increase of present progressives might be due to an increase of direct speech. Even here, we had to go through every concordance line manually and thoroughly check the textual context in each instance. Among the impediments we encountered were the following (focussing only on the American subcorpora of category K to illustrate the methodological challenges):

- Depending on the author of the source text, there are quotation marks that are not closed or not opened (with only one pair of marks before or after the instance of direct speech), which makes the detection of direct speech more time-consuming.
- Direct speech might not be graphically indicated by quotation marks at all in some original texts; thus, if the annotation guideline was to add mark-up only in cases of overt punctuation, these instances would not be annotated.
- Not all passages which are enclosed in the mark-up pair <quote> and <quote/> and not all passages that are enclosed in quotation marks are necessarily direct speech. There are cases of e.g. letters, so-called 'air quotes' and thoughts[14] which are graphically indicated by quotation marks in the source text and consequently annotated by some corpus compilers as <quote>,[15] but are not in fact a representation of spoken language. For our study, we excluded all instances that were not considered unambiguous representations of direct speech. On the other hand, we did include instances that were obviously cases of direct speech even if they were not marked by <quote>. The following passage from the Frown corpus, for instance, though marked with the tag <quote>, really is an example of "direct thought" (Toolan 2006: 703-704) and therefore was not included in our counts:[16]

(6) <quote_>"He's coming for me. I know he is because I know how flat his eyes went when I told him not to. And how they raced afterward. I didn't say it nicely, although I meant to. I practiced the points; in front of the mirror I went through them one by one: the sneaking around, and his wife and all.
[...]
"But he's coming for me. I know it. He's been looking for me all over. Maybe tomorrow he'll find me. Maybe tonight. Way out here; all the way out here.
"When we got off the streetcar, me and Acton and Felice, I thought he was there in the doorway next to the candy store, but it wasn't him. Not yet. I think I see him everywhere. I know he's looking and now I know he's coming. (K03 43-47, 73-79)

Since neither a mark-up code such as <quote> nor the occurrence of quotation marks in the source text guaranteed a case of direct speech, or, on the other hand, a passage of direct speech might not be signalled at all in the surface structure of the text (by corpus annotation or the author of the text), this extensive manual checking on our part seemed indispensable.

Figure 6 illustrates the development of the proportion of progressives in direct speech in general fiction. Our preliminary data do not support the assumption that the increase of the present progressive and the decrease of the past progressive are due to an increase of direct speech in both BrE and AmE; instead, we find a divergent development in the two national varieties. In BrE, we can see a relatively stable proportion of 24.8-27.2% of all progressives that occur in direct speech (the other progressives occurring in narrative passages); in fact, there even is a slight decrease. The progressives in direct speech can thus not be responsible for the general increase of present progressives in BrE. For AmE, however, our data show a development that matches our previous assumptions, as a decrease of progressives in direct speech from the 1930s to the 1960s is followed by a sharp increase from 14.4% to 31.4% in the second half of the twentieth century.

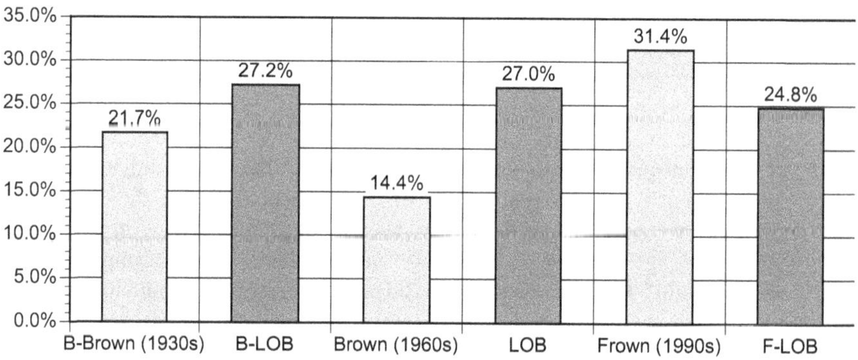

Figure 6. Progressives in direct speech (% of all progressives) in general fiction (Brown family of corpora)[17]

This finding fits in well with the decrease of present progressives and increase of past progressives from the 1930s-1960s in AmE and the increase of present progressives and the decrease of past progressives from the 1960s-1990s in AmE (see Figure 5.3).[18] That the high frequency of present progressives in the 1990s in AmE coincides with a high frequency of progressives in direct speech in the 1990s in AmE (31.4%, n=89) seems to confirm Leech et al.'s (2009: 128) statement, i.e. that "the situational characteristics of colloquial speech, whether genuine speech or speech represented in written form, are conducive to frequent use of the present progressive". Further analysis of the co-occurrence of the progressive with different tenses in relation to direct speech should shed some more light on the question of whether the progressives in direct speech are indeed mostly present progressives and thus the crucial factor for the high frequency of present progressives in 1990s AmE general fiction.

The results for our data for Frown category K are in line with Leech et al.'s (2009: 123) findings (see Figure 7). In direct speech, 70.8% of all progressives are present progressives, while only 14.6% are past progressives. In narrative passages, the situation is rather the reverse, with 62.9% of the progressives in past tense and 22.7% in present tense.

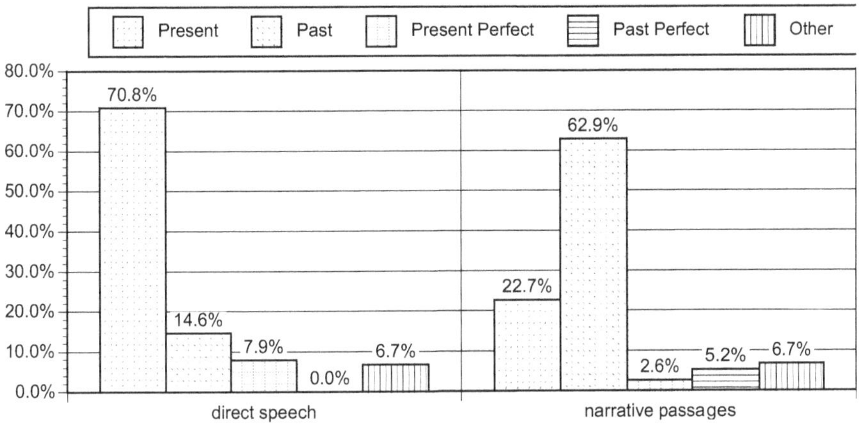

Figure 7. Progressives (proportions) in direct speech (n= 89) and narrative passages (n= 194) according to tense/aspect in category K (general fiction) of Frown (AmE 1991)[19]

The percentage of present progressives in narrative passages, however, is still surprisingly high and deserves further comment. A closer look at these present progressives reveals that a large proportion of them stems from two samples, i.e. K03 and K25. These samples are quite interesting from a stylistic point of view because they show that the type of 'narrative situation' (Stanzel 1984) in fictional texts can have an impact on the results of studies such as ours, which investigate phenomena sensitive to variation in spoken and written language. The narrative passages of texts with a first-person narrator or an 'authorial narrator' (who comments on the action, the characters and his own narration as well as communicates with the readers, see e.g. Stanzel 1984) are stylistically much more 'speech-like' than the narrative passages of a text with a 'figural narrative situation' (especially third-person texts with a limited point of view): in first-person narration there are more representations of thoughts and the narration is often much more immediate and direct, as it were. The following extract from Frown K03 (progressives in italics our emphasis) illustrates the speech-like nature of the narrative, although none of this is direct speech and the quotation marks in the beginning are just a typographic idiosyncrasy:

(7) "Acton has taken his shirt off. People *are blocking* the doorway; some stretch behind them to get a better look. The record playing is over. Somebody they *have been waiting* for *is playing* the piano. A woman *is singing* too. The music is faint but I know the words by heart. (K03 152-156)

Stylistic devices such as 'direct thought' or 'stream of consciousness',[20] either in the form of 'free indirect discourse' or an 'interior monologue', can also have an influence on the results, as the speech-like representation of thoughts makes the use of the progressive (and other phenomena associated with speech, like contractions) more likely, as the following example from the Frown corpus shows:

(8) But recalling the games of his childhood, he thought, who'*s kidding* who? It's one of those illusion things I remember from when I was a kid. In that case I'*m getting* the hell out of here. I can stand maybe mystery but not magic tricks or dealing with a rabbinical magician. (K24 13-17)

Hence, apart from the occurrence of dialogue and thus direct speech in a fictional text, the narrative situation and the individual presentation of character discourse (speech or thought) of a text in the general fiction subcorpus can seriously impact on the frequency of present progressives. For instance, in the case of category K in Frown, 86% of all instances of present progressives in narrative sections were found in texts with a first-person narrator.[21] The fact that a first-person narrative situation also favours present progressives might well be the reason why in our BrE data present progressives increase in general fiction despite the fact that they do not increase in representations of direct speech.

3.2.3 The progressive passive

Another detail that we focussed on is the development of the progressive passive: the overall frequency of this pattern is rather low in our two sub-corpora, so that we will only be looking at the total numbers of both categories together.[22] The trend that emerges from our preliminary evidence (see Figure 8) shows that the two varieties diverge in the usage of the progressive passive in the second half of the twentieth century, a result that fits in with previous findings (Hundt 2004b; Smith and Rayson 2007). We can also corroborate our hypothesis that the progressive passive is used slightly more often in 1930s BrE, even though the difference between BrE and AmE in the 1930s is negligible.

However, we also discovered that Hundt (2004b) was based on a stubbed version of the Brown corpus which contained significantly fewer texts in category K.[23] Our present results thus add an interesting detail to previous studies: Again, we can see that we are not dealing with a linear development in the American corpora; instead we see a sharp increase followed by a sharp decrease. In contrast, the British counterparts display a steady increase of progressive passives from the 1930s to the 1990s. The overall picture is consequently the following: we can identify a somewhat parallel development for the first half of the twentieth century, with AmE in fact using more progressive passives than BrE in the 1960s; in the second half of the twentieth century we see a marked divergence, that is, a decrease in AmE and an increase in BrE. Even though these findings are based on relatively low frequencies in only two sub-sections of the corpora, the divergence fits in well with observations on the overall development of *be*-passive constructions in the second half of the century (see Leech et al. 2009: 148ff.): the declining use of the *be*-passive, overall, is much more advanced in AmE, a finding that may well have to be attributed to the more vigorous attack on the passive in American style guides (ibid.: 151f.).

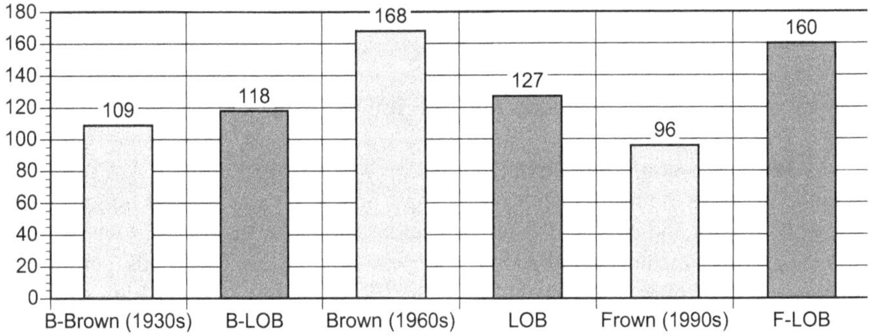

Figure 8. Progressive passives in two sub-corpora – academic writing and general fiction (frequencies pmw)

To sum up, AmE and BrE, as expected, are very similar with respect to tense and aspect combinations of the progressive throughout the twentieth century. The regional fluctuation of present progressives in representations of direct speech in fictional prose is prone to be affected by author styles, especially in small samples. The divergent development in the use of the progressive passive is probably related to the proscriptive influence on the use of the passive voice in American style guides.

4. Conclusion and outlook

The main motivation for including evidence from pre-war corpora in the study of differential change was that evidence from the first half of the twentieth century might add considerably to our view of the whole process. A commonly found hypothesis is that influence from AmE is more likely to have occurred during and after WW II, thus becoming visible in the second half of the century. With respect to overall developments, our pilot study confirms that the two regional varieties converge towards the end of the twentieth century. We did not, however, find evidence that the convergence is due to AmE influence since World War II.

More fine-grained analyses take the possibility of register variation into account. In our pilot study, we have used data from two very different subsections of the corpora: academic writing and general fiction. The former is commonly said to represent a conservative and conceptually prototypical written genre. General fiction, in turn, is more open to influence from the spoken medium: innovations that originate in speech will surface earlier in these texts than in the more conservative text types. In general, the results on the use of the progressive in these two types of text confirm the standard view of academic writing and general fiction as uptight and agile genres, respectively (see Hundt and Mair 1999). At the same time, the American data from the 1930s Brown-prequel lend an interesting twist to the story: American academic writing is more innovative at the beginning of the twentieth century than British academic writing, whereas the writers of fictional texts sampled for B-Brown were more conservative in the 1930s than their British peers. Overall, however, we see the expected long-term convergence of the two regional varieties towards the end of the twentieth century, without obvious evidence of AmE influence during and after the Second World War.

With respect to qualitative differences, we can conclude that AmE is more advanced both in the initial spread of the past progressive in general fiction in the first half of the century but also in the decrease towards the 1990s. Our pre-war data also confirm that the spread of the present progressive in this genre is a relatively recent phenomenon. Although AmE is ahead of BrE in both of these trends, we can identify an overall parallel development in terms of tense and aspect patterns.

A proportional increase of present progressives in direct speech of texts from category K could not be corroborated unequivocally throughout the century for both varieties. Furthermore, the analysis of progressives in fictional dialogue turned out to be a methodologically challenging task.

The progressive passive, finally, is clearly an example of regional divergence which occurred in the second half of the century. It probably has to be attributed to the greater pressure of usage guides on passive constructions, generally, in written AmE.

A major caveat of our pilot study is certainly the amount of data it is based on. Category K alone (at approximately 58,000 words) is not large enough to make generalizations about fictional writing. There are further reasons why results from category K should be treated with caution: developments in general fiction are not necessarily representative of the whole fictional writing section (categories K-R). A comparison with all of the fiction data in our corpora will only be possible once the fiction part of B-Brown has been completed. Moreover, K might not be the ideal starting point because general fiction is more likely to show idiosyncrasies of individual authors. If we take a closer look at e.g. the concordance plot of Frown category K, we see that considerable differences can be found between the individual texts: The numbers of progressives range from 30 instances (Frown K03) to 0 instances (Frown K07). As a result of this imbalance, 3 out of 29 texts (Frown K03, K15, K26) are responsible for 25% of the total number of progressives. It should be emphasized here, though, that this is not a problem only inherent in the sampling of Frown, but a more general problem of relatively small standard reference corpora. It is important to bear in mind that, whereas the Brown corpus as a whole was intended to be representative of written AmE in 1961, this was not the case for the sub-sections of the corpus. In other words, with only 29 samples (i.e. author styles), individual differences are more likely to be a skewing factor in K alone than if the whole fiction section were used, or the number of samples for K increased significantly to, say, 100 extracts (200,000 words). The differential analysis of the much larger academic writing section, on the other hand, yields more conclusive results.

There are various more general conclusions that we can draw from this study. First of all, it provides further proof of how important it is to consider the developments in the different text categories represented in the Brown family of corpora. There appears to be significant variation between the genres, as we could show for academic writing and general fiction.

Secondly, when we look at developments in only two categories against the backdrop of the whole corpora (= categories A-R), we realize that the developments of certain sub-corpora are not necessarily in line with the overall long-term development, i.e. temporarily regressive development in a genre is possible and even likely to occur. A general tendency might thus be marked by rather complicated steps in different directions. For instance, while there is no doubt that the progressive has, overall, been increasing in AmE over the past century, academic prose actually displays a slight decrease, albeit with a temporary increase in between. In other words, our case study has once again shown that variety-internal variation interacts in complex ways with regional variation and variation over time.

Thirdly, and most importantly for the objective we had in mind when we embarked on the project, our pilot study strongly suggests that for the study of differential language change in British and American English, two sampling points are simply not enough. With B-Brown as our new, third reference point in the 1930s for both varieties, we are able to get a much more reliable picture of the – often not quite so straight-forward – developments during the twentieth century. In other words, together with the BrE counterpart B-LOB, B-Brown will certainly provide the basis for more rewarding studies of differential language change in British and American English in the twentieth century.

Notes

1 See also Kranich (2008) for similar results based on a more recent version of ARCHER.

2 Preliminary evidence from the *Time Magazine Corpus* (Mark Davies, personal communication) also shows that the progressive increases steadily throughout the twentieth century.

3 A further addition to the Brown family is currently being compiled that will take us back to the beginning of the twentieth century (Leech and Smith, personal communication).

4 In the design of the Brown family of corpora, the subcorpus K 'General fiction' is only one out of six subcorpora belonging to the genre 'Fiction' or 'Imaginative Prose' (126 samples). See Table 1a in the Appendix for an overview of the different genres and subcorpora in the Brown family of corpora.

5 We allowed for a context word horizon of L7 for those corpora that had additional line numbering which might have intervened, as in *When Alex*

entered his room, the doctor was already K27 0910 preparing a nest in the straw case. [...] (Brown K27).

6 *Clarify* is a transitive verb that, in this context, might also have been used with ellipsis of the object NP. Thus, the example is ambiguous between an (unlikely) verbal interpretation and an adjectival one.

7 For raw frequencies in this and the following figure, see Table 2a in the Appendix.

8 The LL value is 1.17.

9 The LL value is 7.00, i.e. a finding that is significant at $p \leq 0.01$ (1 d.f.).

10 Note that the overall development in fictional writing (categories K-R) in the second half of the century is somewhat different: we see slightly higher frequencies there, especially in the fiction part of the Frown corpus than in our more limited data; but the overall developments in the data are still in the direction of regional convergence.

11 For raw frequencies in this and the following figure, see Table 3a in the Appendix.

12 For all frequencies pmw in this figure, see Table 4a in the Appendix.

13 Strictly speaking, for this and previous analyses it would also be useful to know the total number of verb phrases in order to be sure that any increase in progressives is not related to (or caused by) a general increase in verb density over time (see e.g. Kranich 2008: 13f.) Mair et al. (2002) show that English, in fact, has not become verbier in the second half of the twentieth century, and it is thus unlikely that a significant change in word class frequencies occurred before World War II.

14 Thoughts are not always easily distinguishable from actual spoken utterances. This is particularly true for fictional texts with a first-person narrator, whose narrative representations of thought are often speech-like: *The music bends, falls to its knees to embrace them all, encourage them all to live a little, why don't you? since this is the it you've been looking for* (Frown K03).

15 The general practice in the compilation of B-Brown was to consistently mark all instances of text enclosed in quotation marks with the mark-up <quote> and <quote/>, regardless of what exactly is enclosed by them. Apparently, this was not the practice followed by the compilers of Frown, for example (see e.g. K03).

16 Note that the following examples are quoted in the original format of the Frown corpus, i.e. with category label, line number and mark-up, features that are usually omitted from quotations from the corpus but that we use

here to illustrate the difficulties in obtaining watertight information on the number of words in quotations of direct speech.

17 For raw frequencies in this figure, see Table 5a in the Appendix.

18 The low proportion of progressives in the Brown corpus may possibly be related to less direct speech in general in our 1960s AmE general fiction data, but as mentioned above, this is a factor we cannot control at this point. Since we are dealing with proportions, however, we can at least be sure that the decrease of progressives in direct speech is not due to a decrease in progressives in general. In fact, as discussed in 3.1, there was a significant increase in the overall frequency of the progressive from 1930-1960 in AmE general fiction.

19 For all percentages and raw frequencies in this figure, please see Table 6a in the Appendix.

20 See Toolan (2001: 116-128; 2006) on the fictional representation of character discourse, specifically the narration or presentation of thought, which can create more immediacy in a narrative text.

21 We also noticed that the sample K03 alone accounted for 59% of all present progressives in narrative passages. This shows how stylistic preferences of individual authors in the general fiction sections of our corpora can exert considerable influence on the results, especially since we are dealing with rather low raw frequencies of progressives.

22 For raw frequencies and the number of progressive passives compared to all progressives, see Table 7a and 8a in the Appendix.

23 Hundt (2004b) uses a version of the corpus in which file K.txt was saved on 09.02.90 with a size of 76,693 bytes, whereas the version used for this paper was saved on 20.12.91 with a size of 374,702 bytes. The updated results for the other corpora do not differ significantly from those reported in Hundt (2004b). The search algorithm applied for this case study combined the auxiliary with the participle whereas in the previous paper, the progressive passives were retrieved by searching for *being*.

24 Results for academic writing (category J) from the post-war corpora (Brown, LOB, Frown, F-LOB) are taken from Leech et al. (2009). Note that the raw frequencies for category J in LOB and FLOB have been recalculated backwards, so to speak, by using the same word counts that were used for Leech et al. (2009).

25 Please see Endnote 24.

References

Hundt, M. (2004a), 'Animacy, agency and the spread of the progressive in eighteenth- and nineteenth-century English', *English Language and Linguistics*, 8(1): 47-69.

Hundt, M. (2004b), 'The passival and the progressive passive – a case study of layering in the English aspect and voice systems', in: H. Lindquist and C. Mair (eds.) *Corpus Approaches to Grammaticalisation in English*. Amsterdam/Philadelphia: Benjamins. 79-120.

Hundt, M. and C. Mair (1999), 'Agile and uptight genres. The corpus-based approach to language change in progress', *International Journal of Corpus Linguistics*, 4(2): 221-242.

Hundt, M. and N. Smith (2009), 'The present perfect in British and American English: Has there been any change, recently?' *ICAME Journal*, 33: 45-63.

Hundt, M. and G. Leech (Forthcoming), 'Small is beautiful – on the value of standard reference corpora for observing recent grammatical change', to appear in: E. C. Traugott and T. Nevalainen (eds.) *Handbook on the History of English: Rethinking Approaches to the History of English*. Oxford: Oxford University.

Kranich, S. (2008), *The Progressive in Modern English. A Corpus-Based Study of Grammaticalization and Related Changes*. PhD Dissertation, Freie Universität Berlin.

Leech, G. and N. Smith (2005), 'Extending the possibilities of corpus-based research on English in the twentieth century: A prequel to LOB and FLOB.' *ICAME Journal*, 29: 83-98.

Leech, G., M. Hundt, C. Mair and N. Smith (2009), *Change in Contemporary English: A Grammatical Study*. Cambridge: Cambridge University Press.

Mair, C., M. Hundt, G. Leech and N. Smith (2002), 'Short-term diachronic shifts in part-of-speech frequencies: A comparison of the tagged LOB and F-LOB corpora', *International Journal of Corpus Linguistics*, 7(2): 245-264.

Övergaard, G. (1995), *The Mandative Subjunctive in American and British English in the 20th Century*, Studia Anglistica Upsaliensia 94. Uppsala: Acta Universitatis Upsaliensis.

Smith, N. and P. Rayson (2007), 'Recent change and variation in the British English use of the progressive passive'. *ICAME Journal*, 31: 129-59.

Stanzel, F. K. (1984), *A Theory of Narrative* (transl. Charlotte Goedsche). Cambridge: Cambridge University Press.

Toolan, M. J. (2001), *Narrative. A Critical Linguistic Introduction*. 2nd ed. London: Routledge.

Toolan, M. J. (2006), 'Representation of speech and thought', in: K. Brown (ed.) *Encyclopedia of Language and Linguistics*. Vol. 11. 2nd ed. Oxford: Elsevier. 698-710.

Appendix

Table 1a. Genres and subcorpora in the Brown family of corpora

Genre	Subcorpora		Samples
Press	A-C	Reportage (44), Editorial (27), Reviews (17)	88
General Prose	D-H	Religion (17), Skills and Hobbies (36), Popular Lore (48), Belles Lettres/Biography/Memoirs (75), Miscellaneous (30)	206
Learned (Academic Writing)	**J**		80
Fiction	**K**, L, M, N, P, R	**General Fiction (29)**, Mystery and Detective Fiction (24), Science Fiction (6), Adventure and Western Fiction (29), Romance and Love Story (29), Humor (9)	126

Table 2a. Progressives in two sub-corpora (Brown family of corpora) – figures in brackets give frequencies per million words[24]

	B-Brown (1930s)	B-LOB	Brown (1960s)	LOB	Frown (1990s)	F-LOB
Category J	168 (1041)	149 (922)	197 (1216)	134 (831)	148 (923)	152 (945)
Category K	207 (3544)	265 (4526)	292 (4998)	304 (5199)	283 (4851)	290 (4974)
Total	375 (1706)	414 (1880)	489 (2217)	438 (1993)	431 (1970)	442 (2016)

Table 3a. Distribution of progressives (raw frequencies) according to tense/aspect in two sub-corpora of the Brown and LOB prequels

B-Brown	Present	Past	Pres. Perfect	Past Perfect	Other	Total
Category J	107	34	17	2	8	168
% of all progressives	63.7%	20.2%	10.1%	1.2%	4.8%	100.0%
Category K	33	147	6	12	9	207
% of all progressives	15.9%	71%	2.9%	5.8%	4.3%	99.9 %
Total	140	181	23	14	17	375
% of all progressives	37.3%	48.3%	6.1%	3.7%	4.5%	99.9%

Table 3a (cont.).

B-LOB	Present	Past	Pres. Perfect	Past Perfect	Other	Total
Category J	90	50	1	0	8	149
% of all progressives	60.4%	33.5%	0.7%	0%	5.4%	100.0%
Category K	63	158	7	19	18	265
% of all progressives	23.8%	59.6%	2.6%	7.2%	6.8%	100.0%
Total	153	208	8	19	26	414
% of all progressives	37%	50.2%	1.9%	4.6%	6.3%	100%

Table 4a. Distribution of progressives (frequencies pmw) according to tense/aspect in the Brown family of corpora (Category K, general fiction)

	Present	Past	Present Perfect	Past Perfect	Other
B-Brown	565	2517	103	205	154
B-LOB	1076	2698	120	324	307
Brown	650	3577	120	325	325
LOB	1009	3454	205	274	222
Frown	1834	2297	189	171	360
F-LOB	1646	2590	137	172	429

Table 5a. Progressives in direct speech and narrative passages in general fiction (Brown family of corpora) – figures in brackets give frequencies per million words

Category K	B-Brown (1930s)	B-LOB	Brown (1960s)	LOB	Frown (1990s)	F-LOB
progressives total	207 (3544)	265 (4526)	292 (4998)	304 (5199)	283 (4851)	290 (4974)
in direct speech	45 (770)	72 (1230)	42 (719)	82 (1402)	89 (1525)	72 (1252)
% of all progressives	21.7%	27.2%	14.4%	27%	31.4%	24.8%
in narrative	162 (2773)	193 (3296)	250 (4279)	222 (3796)	194 (3325)	218 (3739)
% of all progressives	78.3%	72.8%	85.6%	73%	68.6%	75.2%

Table 6a. Progressives in direct speech and narrative sections in general fiction (Frown) according to tense/aspect

Frown, Category K	Present	Past	Pres. Perfect	Past Perfect	Other	Total
in direct speech	63	13	7	0	6	89
% of all progressives in direct speech	70.8%	14.6%	7.9%	0%	6.7%	100%
in narrative	44	122	5	10	13	194
% of all progressives in narrative	22.7%	62.9%	2.6%	5.2%	6.7%	100%
Total	107	135	12	10	19	283
% of all progressives	37.8%	47.7%	4.2%	3.5%	6.7%	100%

Table 7a. Progressive passives in two sub-corpora (Brown family of corpora) – figures in brackets give frequencies per million words[25]

	B-Brown	B-LOB	Brown	LOB	Frown	F-LOB
Category J	20 (124)	25 (155)	28 (173)	21 (130)	15 (94)	26 (162)
Category K	4 (68)	1 (17)	9 (154)	7 (120)	6 (103)	12 (206)
Total	24 (109)	26 (118)	37 (168)	28 (127)	21 (96)	38 (173)

Table 8a. Progressive passives in two sub-corpora (Brown family of corpora) in relation to all progressives

	B-Brown (1930s)	B-LOB	Brown (1960s)	LOB	Frown (1960s)	F-LOB
Category J	20	25	28	21	15	26
% of all progressives	11.9%	16.8%	14.2%	15.7%	10.1%	17.1%
Category K	4	1	9	7	6	12
% of all progressives	1.9%	0.4%	3.1%	2.3%	2.1%	4.1%
Total	24	26	37	28	21	38
% of all progressives	6.4%	6.3%	7.6%	6.4%	4.9%	8.6%

"Love is like a stove – it burns you when it's hot": A corpus-linguistic view on the (non-)creative use of love-related metaphors in pop songs[1]

Rolf Kreyer

Philipps-Universität Marburg

Abstract

Pop-song lyrics are often felt to be highly stereotypical and clichéd. The present paper is an exploratory attempt to shed light on the linguistic substance of these stereotypes and clichés by analysing the use of love-related metaphors in a pilot version of the Giessen-Bonn Corpus of Popular Music *(GBoP; see Kreyer and Mukherjee 2007) within the framework of conceptual metaphor theory (e.g. Lakoff and Johnson 1980; Kövecses 2002). In particular, two questions are explored: 1) how much variation in the use of these metaphors do we find in GBoP, and 2) how creatively are these metaphors used in GBoP? The results are surprising in that pop songs show a fair amount of variation as well as creativity. The use of metaphors, therefore, cannot be regarded as the source of clichédness of pop song lyrics. On the basis of a brief comparison of the GBoP data with the poetry section of the* British National Corpus, *the paper suggests an alternative explanation along the lines of the Russian formalists' approach to poetic language.*

1. Introduction

Pop-song lyrics are usually felt to be highly stereotypical and clichéd. This paper explores one possible source of this clichédness, namely the use of love-related metaphors in pop songs. To this end the framework of conceptual metaphor theory (e.g. Lakoff and Johnson 1980 or Kövecses 2002) is applied to the analysis of the 340,000-words pilot version of the *Giessen-Bonn Corpus of Popular Music* (GBoP; Kreyer and Mukherjee 2007). With regard to clichédness, we would assume that either pop song lyrics use the same metaphors again and again, thus showing a lack of variation in the use of metaphors, or that pop songs do not exploit metaphors in a very creative way (or both). The present paper, to my knowledge, is the first attempt to analyse this aspect with the help of an exhaustive corpus analysis.

Following this introduction, Section 2 introduces two important concepts from the field of conceptual metaphor theory. Section 3 describes the corpus and the way in which the data was abstracted. The main part of this paper, Section 4, explores the use of love-related metaphors in pop-song lyrics, focusing on the variation of the metaphors used as well as the creativity with which they are used. Section 5 discusses the results and suggests an explanation for the clichédness of pop songs along the lines of the Russian formalists' approach to poetic language and Section 6 sketches some lines for future research.

2. Conceptual metaphor theory

The main idea of conceptual metaphor theory as described in Lakoff and Johnson's (1980) seminal book is as follows:

> Metaphor is for most people a device of the poetic imagination and the rhetorical flourish – a matter of extraordinary rather than ordinary language. [...] We have found, on the contrary, that metaphor is pervasive in everyday life, not just in language but in thought and action. Our ordinary conceptual system, in terms of which we both think and act, is fundamentally metaphorical in nature. (Lakoff and Johnson 1980: 3)

Furthermore, the authors claim that "[t]he essence of metaphor is understanding and experiencing one kind of thing in terms of another" (5). Usually, a more abstract concept (the 'target domain') is understood by reference to a more concrete – and hence more accessible – one (the 'source domain'). A famous example is the concept LOVE which is often understood in terms of a JOURNEY through the metaphor LOVE IS A JOURNEY. What the metaphor does is to map elements of the target domain onto elements of the source domain, which enables the language user to get a clearer understanding of the concept LOVE. In particular, the target domain contains elements such as the lovers, the love relationship, common goals that the lovers have and difficulties that they encounter in their attempts to achieve their common goals. With the metaphor LOVE IS A JOURNEY, these elements are mapped onto the more concrete elements that are characteristic of journeys, namely the travellers, the vehicle, the destination and impediments on the road.

For the present purposes two kinds of metaphors have to be distinguished, 'structural' and 'ontological metaphors'. The first kind serves to structure one concept in terms of another (Lakoff and Johnson 1980: 14), as is the case in the LOVE IS A JOURNEY metaphor where the concept JOURNEY provides a structure for the concept LOVE. Examples usually cited in this respect are *we are at a crossroads*, *we are spinning our wheels*, or *we have to go our separate ways*. Ontological metaphors are different in that respect. According to Lakoff and Johnson (1980: 27), they "serve a very limited range of purposes – referring, quantifying, etc." With ontological metaphors, the source domain does not have a lot of structure. The purpose of these metaphors is more to help us conceive of feelings, events and emotions as concrete physical objects and substances (see Lakoff and Johnson 1980: 25). A case in point is the metaphor LOVE IS A CONTAINER. The concept CONTAINER in this context makes reference to the most abstract understanding of a container that can be conceived of: it classifies the world in terms of 'inside' and 'outside', i.e. either something is in the container or not. Any linguistic expression which talks about 'being *in* love' testifies to the use of this particular metaphor.

Both kinds of metaphors, as will be seen further below, figure prominently in pop-song lyrics.

3. Corpus data

As said above, the data underlying this analysis is drawn from a pilot version of the *Giessen-Bonn Corpus of Popular Music* (GBoP; see Kreyer and Mukherjee 2007). GBoP is a project which aims at compiling a representative pop-song corpus containing the lyrics of the top 100 albums in the US Album Charts from 2000 to 2010. So far, a pilot version has been compiled which contains all the lyrics of the top 52 albums from 2003. Of these, four did not have any lyrics or no lyrics in English, which means that, at present, the corpus contains 48 albums (namely top 1-6, 8-25, 27-29, 30-48 and 51-52) with a total of 758 songs and approximately 340,000 words.

The corpus merely exists in an orthographic version with no annotation added apart from the addition of line breaks (<br>). The lyrics contained in the corpus, thus, look as in the example below.

(1) After love, after love
 After love, after love
 No matter how hard I try
 You keep pushing me aside
 And I can't break through
 There's no talking to you
 So sad that you're leaving (Cher: *Believe*)

The search for metaphors in this corpus can only be based on lexical queries. A suitable method in this respect is what Stefanowitsch (2006: 66) refers to as 'metaphorical pattern analysis'. A metaphorical pattern consists of "a multi-word expression from a given source domain (SD) into which a specific lexical item from a given target domain (TD) has been inserted". The search for metaphorical patterns in a corpus boils down to a two-step process: 1) search for target-domain lexis in a given corpus, and 2) search for potential source-domain lexis in the concordance lines. Searching for the noun *love* (and the 'deviant' spelling *luv*) in GBoP, for instance, yields the following instantiations of (structural) metaphors.

(2) Blowin me up with her love (JC Chasez: *Blowin' Me Up*)
(3) The spark of love was still burning (Rod Stewart: *That Old Feeling*)
(4) Love will open every door. (Christina Aguilera: *Soar*)

The source-domain lexis in (2) to (4), i.e. *blowin' me up*, *spark/burning* and *open/door* betrays the conceptualisation of love as an explosive, a fire and a key, respectively.

GBoP shows 934 instances of the noun *love*. Of these, 477 occur in metaphorical patterns of the kind illustrated above. Since some of these instantiations are repetitions (for instance in the chorus), we end up with 256 different metaphorical patterns[2]. These are the basis for the following analysis.

4. Love in pop songs

The aim of the following analysis is to get an idea of the extent to which the use of metaphors may contribute to the feeling of clichédness and stereotypicality that many associate with pop-song lyrics. Two hypotheses have been suggested in the introduction: 1) there is too little variation in the metaphors that are used in pop songs, i.e. pop songs use the same metaphors over and over again, and 2) there is too little creativity in the exploitation of the metaphors used, i.e. if pop songs use metaphors, they are always used in a very basic, 'run-of-the-mill' fashion. We will consider each hypothesis in turn.

4.1 Variation in the use of metaphors

To explore the variation in the use of metaphors we first have to get an idea of the number of metaphors that are used to conceptualise love. According to some of the most relevant sources, e.g. Lakoff and Johnson (1980) or Kövecses (2002), we can assume that the twenty metaphors shown in Table 1 are most relevant with regard to love.

Table 1. Love-related metaphors in cognitive linguistics (after Lakoff and Johnson 1980 and Kövecses 2000, 2002) and their frequencies in GBoP

	LOVE IS ...	Example (Lakoff and Johnson 1980; Kövecses 2000, 2002)	Freq.
1	A JOURNEY	*It's been a long bumpy road*	15
2	A NUTRIENT	*I'm starved for love*	2
3	A UNITY OF PARTS	*We're as one*	1
4	CLOSENESS	*they are very close*	0
5	A BOND	*There is a close tie between them*	5
6	A FLUID IN A CONTAINER	*she was overflowing with love*	0
7	A FIRE/HEAT	*I am burning with love*	17
8	AN ECONOMIC EXCHANGE	*I'm putting more into this than you are*	1
9	A NATURAL FORCE	*she swept me off my feet*	5
10	A PHYSICAL FORCE	*I was magnetically drawn to her*	0

Table 1 (cont.).

	LOVE IS ...	Example (Lakoff and Johnson 1980; Kövecses 2000, 2002)	Freq.
11	AN OPPONENT	*she tried to fight her feelings of love*	3
12	A CAPTIVE ANIMAL	*she let go of her feelings*	9
13	WAR	*she conquered him*	2
14	SPORT/A GAME	*he made a play for her*	5
15	A DISEASE/AN ILLNESS	*I am heart-sick*	4
16	MAGIC	*I was entranced by him*	0
17	INSANITY	*I am crazy about you*	0
18	A SOCIAL SUPERIOR	*she is completely ruled by love*	1
19	A RAPTURE/A HIGH	*I have been high on love for weeks.*	1
20	A PATIENT	*love is a sick relationship.*	0
	Sum:		71

A metaphorical expression in GBoP was analysed as instantiating one of these metaphors if it could either be related to the source domain directly (e.g. LOVE being conceptualised as the journey itself) or to an element within the source domain (e.g. Love being conceptualised as the vehicle on the journey). Of the twenty love-related metaphors above, only six are not instantiated in GBoP, namely metaphors 4, 6, 10, 16, 17, and 20. All of the others are instantiated with varying frequencies, as the third column shows. Of the 256 different types of metaphorical expressions, 71 are instantiations of these 14 different metaphors that are found in the corpus.

By way of illustration, consider the following examples from GBoP. These have been classified as instantiating the metaphor LOVE IS A JOURNEY since all of them make reference to conceptual elements that are related to journeys.

(5) We may never meet again <br> on that bumpy road to love
(6) Without love I'd never find a way.
(7) When that love doesn't go the distance.
(8) I thought we had all the love to go for it for the long run.

In example (5) love is conceptualised as the destination of a journey, and in (6) love is understood as the guide that leads the lovers to that destination. Examples (7) and (8) are related to the idea that the lovers use a vehicle on that journey: in (7), love itself is the vehicle and the danger is that it might break down, whereas in (8) love is regarded as the fuel in the vehicle.

All of the above metaphors count as structural metaphors in conceptual metaphor theory. In addition, GBoP also shows a number of ontological metaphors, i.e. metaphors which have a source domain that is not richly structured but merely serves to provide an abstract concept with features of physical entities, substances, etc. GBoP shows three such ontological metaphors, two of which are very frequent in the corpus as Table 2 shows.

Table 2. Ontological metaphors used to describe LOVE in GBoP

	LOVE IS …	Example	Freq.
1	AN OBJECT	*You gave me love* *The love we share* *If we lost true love*	72
2	A CONTAINER	*You fall in love* *I'm in love*	53
3	A PERSON	*My love won't wait* *The sweet breathing of love* *Love is so blind*	3
	Sum:		128

The most frequent ontological metaphor found in GBoP is LOVE IS AN OBJECT with 72 instantiations. The examples show that different characteristics of objects are highlighted, i.e. the fact that objects can be transferred, that they can be used together, or that they can be lost, to name but a few. Second-most frequent is the conceptualisation of LOVE as a container. It is used frequently with 53 different instantiations although basically restricted to variations of the two tokens shown above, i.e. the fact that you fall in love or that you are in love. Finally, love is personified[3] in three cases, all of which are shown in Table 2.

Summing up we can conclude that pop-song lyrics do show variation in the use of metaphors; our assumption that pop songs use the same metaphors over and over again is not supported by the data. Of the twenty love-related metaphors that are listed in the relevant literature, 14 are found in GBoP. In addition, we find that pop song lyrics make use of 3 ontological metaphors. On the whole, we find 17 metaphor types that account for the 256 different metaphorical expressions that we have identified in GBoP. On the basis of these findings our first hypothesis might have to be rejected. The source of clichédness and stereotypicality of pop-song lyrics does not seem to stem from a lack of variation in the metaphors that they use.

4.2 Creativity in the use of metaphors

The second hypothesis is that the locus of clichédness in pop-song lyrics may lie in a lack of creativity in the exploitation of the metaphors that are found in pop-songs. In what sense, according to conceptual metaphor theory, can metaphors be used creatively? Kövesces writes:

> Ordinary metaphors [...] are not things that poets and writers leave behind when they do their "creative" work. On the contrary, there is accumulating evidence that suggests that "creative" people make

> heavy use of conventional, everyday metaphors, and that their creativity and originality actually derive from them. (Kövecses 2002: 46)

In particular, the following four kinds of creativity can be distinguished (cf. Kövecses 2002: 47-49):

- **Extending**: introduction of a new conceptual element or a submetaphor
- **Elaboration**: exploitation of an existing conceptual element in a novel way
- **Combining**: combination of a number of conceptual metaphors in one expression
- **Questioning**: calling into question the appropriateness of our metaphors, i.e. doubting the truth of the proposition conveyed by the metaphor.

On the basis of this view on creativity we might assume that pop-song lyrics tend to make use of 'basic' metaphors only. That is, we do not find a lot of extending, elaboration, combining or questioning in pop songs. What does the corpus say?

The first kind of creativity, extending, is fairly frequent in the corpus. We find that 109 of the 256 metaphorical expressions in the corpus show that kind of creativity. Consider the examples below:

(9) Without love I'd never find a way.
(10) Love lights your way through the night.
(11) K-O, knocked out by technicality
 The love has kissed the canvas.
(12) Ten rounds in the ring with love.
(13) Love is like a stove.
 It burns you when it's hot.

Examples (9) and (10) introduce a new conceptual element into the basic metaphor LOVE IS A JOURNEY, namely the idea that love is a guide on the journey of the lovers. Similarly, (11) and (12) are special instances of the LOVE IS AN OPPONENT metaphor; it introduces the element of the boxing match. The metaphor in (13) is a new submetaphor in the family of fire- or heat-related metaphors: the stove can be conceived of as a special kind of source of fire or heat.

All other kinds of creativity are a lot rarer. Elaboration, i.e. the exploitation of a given conceptual element in a novel way, is attested only 4 times.

(14) You're like a deer who's caught up in the headlights of love.
(15) When that love doesn't go the distance.

Examples (14) and (15) elaborate on the vehicle aspect that is part of the LOVE IS A JOURNEY metaphor, namely the idea that a vehicle has headlights and the idea that it can break down. Similarly rare is the combining of metaphors. It occurs 8 times in the whole corpus.

(16) When it comes to love I may not know the rules.
(17) Bring me your love
 Slowly breaking through the daylight.

Example (16) combines the idea of a journey (with love as the destination) with the conceptualisation of love as a game or a particular kind of sport. In (17), the first clause conceives of love as an object (an ontological metaphor), which can be 'carried' to somebody, and at the same time conceptualises love as the sun or the sunlight (a structural metaphor) – a metaphorical use that can be subsumed under the LOVE IS A FIRE/HEAT metaphor.

The fourth kind of creative use of metaphors is questioning, where the user calls into question the appropriateness of the metaphor, i.e. he or she doubts the truth of the proposition that is expressed through the metaphor. This kind of creativity is very rare, only 2 tokens are attested, one of which is given in (18):

(18) I was naïve, your love was like candy
 Artificially sweet, I was deceived by the wrapping.

This example makes reference to the metaphor LOVE IS A NUTRIENT. Candy can be regarded as a special kind of nutrient since it provides the body with sugar. In this case, however, the piece of candy is artificially sweet and deceptive – it does not seem to be beneficial to the body, i.e. love is not a nutrient in the eyes of the artist.

Table 3. New love-related metaphors in GBoP

	LOVE IS ...	Example	Freq.
1	A VISITOR	*People keep on tellin me your love is here to stay*	13
2	A CONTENT	*To show her the love that he holds inside*	12
3	A SUPPORT	*I feel my love Can give me what I want*	12
4	A PLANT	*The love seeds planted in our souls*	3
5	A WINGED CREATURE	*Love's wings are broken all too soon*	3
6	A BLANKET	*And just leave us wrapped up in this love*	2
7	A FLUID	*More love to flow in between us*	2
8	A CRIME	*If love is a crime baby I'd do my time*	2
9	A CLOUD	*Love is like a cloud And it holds a lot of rain*	1
10	A DRESS	*Just how good your love looks on me*	1
11	AN EXPLOSIVE	*Blowin' me up with her love*	1
12	A GHOST	*Don't you-don't let our love haunt you*	1
13	A ROLLER-COASTER	*Coz in love there's no holding back Tell me that you played it safe Coz you're afraid to hurt your neck On the rollercoaster train,*	1
14	A KNIFE	*Love's like a knife it can cut deep inside*	1
15	THE MOON	*Our love's the moon*	1
16	A CLAIMANT	*You're the only one, with the only love That's strong enough to claim me*	1
	Sum:		57

In addition to the four kinds of creativity mentioned above, there is a fifth kind, namely coming up with new metaphors. So far, we have only concentrated on the structural metaphors listed in Table 1 and the ontological metaphors listed in Table 2. The sums in the bottom rows of these tables only add up to 199 (out of 256), i.e. there are 57 instances of metaphorical expressions left unaccounted for. These are instantiations of 16 metaphors that are not discussed in the literature. Consider Table 3.

These new metaphors can, of course, also be used creatively. A case in point is the idea of love being a support, as shown in line 3 in the above table. Consider the example under (19) below.

(19) Look what love gave us
 A world full of killing, and blood-spilling.

The artist, in this example, uses the metaphor LOVE IS A SUPPORT, which maintains that love provides and gives what is needed. But he calls into question the truth of this metaphor, since love has only given a "world full of killing, and blood-spilling".

Table 4 sums up the frequencies of the five kinds of creative use of metaphors discussed above.

Table 4. Creativity in the use of metaphors in GBoP (n = 256)

Kind of creativity	Freq.
Extending	109
Elaboration	4
Combining	8
Questioning	2
New metaphors	57
Sum:	180 (~70%)

As Table 4 shows, approximately 70% of all metaphorical expressions in GBoP make creative use of existing metaphors or show the use of new metaphors. On the basis of this data, the second hypothesis, namely that the source of clichédness lies in a lack of creativity in the use of metaphors, does not seem to hold either. A number of alternative explanations are discussed in the next section.

5. Alternative explanations: Too much, too simple, too visible?

An obvious first explanation for the clichédness of pop-song lyrics that comes to mind is the mere frequency of occurrence of the noun *love* – there is too much love in pop songs. The impression that pop songs talk about love a lot is supported by a comparison of the GBoP data with the poetry section of the *British National Corpus* (BNC) (W:fict:poetry). In the 340,000 words of GBoP, the noun *love* is instantiated 934 times, which would be 2,747 occurrences of the noun *love* per one million words. In contrast, the 223,683 words of the poetry section of the BNC only shows 178 instances of *love* as a noun, i.e. 796 occurrences per one million words. That is, the noun *love* is 3.45 times as frequent in GBoP than in 'W:fict:poetry'. This might well contribute to an impression of clichédness of pop-song lyrics.

The second and third candidates make reference to ideas discussed by the Russian formalists at the beginning of the last century. According to V. Šklovskij, as van Peer (1986: 1) points out, "[t]he function of art [...] is to make people aware of the world in a fresh way. The device whereby this is achieved is *de-familiarization*, or 'making strange' [...]". This defamiliarisation runs counter to automatisation in processing and interpretation and, thus, leads to foregrounding:

> The task of the poet is to counteract the routine of the reader's attachment to clichés, stock responses and automatized perception [...]. The effect is *density* [...], which hinders ease of communication, hence resulting in *retardation*: the processes of perception and of comprehension are slowed down. The reader is forced to come to grips with the world of the text in a more strenuous and supposedly more rewarding fashion. (van Peer 1986: 2)

According to the Russian formalists, part of the appeal of poetic language lies in the effort one has to put into decoding the message. This view was developed further by Prague School researchers. Havránek (1932 [1964]: 10), for instance, talks of 'foregrounding', i.e. "the use of the devices of the language in such a way that this use itself attracts attention" (see also Jakobson's (1960) 'poetic function of language'). From that perspective, we may expect that pop-song lyrics are too simple and that their language does not draw attention to itself to the same degree as 'real' poems do. In Havránek's terms, popsong lyrics show less 'foregrounding' but more 'automatization'. Let us take a look at two examples. The first is taken from GBoP, the second from the poetry section of the BNC.

(20) I was naïve, your love was like candy
 Artificially sweet, I was deceived by the wrapping. [=(18)]

(21) Some people [...] feel a need to sweeten things – take 'love' in life, tooth-rotting sugar in their tea. (FS5: 1260-1262)

Both examples question the appropriateness of the metaphor LOVE IS A NUTRIENT. In example (20), this questioning is fairly obvious: the reader is told that love is artificially sweet and that it is deceptive. Example (21), in contrast, is more subtle: the reader has to take 'an extra step' to arrive at the same conclusion: love is portrayed as something that can sweeten somebody's life and it is only through analogical thinking that the reader will find out that love can be as detrimental to one's life as sugar can be to one's teeth. The reader has to put more effort into the decoding of the message; the decoding process is de-automatized and the "focus on the message for its own sake" (Jakobson 1960: 356) is stronger.

Related to this aspect is the last possible source of clichédness: love may be too visible in pop songs. This assumption seems plausible in the light of the mere frequency of the noun *love* in GBoP as opposed to its frequency in the poetry section of the BNC. But it also touches on another aspect. In GBoP we find 477 metaphorical patterns, i.e. combinations of target domain lexis (in this case: the noun *love*) and source domain lexis (e.g. *stove* or *candy*). With regard to the decoding of the message, metaphorical patterns are fairly simple in that they tell the reader/listener that the metaphorical expression is about love. Metaphorical expressions that only contain source-domain lexis, e.g. *we are at a crossroads* or *we are spinning our wheels*, are more strenuous to decode and, hence, more artistically rewarding, since the recipient has to discover that such metaphorical expressions tell him or her something about the nature of love. My assumption is that in pop songs the proportion of metaphorical expressions with source and target domain lexis is higher in comparison to those that only contain source domain lexis. That is, pop songs make it easier for the recipient to find out that a string of words is about love than poetry 'proper'. It is in that sense that love is too visible in pop songs.

6. Future research

The present paper is a first case study within a larger project that analyses the use of emotion-related metaphors in pop-song lyrics. For future research, the following three aspects might be taken into consideration.

First, the difficulty of identifying metaphors. In the present study, metaphors were identified in a rather intuitive way on the basis of my own judgements. Recently, the Pragglejaz Group (2007; also see Steen 2007) have suggested a 'Metaphor Identification Procedure' which attempts to operationalise the identification of metaphors. The application of this and similar methods might put the above results on a sounder methodological footing.

Second, the proportion of source-domain lexis metaphors. As sketched out in Section 5, this aspect needs to be taken into consideration if we want to arrive at a clear picture of the use of metaphorical expressions in pop-song lyrics. A useful step in that direction might be the application of Wmatrix, a web-based corpus tool that allows for the automatic semantic tagging of each word in any piece of text (Rayson 2008 and 2009). On the basis of a semantically tagged version of GBoP and 'W:fict:poetry' it would be possible to identify those word forms that are potential candidates for source-domain lexis. For instance, a look at all word forms that are tagged as referring to the semantic field of 'FOOD' might help to identify metaphorical expressions that conceptualise love as a nutrient. In this way, a comparison of GBoP and the poetry section of the BNC as described in Section 5 might be possible.

Third, the applicability of conceptual metaphor theory for the study of creativity. Conceptual metaphor theory, as shown above, understands metaphor not to be an artistic device but to be fundamental to human cognition. One of the main merits of Lakoff and Johnson's book was to draw attention to the all-pervasiveness of conceptual metaphors in everyday language and to illustrate how everyday expressions are fundamentally metaphorical in nature. However, if conceptual metaphors are so elusive that often they are not recognised by the recipient, this approach might not be entirely suitable for the study of creativity, which after all involves drawing attention to a linguistic expression. This becomes most obvious with phraseologies such as '*when it comes to* X', as is instantiated by the string *when it comes to love I may not know the rules* discussed in Section 4.2. If the recipient is not aware of the metaphorical nature of the first clause, perhaps it does not make sense to assume that here we are dealing with a creative use of metaphors, namely combining. Related to that aspect is the question of where to draw the line between non-creative and creative use of a metaphor. A concept like 'extending', which refers to the introduction of a new conceptual element into a metaphor, makes the tacit assumption that there is a consensus among language users and researchers which conceptual elements are 'regularly' associated with a given metaphor. However, it seems doubtful that such a consensus exists; some users may regard a given metaphorical expression as creative while others may not. A case in point is the conceptualisation of LOVE as a GUIDE: while this metaphor is not listed in the sources cited in the present paper, some people might feel that it is a fairly common and, hence, uncreative way of talking about love. More research is needed to get an idea of 'the basic version' of specific metaphors.

Future research will have to show to what extent the consideration of the above aspects can help to arrive at a clearer understanding of the role of metaphors and clichédness in pop-song lyrics.

Notes

1 I would like to thank Jürgen Esser, Harold Fish, Anna Kreyer, Geoffrey Leech, Sebastian Patt, Paul Rayson and Sharmila Vaz for comments on earlier versions of this paper.

2 In some cases different artists use the same metaphorical expression, e.g. *give me love*. Such cases have been counted as different metaphorical expressions since their recurrence is not due to repetition in the chorus.

3 The cases of personification show that the distinction between structural and ontological metaphors is not always easy to draw. The examples *The sweet breathing of love* and *Love is so blind*, for instance, could also be interpreted as making reference to the human body or parts thereof (the breathing apparatus or the eyes). In that case we have a highly structured source domain and the two examples would rather be classified as structural metaphors. In addition, the three metaphors might also be regarded as making reference to animate beings in general, not persons.

References

Havránek, B. (1932 [1964]), 'The functional differentiation of the standard language', in: P.L. Garvin (ed.) *A Prague School Reader on Esthetics, Literary Structure, and Style.* Washington D.C.: Georgetown University Press. 3-16.

Jakobson, R. (1960), 'Closing statement: Linguistics and poetics', in: T.A. Sebeok (ed.) *Style in Language*.. Cambridge, Mass.: M.I.T. Press. 350-377.

Kövecses, Z. (2000), *Metaphor and Emotion. Language, Culture, and Body in Human Feeling.* Cambridge: Cambridge University Press.

Kövecses, Z. (2002), *Metaphor. A Practical Introduction.* Oxford: Oxford University Press.

Kreyer, R. and J. Mukherjee (2007), 'The style of pop song lyrics: a corpus-linguistic pilot study', *Anglia,* 125: 31-58.

Lakoff, G. and M. Johnson (1980), *Metaphors we Live by.* Chicago: Chicago University Press.

Pragglejaz Group (2007), 'MIP: A method for identifying metaphorically used words in discourse', *Metaphor and Symbol*, 22: 1-39.

Rayson, P. (2008), 'From key words to key semantic domains', *International Journal of Corpus Linguistics*, 13: 519-549.

Rayson, P. (2009), 'Wmatrix: a web-based corpus processing environment', Computing Department, Lancaster University. <http://ucrel.lancs.ac.uk/wmatrix/>

Steen, G.J. (2007), *Finding Metaphor in Grammar and Usage: A Methodological Analysis.* Amsterdam: John Benjamins.

Stefanowitsch, A. (2006), 'Words and their metaphors: A corpus-based approach', in: A. Stefanowitsch and S. Th. Gries (eds.) *Corpus-based Approaches to Metaphor and Metonymy.* Berlin and New York: Mouton de Gruyter. 61-105.

van Peer, W. (1986), *Stylistics and Psychology: Investigations of Foregrounding.* London: Croom Helm.

Scare quotes in Norwegian L2 English and British English

Susan Nacey

Hedmark University College

Abstract

This paper presents the findings of a comparative investigation into the use of scare quotes in the English written production of Norwegian university students and the writing of British A-level students. The use of scare quotes usually signifies that the term in quotation marks is somehow inappropriate and that the writers want to distance themselves from it. Motivations for their use vary. Little research has been carried out on scare quotes even though they are a common occurrence in both native speaker and non-native speaker writing. Discussion of scare quotes seems to be primarily restricted to a small number of contributions by linguists in online language blogs or magazines (see e.g. Jacobs 2003; McWhorter 2005; Trask 2000), as well as a few prescriptive admonishments in various language style guides. Taking as its starting point previous research into learner compensation strategies (Poulisse 1993), this paper sets out a taxonomy intended to account for the various possible uses of the quotes. This framework is then utilized in the investigation of the occurrences of scare quotes in essays written by the two groups of students, to discover whether Norwegians and British novice writers employ scare quotes in similar ways. The overall goal is to shed some light on a previously overlooked feature of student writing.

Data for the study comes from approximately 25,000 words of text found in argumentative essays written by Norwegian university and college students and collected in the Norwegian component of the International Corpus of Learner English. *In this study, the Norwegian use of scare quotes is contrasted with British use in roughly 25,000 words of argumentative essays collected in the* Louvain Corpus of Native English Essays *(see Granger 2007a).*

1. Introduction

This paper investigates the use of scare quotes in the English written production of Norwegian university students through a comparative study with the writing of British A-level students. Very little has been written about scare quotes even though they are common features of both native speaker (NS) and non-native speaker (NNS) writing. Indeed, when it comes to novice NS writing R. T. Lakoff claims, "To the extent a writer is insecure, [scare quote] uses tend to proliferate. Therefore, as anyone who has spent time grading freshman themes knows, such writings teem with quotation marks which, to the literate eye, seem inexplicable if not downright execrable" (Lakoff 1982: 246). Nesselhauf makes a similar point about NNS language when she asserts that "the phenomenon deserves to be pointed out, since it can lead not only to unacceptable words or expressions but sometimes even to unintelligibility or misunderstanding" (Nesselhauf 2005: 151).

An investigation into scare quote usage thus meshes well with research concerning learner compensation strategies, and allows for the development here of a framework intended to shed light on many of the various possible uses of scare quotes. This framework is then utilized in the investigation of the occurrences of scare quotes in argumentative essays written by the two groups of students, to discover whether Norwegians and British novice writers employ scare quotes in similar ways.

Data for this study comes from approximately 50,000 words of text found in argumentative essays collected in two corpora of novice writing. The texts written by Norwegian university and college students were collected in the Norwegian component of the *International Corpus of Learner English* (ICLE). The Norwegian component (NICLE) is a computer learner corpus which was specifically designed to facilitate the methodology of Contrastive Interlanguage Analysis, allowing the quantitative and qualitative comparison of NS and NNS language (see e.g. Granger 2007a; Granger 2007 b). In this study, the Norwegian use of scare quotes in roughly 25,000 words of argumentative essays is contrasted with British use in 25,000 words of argumentative essays written by A-level students and collected in the *Louvain Corpus of Native English Essays* (LOCNESS).

2. A taxonomy of scare quote usage

Scare quotes are those quotation marks which are used to enclose expressions which are not direct quotations. They are discussed under various monikers, ranging from the relatively neutral and descriptive *nonstandard quotes* (Schneider 2002) to the deliberately neutralized *s-quotes* (John Swales, personal communication, November 10, 2009) to the "playful" *perverted quotes* (Dillon 1988). In general, they convey that the scare-quoted word or expression is inappropriate for some reason and that the writer desires to distance himself from it. Relatively little has been written about scare quotes other than in prescriptivist handbooks which strongly discourage their use. Pullum (2005), however, notes that that there appear to be two possible pragmatic functions of scare quotes – "secure" and "insecure" usage – and it is this distinction that provides the basis for the following taxonomy of scare quote usage.

Figure 1 offers a summary of the various suggested motivations for the use of secure scare quotes, which are generally used to indicate that the scare-quoted term is for some reason incorrect, but nevertheless employed for the sake of convenience. There are two main divisions, of which the more common presumably consists of those cases where writers overtly attempt to distance themselves from their own wording, catering to the perceived ignorance or carelessness of the average speaker by employing an expression that they feel really should be avoided. Motivations for such "distancing" quotes vary and can be grouped into one of four broad categories. First, the quotes may indicate that there is some disagreement over the accepted term either in general or just on the part of the writer, "so-called" quotes. In essence, so-called quotes conflate several types which Dillon points out: shudder quotes (marking, for instance, a sudden change to an informal register), words not taken at face value (e.g. "living in sin"), expressions used in a figurative sense, and cute quotes (e.g. "poor little rich girl") (Dillon 1988: 64-65, his examples). Second, the scare quotes may mark the introduction of a new or otherwise previously unfamiliar term, thereby endowing it with legitimacy (see e.g. Trask 2007). Third, the writer is expressing irony or sarcasm using "sneer" quotes (see e.g. Jacobs 2003). And finally, the scare quote is part of a so-called mixed quote, "mixed" in the sense of being an actual citation (unlike the typical scare quote) from which the writer desires - for whatever reason - to distance himself (see Cappelen and Lepore 1997). These categories are not absolute, as there could be some overlap. For instance, irony is often the intended distancing effect rendered by mixed quotes. Moreover, motivations may sometimes be difficult to determine without recourse to interviews with the writers after the fact. In interpreting factors explaining the use of a particular scare quote, for example, disagreement may be confused with irony and indeed, the two may often go hand in hand. Still, the motivations seem distinct enough to warrant separate categories. The second main division involves a deviation from the standard function(s) of quotation marks to that of adding emphasis only rather than distance, and is typically found on signs. By typographically marking off a string of text, such emphatic quotes are intended to highlight a particular message (see Keeley 2008; McWhorter 2005; Trask 2000).

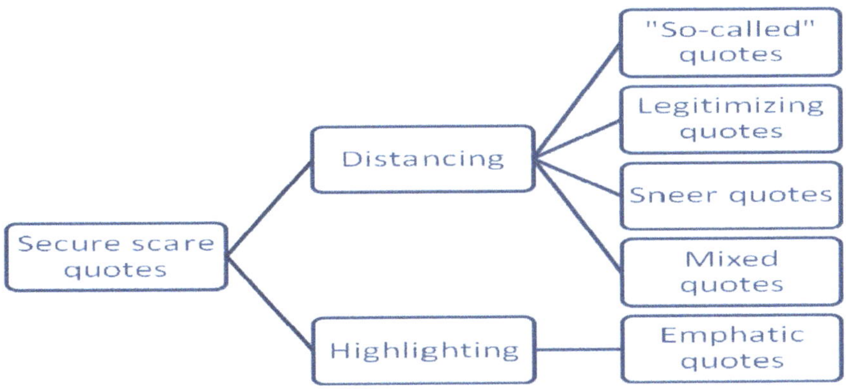

Figure 1. The pragmatic motivations of secure scare quotes

Figure 2 offers details about insecure scare quotes. In contrast to secure scare quotes with their varying motivations, there is only one primary motivation for insecure scare-quoting, that is, the writer's perception of a gap in his own lexicon.

In other words, this scare-quoting marks the writer's contention that his chosen term is somehow wrong, perhaps due to inaccuracy, sudden change in register, or possible unfamiliarity as when the term is, for instance, foreign. In effect, insecure scare quotes overtly mark a deliberate employment of a learner compensation strategy used to bridge a perceived lexical gap. For the purposes of this study, the following terms for compensation strategies from Poulisse (1993) have been adopted. The first two main categories along with their related subcategories involve linguistic strategies, whereas the last category is conceptual:

Substitution: the replacing of the intended word with another

- **Approximation**: replacement of general item for specific item, e.g. *animal* for *rabbit*
- **Pure borrowing**: transfer of an unaltered L1 word into the L2 (code switching), e.g. *I'm going to a dugnad tonight* (*dugnad* being a Norwegian term referring to a voluntary community work)

Substitution Plus: substitution plus some alternative coding (word coinage)

- **Foreignizing**: "when an L1 word is phonologically or morphologically adapted to the L2" (Poulisse 1993: 172), e.g. *brain curtain* from Norwegian *jernteppe/hjerneteppe* to express *mental blackout*
- **Alteration of known TL term**:[1] substitution of an altered (already acquired) TL term for the unknown item, e.g. *to ironize*, from known noun *iron* and known English suffix *–ize*

Conceptual compensation: description of the unknown term

- **Analytic**: describes features of the target lexis, e.g. *it's made out of wood, has drawers, and it's in your office* (for *desk)*
- **Holistic**: creates an analogy between the target lexis and another item that is perceived to be similar, e.g. *a table in your office* (for *desk*)

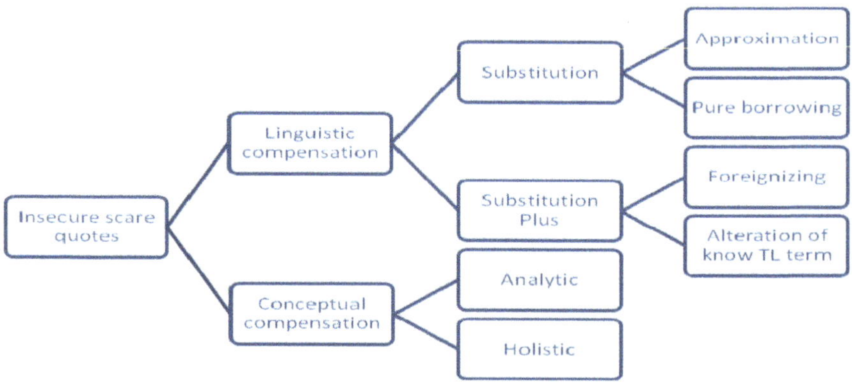

Figure 2. Insecure scare quotes and learner compensation strategies

Given the different functions and underlying motivations of scare quotes, questions arise concerning the extent to which native speakers of English and non-native speakers of English employ them, both in terms of quantity and quality. Do the two groups favour their use equally or does one group use them in a comparatively disproportionate fashion? Are they used to accomplish the same pragmatic functions?

3. Scare quote frequency and distribution in NICLE and LOCNESS

As can be seen in Table 1, the frequency of scare quote usage by the British and Norwegian students is remarkably similar. For the purposes of this study, nearly 50,000 total words of text are examined, evenly divided between NS and NNS prose. The Norwegian essays, however, are longer on average and consequently fewer are included in this study. Still, given the same amount of text, the extent of scare-quoting is almost identical: 64 instances in the Norwegian sample and 65 instances in the British sample. Not every essay examined contains scare quotes, of course, but here too the numbers are close. 56% (20) of the Norwegian essays contain scare-quoted expressions while 58% (28) of the British essays contain them. For both groups, writers who succumb once to the temptation of scare-quoting tend to repeatedly employ the same tactic. Of those essays that contain scare quotes, 65% (13) of the Norwegian essays and 67% (19) of the British essays contain more than one instance. The number of scare quotes in each individual text with multiple quotes varies, the maximum in a single text being 11 for the Norwegian material and 8 for the British material. These figures provide testimony for Jacob's (2003) contention that scare-quoting can become endemic, something which holds true for both NS and NNS writing.

Table 1. Overview of material and scare quote distribution, NICLE and LOCNESS

	Norwegian (NICLE)	British (LOCNESS)
Number of words	24,800	24,811
Number of essays	36	48
Average number of words per essay	689	517
Total number of scare quote instantiations	64	65*
Number of essays with scare quotes	20 (56%)	28 (58%)

*minus three incomplete scare quotes, lacking the end quote

Table 2 presents an overview of the distribution of scare quote types in the Norwegian and British material, divided into the three main categories of "Secure", "Insecure" and "Borderline tokens", the last category compensating for the fact that determination of motivation based on the written word alone can be challenging. Because categorization of scare quote usage depends upon individual interpretation, I follow Schneider's example and consider my coding a means of shedding light on the multiple purposes to which scare quotes are put, rather than a completely reliable, ironclad classification procedure (see Schneider 2002: 195).

Table 2. Overview of scare quote distribution in Norwegian and English texts

		Norwegian (NICLE)	**British (LOCNESS)**
SECURE:			
	"So-called"	7	25
	Sneer quotes	8	4
	Mixed quotes	4	2
	Legitimizing	1	9
	Highlighting	1	0
	Ambiguous	3	5
	Subtotal	**24**	**45**
INSECURE:			
	Substitution	16	2
	Approximations	15	2
	Pure borrowing	1	0
	Substitution Plus	7	5
	Foreignizing	1	0
	TL alteration	5	5
	Conceptualization	7	7
	Analytic	6	6
	Holistic	1	1
	Ambiguous	3	0
	Subtotal	**32**	**14**
	Borderline tokens	**8**	**6**
TOTAL		**64**	**65**

In Table 2 it can be seen that although the Norwegians and English students employ scare quotes in roughly the same frequencies, they use them in different ways. Namely, Norwegian students are much more likely to employ insecure scare quotes than secure ones when they write in English as compared to the British students. The differences noted here are statistically significant ($\chi^2 = 13.37$ (df = 1), $p = 0.0002$). In the following sections, actual tokens of scare-quoting from NICLE and LOCNESS are discussed in order to cast further light on the individual categories outlined in Figures 1 and 2, and to highlight the main differences between the NS and NNS scare quote usage.

4. Secure scare quotes

Because the dividing line between scare quotes which for instance exemplify the "so-called" quotes and sneer quotes is a thin one, one should not overestimate the possible significance of the numerical differences between these two types. The two categories are meant to be indicative only, rather than absolute. Closer inspection of the instantiations of secure quotes when taken as a whole does, however, reveal some differences. First, some of the British students display a sense of political correctness, scare-quoting expressions that may possibly be deemed controversial in their contexts, as in (1) where some might object to the characterization of any natural creation as a *flaw*. Moreover, the British sometimes employ scare quotes to enclose idioms and set phrases, such as *wear and tear, carrot and stick [approach],* and in the case of three separate writers, *playing God*. Instances where factual accuracy may be questioned also seem to promote the use of scare-quoting as in (2) where the use of black might be considered a misnomer because no truly black rose yet exists.

(1) Most people believe that the ability to erase genetic 'flaws' is a good thing, but the key to the problem is knowing when to stop. (ICLE-ALEV-0011.8)[2]

(2) The flowers themselves are manipulated for varying colours, which couldn't be done before such as a "black" rose. (ICLE-ALEV-0026.8)

The Norwegians, by contrast, only employ scare quotes in connection with one particular set phrase, *good old days* which is scare-quoted by three separate writers. The Norwegian material contains no scare-quoted expressions which cater to concerns of either political correctness or factual accuracy, but does include several instances of obviously exaggerated generalizations which are enclosed in scare quotes, as in (3).

(3) The main worry is that the choice of sex will lead to other specifications which result in parents being able to choose the 'perfect child' and natural variation going out of the window. (ICLE-ALEV-0029.8)

Furthermore, the Norwegians have a tendency to scare-quote terms which are seemingly appropriate in context. Therefore, the motivations behind the scare-quoting of some expressions are not immediately obvious. Examples include the following:

(4) Some people will always have hard lives and try to "escape" from them by dreaming, and most people will meet problems in life and handle them by dreaming away. (ICLE-NO-AG-0007.1)

(5) Next to the terrorists-experts and politicians, the "philosophers" and writers were the next to be interviewed by news reporters, seeking their opinion on this; the New World Order. (ICLE-NO-HO-0036.1)

Escape in (4) could well be scare-quoted in part due to recognition of the metaphorical nature of said "escaping", were it not for the fact that the same term is utilized in a nearly identical context, but minus the scare quotes, in an earlier portion of the same essay. Similarly, *philosophers* in (5) is an apt term, which therefore causes one to question the need for scare quotes. Is the writer expressing his sense of disdain for the profession? Does the writer not mean to refer to philosophers at all, but lacks the actual target vocabulary and hopes that readers will somehow infer what is really meant? Although it is almost always possible to come up with some semi-plausible explanatory motivation, the primary effect of these scare quotes seems to be that of misdirecting the reader to an unintended alternative reading or adding undue emphasis. In such cases, one might perhaps do better to heed the prescriptivist advice of allowing the word to carry its own meaning without the added quotation marks.

One further area in which the NICLE and LOCNESS practice appears to differ lies in the use of legitimizing quotes, a practice by which the initial mention of an unfamiliar term is scare-quoted in order to establish its contextual sense for the reader (see Kenyon 1994; Trask 1997). The British students avail themselves of this potential to a far greater degree than do the Norwegians, appropriating words which are potentially unfamiliar to the reader. In (6), for example, the writer encloses the term *fractal* in scare quotes, thereby highlighting a break in register through the use of a technical term from medical jargon. In such cases, the scare-quoted expressions are conventional in the sense that they are included in standard lexicons.

(6) Computer generated pictures, including 'fractal' pictures, drawn from equations, seem to be more popular than hand printed images from an artist's imagination, and computer games seem to provide more entertainment than any game or activity that takes place in the real, physical world. (ICLE-ALEV-0005.6)

5. Insecure scare quotes

When it comes to the types of insecure scare-quoting, it is hardly surprising that the British students in my study never resort to the strategies of either pure borrowing or foreignizing, as the target language is their L1. What is perhaps more surprising is that the Norwegians rarely take advantage of these strategies either. Pure borrowing, which is likely to be the least successful strategy in terms of communicative success, is found only once in my material when a student scare-quotes the Norwegian phrase *Ola Nordmann*, in reference to the average person, the equivalent of the English *John Smith*. The clearest case of foreignizing is found in example (7). Here, the use of *strong* in exemplifies foreignizing due to the NNS shift in meaning away from the denotation of words that induce a powerful effect to swear words.

(7) When their parents think they're watching cartoons, they're actually watching cartoons with porn, violence and "strong" words. (ICLE-NO-AC-0009.1)

Indeed, *strong words* and its direct Norwegian equivalent *sterke ord* originally had the same meaning, referring to words which induce a powerful emotional effect but not swear words. Internet searches reveal, however, that many have begun to use the term *sterke ord* to refer to swear words, while the same tendancy does not appear to apply to the collocation *strong words*. It is quite possible then that the writer simply foreignized the Norwegian lexeme *sterk* to the English *strong*, perhaps influenced by awareness of the metaphorical extension from the basic physical sense of *strong*.

Other potential cases of foreignizing have been classified as borderline tokens rather than clear-cut cases of insecure usage. For example, *soap* in (8) could very well constitute a case of foreignizing from Norwegian *såpe*, an insecure use of scare-quoting where the writer is unsure of whether the same term can be applied in English to a particular type of television series:

(8) An example which illustrates this is the "soap" on Norwegian TV these days: "Hotel Caesar". (ICLE-NO-BU-0002.1)

On the other hand, this use of scare-quoting could simply represent a case of secure scare-quoting, an instantiation of the "so-called" function. This second hypothesis is not unlikely, given that the term *soap/såpe* is actually just an abbreviation for *soap opera/såpeopera*. In any case, foreignizing as a source of motivation for scare-quoting rarely appears in my material and is in any case difficult to determine with any certainty, based on the written word alone. Both English and Norwegian are Germanic languages, so there are often similarities between words in the two languages. An expression might be chosen because the writer is uncertain and adapts the term to make it resemble English, being lucky enough to hit upon the appropriate term. In other cases, the writer might be genuinely certain of the correctness of his chosen lexis, a version of which just happens to appear in both languages.

A further notable discrepancy between Norwegian and British use of insecure scare quotes lies in the much greater tendency for Norwegians to substitute some sort of general expression to compensate for the lack of a more precise term. The actual approximations result in varying degrees of success, but the very fact that they are scare-quoted serves to safeguard the writers from criticism of their lexical choice. Why bother to direct criticism at something the writer is already aware of, particularly when in many cases there are other more basic issues that need addressing, such as the formation of plurals or subject-verb concord? Still, scare-quoting of such generalized expressions often directs the reader's attention to weaknesses that might otherwise have passed unnoticed:

(9) So of course we too use our imagination and dream about how it looks like on other planets and what kind of "creatures" that exist there for instance. Nowadays we do not have realistic stories about trolls and witches anymore, but of UFO's and aliens. (ICLE-NO-HE-0005.1)

(10) There are two main "subjects" that often are discussed, censorship according to sexual exploitation and violence. (ICLE-NO-HO-0039.1)

In (9), the word *creatures* is used as a superordinate term to refer to trolls, witches, UFOs and aliens. Granted, UFOs are not creatures as such, a fact which might have prompted the scare-quoting. Still, the word is not so inappropriate as to necessarily have caught the reader's notice had it not been for those scare quotes. Similarly, *subjects* in (10) might be scare-quoted due to the writer's uncertainty about whether sexual exploitation and violence can properly be considered "subjects", the same term used to refer to academic disciplines. Chances are, however, that this use of *subjects* would have been considered unremarkable had its use not been orthographically highlighted. Indeed, scare-quoting of such approximations arguably has the effect of drawing undue notice to lexical choice.

The Norwegian and British writers display some similarity when it comes to modifying the standard lexicon of the English language in order to express their thoughts. The strategy of TL alteration is evident in 5 of the 32 Norwegian insecure scare quotes, as well as in 5 of the 45 corresponding cases in the British material. The word *organisators* in (11), for example, constitutes a prototypical instantiation of TL alteration, where the writer in this case takes a known verb, *organize*, and adds a common English suffix, *-ator*, to create a lexeme which is certainly understandable albeit incorrect.

(11) And what if everybody expects an easy, well-organised society where everything is set up for them, – somebody has to be the "organisators". (ICLE-NO-HO-0032.1)

The predominant means of TL alteration in both the Norwegian and British material, however, involves the development of new compounds such as *fantasy harming* in (12), where the writer first discusses the types of experiences which may successfully activate a child's imagination but lacks a satisfactory means to express the opposite concept:

(12) We should take care in how our children spend their time and limit the use of "fantasy harming" experiences, the point isn't supposed to be keeping the children busy until they have to go to bed! (ICLE-NO-AG-0019.1)

Two of the British writers who utilize this same strategy of creating novel compounds, however, do so for the purpose of labelling a phenomenon which they then proceed to define, illustrated in (13). Here the scare-quoted term *stay-ripe* serves as a cataphoric device, allowing the writer a concise means by which to refer to an item which would otherwise require lengthy explication. This particular type of usage is similar in its defining function to many of the secure legitimizing quotes, the difference being the non-standard nature of the scare-quoted term.

(13) The story that hit the scientific press about two years ago was about the "Stay-ripe" tomato. It was an ordinary tomato which had genes from a wheat variety added to it creating a tomato that, once ripe, stayed red for weeks. (ICLE-ALEV-0025.8)

In a similar vein, other writers employ newly-coined compounds to refer to concepts for which they otherwise lack a label, but choose not to explicitly define their scare-quoted newly-coined compound, perhaps feeling that the meaning of the term is self-evident. An example is given in (14).

(14) The first case is if the ovum comes from the 'mother to be', this is usually because her partner has a low sperm count or is infertile; if he is infertile a donor's sperm will be used instead. The second case is when the 'mother to be' is post-menopausal or infertile, it is then that a donor's ovum would be used. (ICLE-ALEV-0029.8)

The LOCNESS example of *mother to be* is paralleled in NICLE by the use of *consumer* in (15). Here the writer chooses to implicitly introduce a term, being unsure of whether patrons of the arts can be called *consumers*. Not content with a single scare-quoting, however, this student feels compelled to continue scare-quoting the term. As a consequence, undue focus is placed on each occurrence of the word. Convention has it that the scare quotes should be dropped upon any subsequent mention of the term, as it is claimed that failure to do so may annoy the reader (Trask 1997). This text provides a good example of the potentially irritating effect of duplicate scare-quoting, especially as the last two instances of the word follow so hard upon the first.

(15) As a "consumer" of the art, to reflect upon work of art you need to be creative, so the "consumer" also has to be imaginative. We (as "consumers" of art) have to be able to compare what is expressed to us with experiences we have for ourselves, and to be able to relate to the work of art. (ICLE-NO-HO-0029.1)

The double scare-quoting of *mother to be* in (14), by contrast, is arguably somewhat less annoying for the reader. Here, the writer struggles to find a term not for a prospective mother who is already pregnant, but for a woman who has not yet undergone the IVF treatment, a "prospective prospective mother". The initial scare quotes help alert the reader that the woman in question is not truly a mother-to-be. The second set of scare quotes serve to effectively isolate the three individual words in the text and bind them as a single unit. This is a potentially effective tactic given that the writer is unaware of the use of hyphens in the standard spelling of the compound in its lexically conventionalized sense.

In any case, examples such as those in (14) and (15) mark both the British and Norwegian contributors as the novice writers they are. In her comparative study on the use of scare quotes by novice and professional writers, Schneider comments that this type of quote which marks invented language is "used in just those places where students either lack the disciplinary language that would supply them with the vocabulary for which they appear to be searching or the argumentative strategy that would allow them to make a claim in ordinary language" (Schneider 2002: 204). In such cases, these students "abdicate their linguistic responsibility",[3] something which professional writers rarely permit themselves.

6. Summary and conclusions

The primary finding of this study is that although Norwegian learners of English and novice British writers employ roughly the same number of scare quotes, they do so for quite different reasons. In brief, Norwegian writers more often resort to insecure scare quotes than do British writers. As previously noted, Nesselhauf claims that scare quote usage can lead to the use of "unacceptable words or expressions" (Nesselhauf 2005: 151). By contrast, I would contend that scare-quoting provides a strategy which effectively contributes to the legitimization of what otherwise would be judged an inappropriate term. In other words, scare quotes make the "unacceptable" acceptable.

Due to the methodological challenges of determining the underlying motivations for scare-quoting, attempts were made to give each quote the widest possible interpretation. Even so, the greater extent of insecure scare-quoting in the Norwegian material is an inescapable conclusion. These findings are intuitively satisfying, as one would expect NNS writers to experience more lexical gaps and thus exude less confidence in the appropriateness of their lexical choice. A further study is planned to investigate the use of scare quotes in argumentative essays written by Norwegian university and college students in their native Norwegian, in order to discover whether they then employ a greater percentage of secure scare quotes when the target language is their L1.

Any word is associated with a degree of subjectivity. Such variation is particularly apparent in learner language where writers are quite often on shaky territory as to the conventional meanings and associations of words. Inappropriateness is in the eyes of the beholder, such that Norwegians seem to more often scare-quote expressions which are apparently appropriate in context, with the consequent unfortunate effect of placing undue emphasis on a particular expression. This could explain, for instance, cases where Norwegians enclose conventional metaphors in scare quotes. As foreign speakers of English, they may very well remain sensitive to the metaphorical nature of such terms and employ scare quotes to mark the semantic stretching of a word away from its basic sense.

As for the links between compensation strategies and scare quotes, it would appear that Norwegians resort only infrequently to either the strategies of foreignizing or pure borrowing, or alternatively, that Norwegian students are usually careful not to highlight the use of such compensation strategies with scare quotes. If it is indeed the case that less proficient writers of an L2 tend to find inspiration for unknown lexis in their own L1 as Poulisse (1993: 184) claims, then the lack of scare-quoted L1 variations could testify to the overall advanced level of English in the Norwegian essays. It might prove interesting to investigate the use of scare quotes in the English of other language groups as well, in order to investigate whether there tends to be any link between scare-quoting and L1-inspired learner compensation strategies on the one hand, and proficiency level in English on the other hand.

Finally, a number of other minor differences in the use of scare quotes in Norwegian and British English have also been noted. These include the greater tendency apparent in the Norwegian material to scare-quote approximations of the target vocabulary as well as exaggerated generalizations. The British texts, by contrast, display an increased proclivity towards the use of scare quotes which mark set phrases or introduce specialized terms. Additionally, concerns relating to political correctness and factual accuracy also appear to motivate scare quote usage by the British authors. Such phenomena merit further investigation in larger samples of novice writing to discover whether these tendencies may be confirmed.

Notes

1 For the present study, the target language (TL) is English, which is the first language (L1) of the British students and the second language (L2) of the Norwegian students.

2 The British material is coded with *ALEV* (A-levels), whereas the Norwegian material is coded with *NO* (Norwegian). All examples from LOCNESS and NICLE are quoted verbatim, including any errors.

3 Schneider's conclusion (2002: 204), borrowing a phrase from Robin Lakoff.

References

Cappelen, H. and E. Lepore (1997), 'Varieties of quotation', *Mind,* 106: 429-50.

Dillon, G. L. (1988), 'My words of an other', *College English*, 50(1): 63-73.

Granger, S. (2007a), 'A bird's-eye view of learner corpus research', in: W. Teubert and R. Krishnamurthy (eds.) *Corpus Linguistics: Critical Concepts in Linguistics*. London: Routledge. 44-72.

Granger, S. (2007b), 'The computer learner corpus: A versatile new source of data for SLA research', in: W. Teubert and R. Krishnamurthy (eds.) *Corpus Linguistics: Critical Concepts in Linguistics.* London: Routledge. 166-82.

Jacobs, A. (2003), 'The war in quotes: Journalists who don't like the war – and like thinking even less – have a little trick they use to tell us how they really feel', *Weekly Standard,* 14 April 2003, <http://www.weeklystandard.com/Content/Public/Articles/000/000/002/548bpdrs.asp>, accessed 15 September 2008.

Keely, B. (2008), *The "Blog" of "Unnecessary" Quotation Marks,* <http://www.unnecessaryquotes.com/>, accessed 30 October 2008.

Kenyon, R. E., Jr. (1994), 'On the use of quotation marks', *Etc: A Review of General Semantics,* 1: 47-50. Available online <http://www.xenodochy.org/gs/quotes.html>, accessed August 26, 2008.

Lakoff, R. T. (1982), 'Some of my favorite teachers are literate: The mingling of oral and written strategies in written communication', in: D. Tannen (ed.) *Spoken and Written Language: Exploring Orality and Literacy.* Norwood, NJ: Ablex. 239-260.

McWhorter, J. (2005), 'Air quotes in New York', *Language Log,* <http://itre.cis.upenn.edu/~myl/languagelog/archives/001862.html>, accessed 15 September 2008.

Nesselhauf, N. (2005), *Collocations in a Learner Corpus.* Amsterdam/Philadelphia: John Benjamins Publishing Company.

Poulisse, N. (1993), 'A theoretical account of lexical communication', in: R. Schreuder and B. Weltens (eds.) *The Bilingual Lexicon.* Amsterdam and Philadelphia: John Benjamins Publishing Company. 157-89.

Pullum, G. (2005), 'Secure and insecure scare quotes', *Language Log,* <http://itre.cis.upenn.edu/~myl/languagelog/archives/002188.html>, accessed 7 October 2011.

Schneider, B. (2002). 'Nonstandard quotes: Superimpositions and cultural maps', *College Composition and Communication,* 54(2): 188-207.

Trask, L. (2007), *Scare Quotes,* <http://www.informatics.sussex.ac.uk/department/docs/punctuation/node31.html>, accessed 31 May 2007.

Trask, L. (2000), 'The Jawbone of a scare quote', *Suck,* <http://www.suck.com/daily/2000/03/20/1.html>, accessed 5 June 2008.

NEED TO and the domain of Business in spoken British English[1]

Soili Nokkonen

University of Helsinki

Abstract

In the Business domain of the British National Corpus, *NEED TO has a much higher frequency than in the other spoken BNC contexts. To find out why, I first explore the semantic variation of NEED TO and its distribution in the Business genres of Meeting, Training session, Unscripted speech, Scripted speech and Interview, and then study it in connection with the sociolinguistic variable of gender. The results show that deontic instances are prevalent, and that the argumentative/persuasive genres offer numerous communicative situations for the various semantic domains of NEED TO. Interactivity further increases the use of NEED TO: Meeting and Training session have the highest frequencies and the most versatile instances. Considering gender, men express an obligation with NEED TO more than women do in the dialogic genres, while in speeches women lead men with many weaker deontic instances.*

1. Introduction

This paper explores semi-modal NEED TO and its meanings in the Business domain of the spoken context-governed part (CG) of the *British National Corpus* (BNC). NEED TO has a much higher frequency in this social context than in the other CG domains, and, in comparison to the more informal encounters of the demographically sampled part (DS), it is four times more frequent here (Nokkonen forthcoming). These intriguing patterns probably have to do with the argumentative and persuasive nature of many of the texts in CG – such texts always include a great many necessity modals. Therefore, the business encounters are worth studying in detail.

So far, corpus-based studies have shown that semi-modal NEED TO has been spreading, and its meanings/uses have been changing (e.g. Krug 2000; Leech 2003; Nokkonen 2006; Smith 2003). These changes involve the whole field of obligation. Semi-modals HAVE TO, HAVE GOT TO and NEED TO have been rising, while central modal MUST in its strong obligation meaning has been declining. These shifts have been associated with a tendency to avoid overt claims to authority by the speaker, i.e. democratization (see Myhill 1995). By using NEED TO, the speaker can downplay his/her authority and claim that the action is recommended for the doer's own sake.

Nevertheless, NEED TO has received the least attention of the obligation/necessity modals. It therefore merits an independent study of its semantic profile and its spread in society. Hence, this paper is part of my continuing research on NEED TO. According to Nokkonen (2006), NEED TO covers all the semantic domains of a necessity modal. While its basic internal meaning is still important, a third of the instances are deontic. As regards its sociolinguistic variation, NEED TO seems to be undergoing change from below (Nokkonen 2010). In the DS part of the BNC, it shows increasing frequencies down the age scale, i.e. monotonic distribution (cf. Labov 2001: 460), but men use it slightly more than women and the leading social class is the upper middle class.

In this paper, my goals are twofold. I study NEED TO in the spoken Business domain by means of its semantic variation and its distribution in Lee's genres (2001), and from the viewpoint of the sociolinguistic variable of gender. This enables me to reflect on the reasons why NEED TO is so frequent in the Business domain, and to compare the findings with my previous studies. The ultimate goal is to trace the spread of NEED TO in present-day British English.

2. The semantic domains of NEED TO

The semantic differences between true obligation modals and semi-modals have been described in terms of subjective and objective necessity (Leech 1971/1987/2004: 96; Perkins 1983: 62-63; for a summary see Nokkonen 2006). When obliging with MUST, the speaker is clearly advocating a certain behaviour, e.g. *you* ***must*** *get a hair-cut.* The same example with NEED TO requires a clear authority structure between the speaker and the addressee for a similar interpretation as with MUST – the directive element is provided by the context or co-text.

In order to analyse the semantic variation of NEED TO in real corpus data, I developed a frame which would take account of the pragmatic interpretation as well (Nokkonen 2006). This frame is based both on the study on central modals by Coates (1983) and the cross-linguistic studies on modality by Bybee et al. (1994) and van der Auwera and Plungian (1998). Figure 1 illustrates my framework. The arrows indicate the direction of historical change.

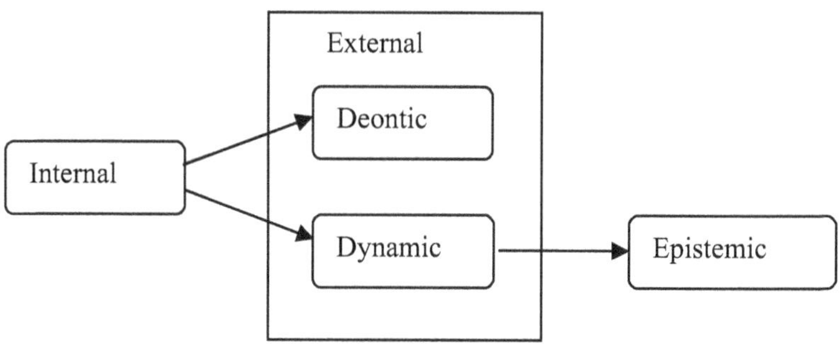

Figure 1. The different meanings of NEED TO

The semantic domains in Figure 1 are described next. The examples are from the primary material, the spoken Business domain of the BNC.

Participant internal instances express the basic/lexical meaning of NEED TO, i.e. an internal compulsion which originates in the human agent – see example (1). With *I* as the subject, the speaker is communicating a necessity concerning him/herself. Other subjects are possible especially in questions and conditionals.

(1) Internal
Erm most of the writing letters and things are follow-ups so I *need to* dothose myself cos I did the originals. (F8U 1076)

Participant external examples are those that within the contextual frame express different degrees of imposed obligation. These instances contain a mixture of internal and external compulsion, as the speaker is both appealing to the assumed needs of the addressee and expressing an obligation. The participant external domain includes the deontic and dynamic domains. For the spoken primary material of this paper, I have divided the deontic domain into two. I usc the term **Deontic 1** for the strongest instances, such as (2). The speaker, who is in authority, is instructing the listener directly with *you* as a subject. The main verb is typically agentive and an activity verb. Instances in **Deontic 2** are less strong, since the participants are equals and the directive is more hidden and hedged – see (3). The subject is typically *we*. The main verbs also include mental verbs and verbs of existence. Some instances have only a weak directive function, since the speaker is talking about people in general with impersonal *you* or *we*, or the instances are in the passive voice – see (4).

(2) Deontic 1
Erm Jim you, you *need to* present it in a certain way to your staff, and after you've considered that, if you don't feel it's workable then I think you *need to* talk to David and I. (FUL 956)

(3) Deontic 2
But we *need to* no we *need to* sort that out. Er I don't see that it's a big problem. And we ought to make a very definite point of putting our heads together … (JP0 920)

(4) Deontic 2
But I think there are a number of things er which would *need to* be taken into account. (F7A 843)

Dynamic examples, such as (5), express vague necessity, which usually has to do with the necessary qualities of the subject in certain circumstances. Most instances have an inanimate subject and a stative main verb. Some imply an epistemic meaning as well. In fact, it seems as if NEED TO is sliding through the Dynamic domain into **Epistemic** meaning. The term epistemic is used in its standard meaning here. In typical instances the subject is inanimate and the main verb stative (6).

(5) Dynamic
As there will *need to* be more campaigning before we see the expansionable description in the theatre … (J8B 387)

(6) Epistemic
Sue: It's, it's the, the
Kevin: it's the follow up it's the phone calling
Sue: Yeah.
Kevin: and the follow up of cases.
Sylvia: Yeah.
Kevin: that *needs to* be time consuming (H5E 707)

The distribution of the semantic domains varies depending on the register in question. In spontaneous informal conversation, the internal domain covers about half the instances (Nokkonen 2010). The deontic domains are the most common in more formal encounters where NEED TO is used to oblige politely (Nokkonen forthcoming). In dynamic and epistemic instances, NEED TO resembles central modals by accepting any kind of a subject – see (5) and (6). However, it does not entail the speaker's subjective opinions on its own, but the context plays a crucial role in deciding the semantic domains.

3. Primary material

The data come from the Business domain of the spoken context-governed component (CG) of the BNC.[2] The 1.3 million word Business domain is one of the four equal-sized domains based on the social context in which they were produced (Hoffmann et al. 2008). In comparison with the DS part of the BNC with private spontaneous encounters, the CG part has more formal encounters in public contexts.

The Business domain was chosen because of its highest frequency of NEED TO among the spoken BNC contexts (Section 4, Figure 2). The domain is divided into dialogues and monologues, but I have chosen to apply the more fine-grained categories of use devised by Lee (2001).[3] His genres in the Business domain include Meeting, Training session[4], Unscripted speech, Scripted speech, Interview, Consultation, and Broadcast discussion. The last two genres are left out because of their low number of words and few instances of NEED TO (only 12 and 6 respectively).

The Business genres represent the business world in a broad sense. The texts in Meeting range from get-togethers of, e.g., the Tyneside Cinema Board, Nottingham Constabulary and York Green Party to more formal annual general meetings. The texts in Training session and Unscripted speech come from the same training sessions/seminars, but Training session has more interactive texts. Scripted speech mostly consists of speeches at a Trade Union Annual Congress. Interview includes job or market research interviews.

In the Business domain, only the sociolinguistic variable of gender is marked extensively enough for investigation – 80% of the instances of NEED TO have this mark-up. The domain is dominated by men (77% of the words). Hence in smaller categories, the number of female speakers is quite low, and the results are, therefore, tentative.

As regards data retrieval, BNCweb was used to provide the concordance lines. Each occurrence of NEED TO was, subsequently, coded for meaning. I went through the concordance lines manually three times checking the wider co-text and the extra-linguistic context. Even so, semantic categories are hazy, and there is, admittedly, a subjective element present. Especially the examples on the borderline between the non-epistemic and the epistemic field are fuzzy, and sometimes both a dynamic and an epistemic interpretation are possible. For such unclear instances, I chose the dynamic domain.

4. Register variation – background and hypotheses

The starting point for exploring the register variation of NEED TO is that modal use can vary across registers, and that the study of modal meaning requires an understanding of the wider context of use. Therefore, it seems relevant to widen the study of NEED TO to a full range of spoken registers, also of a more public and formal kind.

The use of NEED TO, indeed, varies in different registers, i.e., in written and spoken language (Nokkonen 2006) and in the informal DS part and the more formal CG part of the BNC (Nokkonen 2010 and forthcoming). The CG part has a much higher frequency of NEED TO than the DS part (about 500 and 200 hits per million words respectively). These differences can be explained by the nature of many of the CG texts: they can be classified as argumentative or persuasive (cf. Biber 1988). Typical features include prediction, necessity and possibility modals and conditional clauses. In these texts, necessity modals can mark the speaker's attempts to persuade the addressee that certain events are desirable or probable. In contrast, ordinary conversation such as in DS is not particularly persuasive in nature. In addition, the distributions of the semantic domains differ a great deal in the CG and the DS parts. More than 60% of the CG instances are deontic, while the percentage is only 40 in DS. Hence, the public CG encounters seem just the right kind of territory for NEED TO especially in its personal obligation meaning.

There are also large differences between the four CG domains (Nokkonen, forthcoming), as illustrated in Figure 2. The Business domain is different not only because of its high frequencies but also because the dialogues and monologues have an equally high frequency unlike the rest of the domains. They behave more as expected, since, in general, one could assume that dialogues, i.e. conversation even though of a more formal kind this time, have more modals than monologues especially as most of them in CG are written to be spoken (see Biber 2004 for written and spoken language). As for NEED TO, it is more common in speech than in writing according to Nokkonen (2006). This paper investigates what lies behind this puzzle.

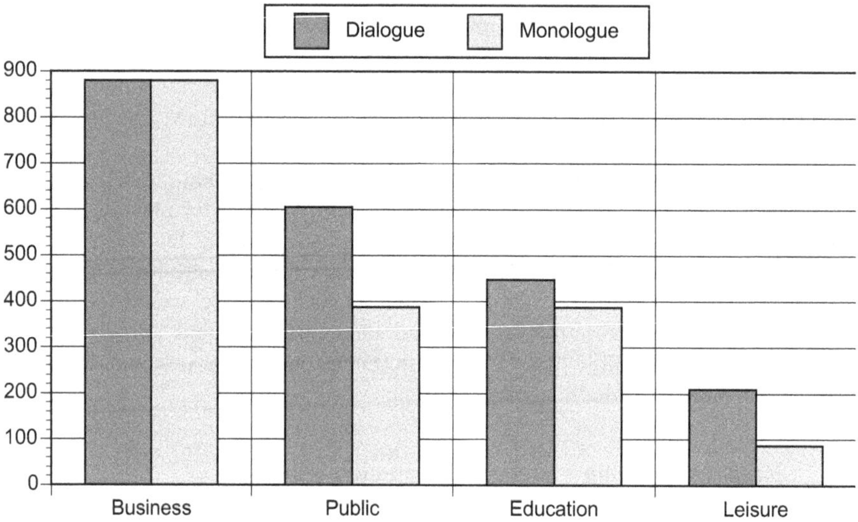

Figure 2. Frequencies of NEED TO in the CG domains (per million words)

In this paper, the Business domain is approached from the point of view of Lee's genres, or situations of use, i.e., Meeting, Training session, Unscripted speech, Scripted speech, and Interview. The first set of hypotheses concerns the differences between these genres and the distribution of the semantic domains in them. First on the basis of previous research, in persuasive texts, the interactive and interpersonal nature of conversation increases the use of polite hedges such as NEED TO. Conversations in the workplace are known to have a great deal of polite hedges (Holmes and Stubbe 2003), while interviews a great deal less (see Biber 1988). In university language, necessity modals are clearly preferred in registers that give advice or regulation (Biber 2006). As regards training, teacher talk is heavily marked by the instructor's sense of responsibility to transmit information, and it contains linguistic features such as conditionals and directives (Heath and Langman 1994). In sum, Meeting and Training session must have high frequencies with many deontic instances, also in the strongest domain. Considering speeches, the more dialogic genre of Unscripted speech probably has a higher frequency of NEED TO than Scripted speech. The first set of hypotheses is as follows: The dialogic genres of Meeting and Training session have the highest frequencies with numerous deontic instances. Unscripted speech has a higher frequency than Scripted speech, and deontic instances are more frequent in it.

The second set of hypotheses concerns the relationship between social and register variation, i.e. inter-speaker and intra-speaker variation. Relying on the findings in Biber and Finegan (2001: 244), many patterns of register variation can be explained by the communicative functions of particular features across the situations of use. The social dialect patterns for those features derive both from their communicatively motivated distributions across registers and the differential access of social groups to praxis in those registers.

Considering NEED TO, these findings may be applicable to its social and register variation. The data from DS suggests that upper middle class people, many of whom have positions with some authority, have the highest frequencies of NEED TO in their private lives (Nokkonen 2010). Originally the idea was to investigate whether similar patterns could be seen in public contexts, and middle-aged professionals seemed well represented in the CG part. Unfortunately, CG is poorly marked for social class. Nevertheless, the social variable of gender is well marked in the Business domain. As the public CG encounters are dominated by men, in this data men have more access to the communicative situations with NEED TO in high frequencies.

According to Labov (2001: 367), in linguistic changes women use the incoming form more than men do. In the private DS encounters, NEED TO is slightly more frequent among men in contrast to Labov's findings (Nokkonen 2010). Especially the deontic instances are more frequently uttered by men. Nevertheless, the 25-34 year old women are among the three top user groups due to their nurturing roles: they guide children with NEED TO.

To conclude, the second set of hypotheses is as follows: Men use NEED TO more than women do in the Business genres, and they have more deontic instances than women.

5. Empirical results

5.1 The Business genres

The frequencies of NEED TO in the genres are presented in Table 1 which is organised according to order of frequency.

Table 1. Distribution of NEED TO across Business genres

Category	*Words*	*RF*	*NF*	*Dispersion*
Meeting	526,441	496	942.2	46/53
Training session	214,009	197	920.5	18/18
Unscripted speech	228,530	202	883.9	19/22
Scripted speech	176,226	147	834.2	14/20
Interview	94,399	51	540.3	9/9
total	1,239,605	1,093	881.7	106/122

Note. Words = number of words, RF = raw frequency, NF = normalized frequency per million words, Dispersion = dispersion over files.

The first two genres – Meeting and Training session – are both interactive and dialogic. Nevertheless, the Speech genres do not lag much behind in frequency. In contrast, Interview has a much lower frequency. These results are largely along the lines of the first set of hypotheses (see Section 6 for discussion). The distribution of the semantic domains is illustrated in Figure 3.

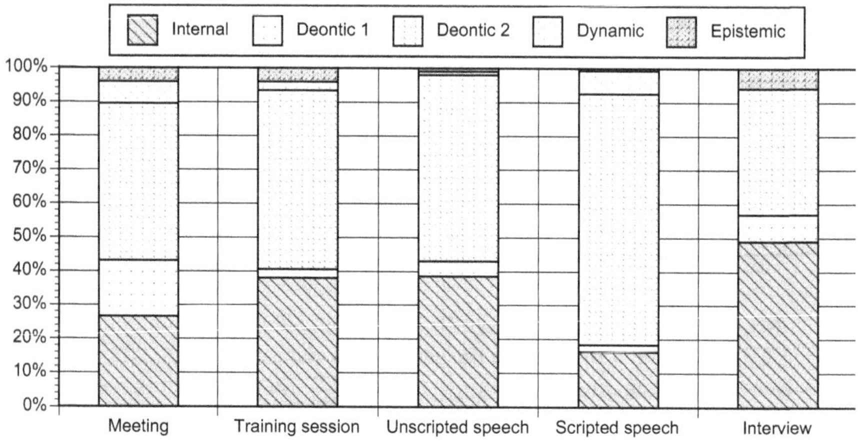

Figure 3. Distribution of NEED TO across semantic domains in Business genres

There is statistically significant variation in the distribution (for chi-squared results see Appendix, Table 2). First, the internal domain has the largest proportion in Interview (50% of the instances), while smallest in Scripted speech (16%). Second, the two deontic domains together cover the largest proportion in Scripted speech (76%), and Meeting comes next with many strong deontic instances. Third, Meeting and Scripted speech have the largest proportions of the dynamic domain, while the epistemic domain is favoured by the dialogic genres of Meeting, Training session and Interview. With the exception of Interview, the proportions reveal the rankings in frequencies quite well. Next, the genres are discussed in turn with typical examples.

In Meeting, typical instances are deontic (63%). The strongest deontic instances have the highest frequency of all the genres, the weaker ones the second highest. In a typical example of the strongest kind, the manager obliges his subordinates in a straightforward fashion, consider (7). Most instances are, however, less strong and of a more general kind – *we* is the typical subject in them, see (8).

(7) Deontic 1
Roger, Terry and David, er *need to* take this away, have a look at it and at the next meeting we either then draw some conclusions and again what I'm looking for (FUJ 230)

(8) Deontic 2
I mean it's exactly what Iris is saying it's a meeting with minds in a way because we *need to* know that … (F7C 104)

Both dynamic and epistemic instances have the highest frequencies in this genre. The dynamic instances may have deontic overtones: in (9) the speaker tells everyone to pass around the sheets of information. With NEED TO, *there*-construction is possible in both dynamic and epistemic domains. In example (10), the dynamic interpretation 'it is necessary that there is a budget' is more natural, whereas (11) is epistemic with some typical features (*would, presumably*).

(9) Dynamic
You can see on the front what is on offer. They *need to* go right round. (F7A 234)

(10) Dynamic
And then of course there *needs to* be a a budget for the rest of the year doesn't there? (FUJ 1889)

(11) Epistemic
I was just gonna say th- th- there's there *would need to* be a tiebreaker of some sort presumably. (JP0 456)

In the genre of Training session, most instances are spoken by the trainer. The internal domain has the second highest frequency of the Business genres. Example (12) performs the function of a polite hedge, as the trainer appeals to his/her own needs instead of telling the trainees to give information more directly. Many of the internal instances are hypothetical questions or conditionals often with *you* as a subject, see (13). These examples are part of a teaching strategy.

(12) Internal
I *need to* take down one or two details, will that be alright. (J3U 306)

(13) Internal
I mean, in a real life situation, think about, ought you think about, imagine what how much do you know about, do you *need to* use your network, to find out what … (JJ8 735)

Typical instances in Training session are, however, shaded by weak deontic meaning. In (14), the trainer advises with *you* as a subject.

(14) Deontic 2
So, you *need to* make your colleague work for what they get, without being totally sort of bloody minded. (JJ8 749)

The genre of Unscripted speech resembles Training session in many ways – their context of use is very much the same (see Section 3). The style in the speeches is more formal, and in the deontic instances subject *we* is more common than in the two previous genres. The trainers/managers want to create the right kind of spirit in the firm, see (15).

(15) Deontic 2
We act as separate cells, we *need to* act as a team. (H47 595)

Scripted speech mainly consists of speeches at a Trade Union Annual Congress: NEED TO often has a rhetorical function as well. The internal instances are not frequent, but they have some particular features: they introduce a new topic or stress a point, as in (16). The most typical domain is the weaker deontic one with a frequency of 619 hits per million words, which is the highest frequency of any of the semantic domains in the genres. Typical instances appeal to the audience in an argumentative way – notice the repetition in (17). Unlike in the other genres, there are only few deontic instances with *you* as a subject – most have *we* as a subject, and the passive voice is also common. Dynamic instances are equally persuasive, see (18).

(16) Internal
The privatization which handed over administration of benefit payments to employers was the brainchild of Sir Norman [pause] do I *need to* say more? (HDP 216)

(17) Deontic 2
We *need to* invest [pause] we *need to* encourage research and development [pause] we *need to* provide quality training. (HDP 245)

(18) Dynamic
And that's why it's important that there *needs to* be an open debate, both within the union, and there *needs to* be a proper flow of information from the Executive in these discussions to the branches and to the members to tell them what's going on. (HLW 162)

In contrast to the other Business genres, Interview has its highest frequency in the internal domain, and most of the internal instances have *I* as a subject. In (19), the interviewer is describing the practices of the trade, whereas in (20) the interviewee is hypothesising his/her actions. The deontic instances by the interviewer appear in between, see (21).

(19) Internal
And then of course they'll always retain the one that appeals. I'll keep this cos I *need to* keep that guy's. (JA4 355)

(20) I mean first of all I would *need to* believe in the company the product and that the quality is saleable. (JA0 115)

(21) Deontic 1
Okay? and do *need to* be reassured about the car. (JA0 479)

5.2 The sociolinguistic variable of gender

In the Business domain, 75% of the instances of NEED TO marked for gender are uttered by men. However, the fewer women use NEED TO more than men do as regards the frequencies: 955 hits per million words versus 851 hits. This result disagrees with the second set of hypotheses, although the difference is not statistically significant.[5] In the genres, the situation is more complex, as can be seen in Figure 4.

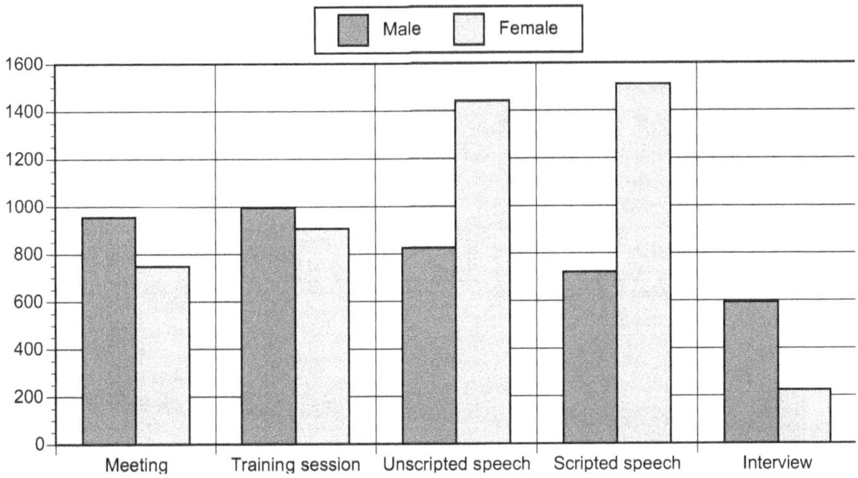

Figure 4. Frequencies of NEED TO for men and women across Business genres (per million words). (Appendix, Table 3)

In the dialogic genres of Meeting, Training session and Interview men lead women in the use of NEED TO, whereas in the Speech genres, the situation is the opposite.[6] In Scripted speech, women have the top frequency of 1510 while men only 721. As Meeting and Scripted speech are at the opposite ends of the scale, the distribution of the semantic domains across gender is only studied in them. Figure 5 illustrates the proportions of the semantic domains in Meeting.

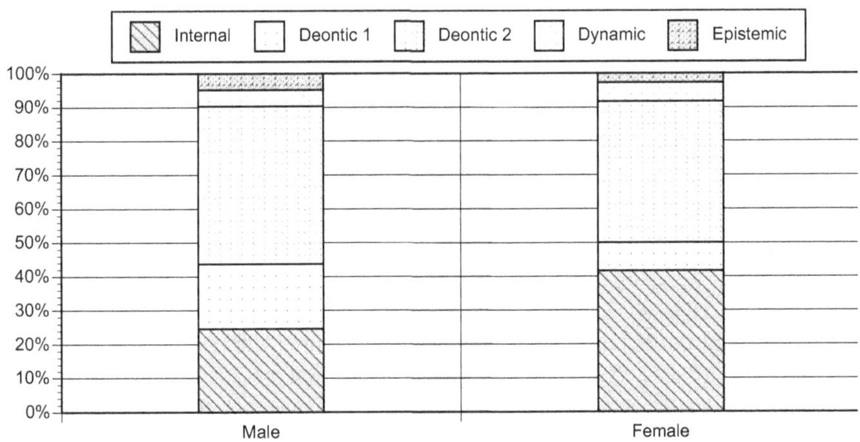

Figure 5. Men vs. women. Semantic domains in Meeting (Appendix, Table 4)

There are statistically significant differences in the distribution. The internal domain covers 25% of men's instances, whereas 42% of women's. The difference is equally large in the deontic instances: 66% of men's and 50% of women's instances are deontic. In terms of frequencies, men have 628 deontic hits per million words, while women 374. Especially the strongest instances are rare among women. These figures suggest that men express an obligation with NEED TO much more than women in interactional situations.

Scripted speech shows very different proportions for the semantic domains as illustrated in Figure 6.

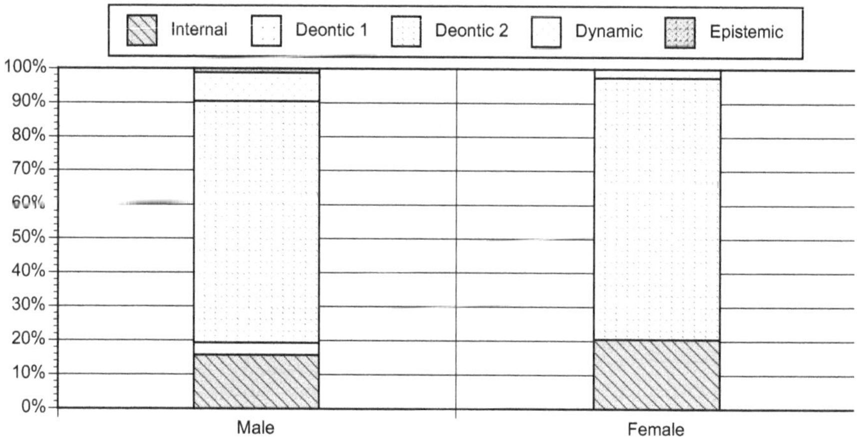

Figure 6. Men vs. women. Semantic domains in Speech scripted (Appendix, Table 5)

The distribution is not statistically significant: men and women have similar proportions in the semantic domains. For both genders, the weaker deontic instances are the most common ones. Concerning the frequencies, the largest difference is also in the weaker deontic instances – women have 1,162 hits per million words, whereas men only 512 hits. Women's high frequency in a deontic domain is quite unexpected.

6. Discussion

This paper has presented an empirical account of NEED TO in the spoken Business domain of the BNC. It now remains to draw conclusions from the findings.

As regards the differences between the genres, the results presented in Section 5.1 are largely along the lines of the first set of hypotheses. First, interactivity and the spontaneous spoken nature of a genre increase the use of NEED TO. The dialogic genres of Meeting and Training session have higher frequencies than the Speech genres. They also have the most versatile deontic instances ranging from strong to weak, and there are both dynamic and epistemic instances. Second, the genre must also possess persuasive functions in order to have many obligation modals. This explains why the dialogic genre of Interview has the lowest frequency and the fewest deontic instances of NEED TO. The patterns are, however, more complicated than expected. The differences in frequencies between Meeting, Training session, and the Speech genres are quite small, and the highest frequency of deontic instances is in the monologue genre of Scripted speech. Undoubtedly, these findings are related to the distribution of various communicative functions across the situations of use, and the semantic domains of NEED TO reflect these patterns.

In all the Business genres, most speakers that employ NEED TO hold a position of power in the context of use. Managers in Meeting negotiate power in a similar fashion as they do in the workplaces of Holmes and Stubbe (2003). In Training sessions, the trainers employ typical teaching strategies (cf. Heath and Langman 1994), and this can be seen in the various conditionals and directives with NEED TO. In sum, NEED TO is useful when addressing subordinates politely, discussing business with colleagues, training, giving speeches, lecturing and interviewing. The versatility of NEED TO is, obviously, the main reason for its high use in the domain of Business.

Considering the variable of gender, the results of Section 5.2 do not, as such, confirm the second set of hypotheses, which assumed that NEED TO is employed more by men. In the Business domain, women have a slightly higher frequency than men, but the situation varies in the genres. In the dialogic genres of Meeting, Training session and Interview, men have higher frequencies. In Meeting, men use the two deontic domains much more than women do (see Figure 5), i.e. they express an obligation more with NEED TO in interactive situations. In these situations, the roles of men and women are obviously different in the corpus data. In the Speech genres, the situation is quite different: women lead men in frequency. In Scripted speech women have the highest frequency of this study with numerous weak deontic instances. Hence, one may speculate that whenever women are in a clear position of authority – when giving a speech or lecturing – the obligation meaning of NEED TO expresses their assertiveness well.

The above finding corroborates the finding that, in the DS part of the BNC, the 25-34 year old women are among the top users (Nokkonen 2010). In the private DS encounters women typically employ the deontic instances when directing children. Both these findings suggest that women play an important role in the rise of NEED TO. Consequently, Labov's idea about women being leaders in linguistic changes may be applicable even to a variant such as NEED TO.

Finally, from a historical perspective the Business genres favour the newer semantic domains of NEED TO. The deontic domains cover 62% of the instances, while the percentage of the internal domain is only 31. The situation is the opposite in private conversations (cf. Nokkonen 2010). The obligation meaning of NEED TO expresses a new, less authoritarian attitude towards the addressee, and such an attitude is, without doubt, important in working life. On this basis, one may speculate that the communicative situations of the Business genres have contributed to the rising use of NEED TO. This conclusion is further strengthened by the highest frequencies of NEED TO and the most versatile instances within the semantic domains.

7. Conclusions

In this paper, I have analysed NEED TO and its semantic variation in the spoken Business genres of the BNC, i.e. Meeting, Training session, Unscripted speech, Scripted speech and Interview, and I have studied it in connection with the sociolinguistic variable of gender.

There are several factors that bear upon its use in the genres. The interactive and persuasive contexts of use explain why Meeting and Training session have the highest frequencies: NEED TO is employed most in its polite obligation meaning. Unscripted speech and Scripted speech have high frequencies due to their argumentative contexts: the weaker deontic instances are prevalent. NEED TO is the least frequent in Interview, where the internal domain covers half the instances. In sum, NEED TO is useful when negotiating power in various communicative situations, and this versatility explains the high use of NEED TO in the Business domain.

Concerning gender, women have a small lead in the whole Business domain, but the situation varies in the genres. In the dialogic genres of Meeting, Training session and Interview, men have higher frequencies, and they express an obligation with NEED TO much more than women do. In these situations, the roles of men and women are different in the corpus data. In contrast, in the Speech genres women lead men in frequencies with many weak deontic instances.

To conclude, the patterns concerning NEED TO in the spoken Business encounters are highly complex. This paper also leaves many questions unanswered. Further studies in various spoken registers would give wider insight into the present uses of NEED TO, and, without doubt, studies that compare several modals of obligation in similar communicative situations would clarify the underlying patterns of usage.

Notes

1 I would like to thank Professor Terttu Nevalainen and Dr. Arja Nurmi for their valuable feedback on an earlier version of this article. I am also grateful to the two anonymous reviewers for their helpful comments. All the remaining mistakes are mine.

2 I had access to the XML version of the corpus through the BNCweb Query program.

3 The division into dialogues and monologues does not coincide with Lee's genres. Unscripted speech and Interview include both dialogues and monologues. Scripted speech is the only monologue genre, the rest are dialogues.

4 I have renamed Lee's original genre of Unclassified as Training session, since all the texts come from various training sessions.

5 The goodness of fit test was applied to the raw frequencies of the two genders. The result is only significant at the 0.20 confidence level (chi-square = 2.20; df = 1).

6 According to the goodness of fit test, the result concerning the two genders in Meeting is only significant at the level of 0.1 (chi-square = 3.48; df = 1). In Training session, the result is not significant. In contrast, the results for Unscripted speech (chi-square = 11.38; df = 1; $p < 0.001$) and Scripted speech (chi-square = 15.20; df = 1; $p < 0.001$) are statistically significant.

Corpus

The *British National Corpus*, version 3 (BNC XML Edition). 2007. Distributed by Oxford University Computing Services on behalf of the BNC Consortium. URL: <http://www.natcorp.ox.ac.uk/>

References

Biber, D. (1988), *Variation across Speech and Writing*. Cambridge: Cambridge University Press.

Biber, D. (2004), 'Modal use across registers and time', in: A. Curzan and K. Emmons (eds.) *Studies in the History of the English Language II: Unfolding Conversations*. Berlin: Mouton de Gruyter. 189-216.

Biber, D. (2006), *University Language: A Corpus-based Study of Spoken and Written Registers*. Amsterdam: John Benjamins.

Biber, D. and E. Finegan (2001), 'Register variation and social dialect variation: the Register Axiom', in: P. Eckert and J. Rickford (eds.) *Style and Sociolinguistic Variation*. Cambridge: Cambridge University Press. 235-267.

Bybee, J., W. Pagliuca and R. Perkins (1994), *The Evolution of Grammar. Tense, Aspect and Modality in the Languages of the World*. Chicago: University of Chicago Press.

Coates, J. (1983), *The Semantics of the Modal Auxiliaries*. London: Croom Helm.

Heath, S. and J. Langman (1994), 'Shared thinking and the register of Coaching', in: D. Biber and E. Finegan (eds.) *Sociolinguistic Perspectives on Register*. New York: Oxford University Press. 82-103.

Hoffmann, S., S. Evert, N. Smith, D. Lee and Y. Berglund Prytz (2008), *Corpus Linguistics with BNCweb – a Practical Guide*. Frankfurt: Peter Lang.

Holmes, J. and M. Stubbe (2003), *Power and Politeness in the Workplace: A Sociolinguistic Analysis of Talk at Work*. Harlow: Pearson Education.

Krug, M. (2000), *Emerging English Modals: A Corpus-based Study of Grammaticalization*. Berlin: Mouton de Gruyter.

Labov, W. (2001), *Principles of Linguistic Change: Social factors.* Oxford: Blackwell.

Lee, D. (2001), 'Genres, registers, text types, domains, and styles: Clarifying the concepts and navigating a path through the BNC jungle', *Language Learning & Technology,* 5(3): 37-72.

Leech, G. (1971/1987/2004), *Meaning and the English Verb.* London: Longman.

Leech, G. (2003), 'Modality on the move: The English modal auxiliaries 1961-1992', in: R. Facchinetti, M. Krug and F. Palmer (eds.) *Modality in Contemporary English.* Berlin: Mouton de Gruyter. 223-240.

Myhill, J. (1995), 'Change and continuity in the functions of the American English modals', *Linguistics,* 33: 175-211.

Nokkonen, S. (2006), 'The semantic variation of NEED TO in four recent British English corpora', *International Journal of Corpus Linguistics,* 11(1): 29-71.

Nokkonen, S. (2010), '"How many taxis there needs to be?": The sociolinguistic variation of NEED TO in spoken British English', *Corpora,* 5(1): 45-74.

Nokkonen, S. (Forthcoming), 'The register variation of NEED TO in spoken British English'.

Perkins, M. R. (1983), *Modal Expressions in English.* London: Frances Pinter.

Smith, N. (2003), 'Changes in the modals and semi-modals of strong obligation and epistemic necessity in recent British English', in: R. Facchinetti, M. Krug and F. Palmer (eds.), *Modality in Contemporary English.* Berlin: Mouton de Gruyter. 241-266.

van der Auwera, J. and V. Plungian (1998), 'Modality's semantic map', *Linguistic Typology,* 2: 79-124.

Appendix

Table 2. Distribution of NEED TO across semantic domains in Business genres

	Data type	*Internal*	*Deontic 1*	*Deontic 2*	*Dynamic*	*Epistemic*
Meeting	RF	132	82	230	32	20
	NF	250.7	155.7	436.9	60.8	38.0
Training session	RF	75	5	104	5	8
	NF	350.5	23.4	486.0	23.36	37.4
Unscripted speech	RF	78	9	111	2	2
	NF	341.3	39.4	485.7	8.8	8.8
Scripted speech	RF	24	3	109	10	1
	NF	139.2	17.0	618.5	56.8	5.7
Interview	RF	25	4	19	0	3
	NF	264.8	42.4	201.3	0	31.8
total	RF	334	103	573	49	34

Note: Df = 16, chi-square = 119.910, $p < 0.0001$.

Table 3. Men vs. women. Distribution of NEED TO in Business genres

	Male				*Female*			
Category	*Words*	*RF*	*NF*	*Disp.*	*Words*	*RF*	*NF*	*Disp.*
Meeting	323,432	309	955.4	81/192	96,153	72	748.8	23/67
Training session	116,497	116	995.7	23/70	60,691	55	906.23	14/37
Unscripted speech	126,102	104	824.7	18/56	37,468	54	1441.2	15/33
Scripted speech	115,176	83	720.6	43/93	25,822	39	1510.3	13/22
Interview	94,228	48	593.8	10/15	13,395	3	224.0	2/4
total	775,435	660	851.1	175/426	223,529	233	954.9	67/163

Note 1: Disp. = dispersion over speakers.
Note 2: Df. = 4, chi-square = 32.196, $p < 0.0001$.

Table 4. Men vs. women. Distribution of NEED TO across semantic domains in Meeting

Gender	*Data type*	*Internal*	*Deontic 1*	*Deontic 2*	*Dynamic*	*Epistemic*
Male	RF	76	59	144	15	15
	NF	234.9	182.4	445.2	46.4	46.4
Female	RF	30	6	30	4	2
	NF	312.0	62.4	312.0	41.6	20.8

Note: Df. = 4, chi-square = 11.013, $p < 0.05$.

Table 5. Men vs. women. Distribution of NEED TO across semantic domains in Scripted speech

Gender	*Data type*	*Internal*	*Deontic 1*	*Deontic 2*	*Dynamic*	*Epistemic*
Male	RF	13	3	59	7	1
	NF	112.9	26.1	512.3	60.8	8.7
Female	RF	8	0	30	1	0
	NF	309.8	-	1161.8	38.7	-

Note: The distribution is not statistically significant.

Perfect problems: A corpus-based comparison of the perfect in Bulgarian and German EFL writing

Svetla Rogatcheva

Justus-Liebig Universität Giessen

Abstract

The English perfect aspect is an area of English grammar which has proven a traditional stumbling block for non-native speakers of English from a variety of mother-tongue backgrounds (Swan and Smith 1987). The present perfect in particular has been characterized as notoriously difficult for EFL learners, on the one hand because of its partial semantic overlap with both the simple present and the simple past, and on the other because of the discrepancies in its representation in grammars and ELT textbooks (Schlüter 2002a, 2002b). Although research on the perfect and its problematic delineation abounds, there have been few corpus-based studies on its authentic use in spoken and written English and hardly any on second language use of the perfect (e.g. Granger 1999; Biber et al. 1999; Mindt 2000).

The present report investigates second language use of the perfect aspect in argumentative writing produced by advanced Bulgarian and German learners of English and contrasts it with non-professional British and American writers' use. The comparison is based on two learner subcorpora drawn from the Bulgarian and German components of the International Corpus of Learner English *(ICLE), and two control corpora drawn from the* Louvain Corpus of Native English Essays *(LOCNESS) (Granger et al. 2002, 2009).*

The pilot study results confirm previous corpus-based findings in terms of the preference of the present perfect in the British subcorpus; however, they show remarkable differences between the Bulgarian and the German learner subcorpus. Whereas Bulgarian EFL learners have similar frequencies of use of the perfect to those of British novice writers, German EFL learners' frequencies of the perfect resemble American novice writers' frequencies. A further analysis shows that both learner populations fail to employ the perfect in a target-like manner; however, the differences between the German and the Bulgarian learner subcorpus can be attributed to variables like the native language influence and the target language exposure on the one hand, and to the effects of register awareness on the other.

1. Introduction

The perfect is an area of English grammar which has been identified as equally problematic for EFL learners and grammarians for a variety of reasons, ranging from the ongoing debate about its exact nature as a verbal category, to the delineation of its central meanings from the peripheral ones. The first part of the problem refers to the controversy whether the perfect should be treated as a tense or an aspect. Comrie points to the fact that the perfect is "an aspect in a rather different sense from other aspects" (Comrie 1976: 52), since it does not represent the internal temporal constituency of a situation as traditional aspects like the progressive do, but relates "some state to a preceding situation" (Comrie 1976: 52). Other researchers (see Kortmann 1995 for a review) define the perfect as a verbal category of its own, different from both tense and aspect, and term it "anterior" (cf. Kortmann 1995). However, the present study will not deal with the controversy over the exact semantic nature of the perfect and will adopt Comrie's (1976) and Quirk et al.'s (1985) definitions of the perfect as an aspect rather than a tense or a third type of category.

1.1 The perfect in English – meanings and frequency distribution

Quirk et al. (1985) characterise the perfect aspect as "time preceding whatever time orientation is signalled by tense or other elements of the sentence or its context" (Quirk et al. 1985: 190); whereas more recent corpus-based grammars like Biber et al. (1999) define the perfect as referring to "events or states taking place during a period leading up to the specified time" (Biber et al. 1999: 460). With respect to the present perfect, most grammars summarise its core meaning as "past with current relevance" (Quirk et al. 1985: 189-190). Although the present perfect overlaps with the simple past in terms of the same semantic "past time territory" (Comrie 1976: 54), it is not tied to a specific reference point in the past and cannot be combined with definite past-time adverbials signifying such a point (cf. Comrie 1976: 54; Quirk et al. 1985: 191).

Formally, the perfect in English consists of the auxiliary verb *have* followed by the past participle of the main verb. In terms of its most common functions and in particular the functions of the present perfect, it signifies "a state leading up to the present", "indefinite event(s) in a period leading up to the present", or "a habit in a period leading up to the present" (Quirk et al. 1985: 192). Some of the most recent corpus-based grammars such as Mindt's grammar (2000) enumerate as many as five different meanings for the present perfect and seven different meanings for the past perfect, ranging from definite pasts (resultative and non-resultative), to recent pasts and continuative pasts. (cf. Mindt 2000). The present study will focus on learner and native use of the two major tensed perfects only – the present and the past perfect – and will ignore other forms of the perfect in view of their relative infrequency in both the learner and native-speaker data.

In terms of its frequency of occurrence in spoken and written English, the perfect aspect has been analysed in several recent corpus-based studies (e.g. Biber et al. 1999; Mindt 2000; Schlüter 2002a etc.). Biber et al. specify that the perfect accounts for 5 - 10% of all verb phrases and is thus much less frequent than the simple aspect (cf. Biber et al. 1999: 461). In terms of its distribution across different registers of English, the present perfect is most common in news, followed by conversation and academic prose, and least common in fiction, whereas the past perfect is most common in fiction, followed by news and academic prose, and least common in conversation (cf. Biber et al. 1999: 461).

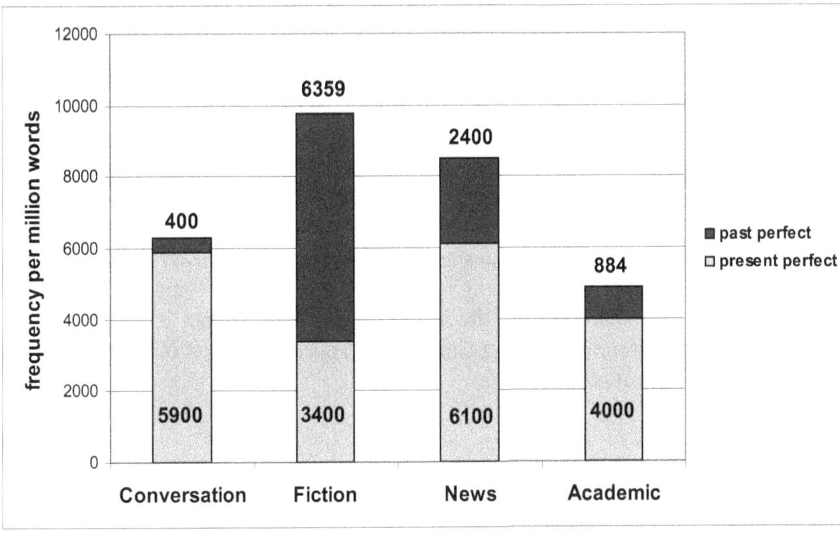

Figure 1. Frequency of the present and past perfect aspects across registers (adapted from Biber et al. 1999: 461)

In terms of the distribution of the perfect across native varieties of English, all corpus-based studies (e.g. Biber et al. 1999; Schlüter 2002a etc.) agree on the fact that the perfect is much more frequent in British English than in American English. This tendency towards 'non-use' of the perfect in American English has been variably explained with the replacement of the present perfect by the simple past or the so-called "colloquial preterite" in less formal communicative situations and in certain linguistic contexts featuring adverbials such as *just*, *yet* and *already* (Marshall 1989: 298-299).

1.2 Contrastive remarks on the perfect

Although research on EFL learners' problems with the present perfect abounds (cf. Swan and Smith 1987), few studies have taken into consideration the influence of the tense-aspect systems of the learners' native languages. Swan and Smith (1987) identify the present perfect as a stumbling block for learners from various mother-tongue backgrounds, including German learners of English. Formally, the perfect in German is deceptively similar to the English perfect (auxiliary *have* + past participle); functionally, the present perfect in German (*Perfekt*) is used in instances where English requires the simple past, such as the narrative use of the perfect in German (cf. König and Gast 2009: 86). Conversely, experiential uses of the present perfect in English are mostly rendered by the preterite (*Präteritum*) in German, whereas other uses such as the continuative perfect are normally rendered by the German simple present tense (cf. Klein and Vater 1998). Furthermore, the perfect has almost fully supplanted the preterite in many varieties of German and in southern German in particular, and is thus increasingly used in all past-time contexts (cf. Löbner 2002).

The perfect in Bulgarian is both formally and functionally different from the English perfect, although there are some functional overlaps between the two: both the English and the Bulgarian perfect can convey the current relevance meaning and the experiential meaning relating an action that has happened at an indefinite point in time (cf. Scatton 1984: 323-324). In contrast to the English present perfect and similar to the German *Perfekt*, the present perfect in Bulgarian can also be used as a narrative tense (cf. Scatton 1984).

Thus, the task of both Bulgarian and German EFL learners consists of an adequate "form-to-function mapping" (Housen 2002: 156), which involves not only the acquisition and use of the form of the English perfect, but also an acquisition of its different meanings and its appropriate use in context, observing its temporal and discourse properties.

2. The study

The present study is a pilot-study report based on learner data extracted from the *International Corpus of Learner English* (ICLE) and native-speaker data extracted from the *Louvain Corpus of Native English Essays* (LOCNESS) (Granger et al. 2002, 2009). ICLE is one of the most widely-used learner corpora comprising advanced learners' academic writing which provides a resource for "large-scale comparative studies of the interlanguage of advanced EFL learners with significantly different native language backgrounds" (Pravec 2002: 83). These studies fall under the Contrastive Interlanguage Analysis (CIA) framework (Granger 1996), which involves a cross-comparison between native and non-native varieties of English, as well as different English interlanguages with each other. The two learner corpora which have been used for this study are subcorpora of the Bulgarian and German components of ICLE, and the control corpora are a British and an American subcorpus of LOCNESS. LOCNESS provides an excellent basis for a comparison between non-native and native writing, since the essays in the corpus have been written by British and American school and university students with little or no previous experience in academic writing. For the sake of convenience, the Bulgarian and German learner subcorpora have been named BUCLE_part and GICLE_part; likewise, the British and American subcorpora of LOCNESS have been called BRSUR3 and USSCU2 in turn. The composition of the learner and native subcorpora used for this study is presented in Table 1.

Table 1. Subcorpus design

Subcorpus	#Words	Essays
1. BUCLE_part	18,752	37
2. GICLE-part	19,009	47
3. BRSUR3	19,019	33
4. USSCU2	18,630	17
Total	75,410	134

The four subcorpora were automatically tagged for parts of speech with the CLAWS7 tagset via the online tool Wmatrix (Rayson 2008), which helped to determine the total verb tag frequencies in each subcorpus. Next, the number of finite verb phrases in the four subcorpora was carefully calculated following Quirk et al.'s finite verb phrase model (cf. Quirk et al. 1972: 73). In addition, the learner subcorpora were manually tagged for errors on all verb phrases by an American informant (professional writer), following the problem-oriented annotation approach (cf. McEnery et al. 2006). Subsequently, WordSmith concordances (cf. Scott 2004) were run in search of the perfect verb phrases on the basis of the auxiliary forms *have*, *has* and *had*, followed by anything and were carefully matched with the Wmatrix frequencies for the verb tags VH0, VHZ and VHD. All non-perfect verb forms, as well as all modal perfects resulting from the WordSmith concordances were manually discarded. Finally, concordances were run for the error tags in the learner subcorpora.

3. Quantitative results

Two types of measurements were used to compare the frequencies of use of the perfect in the learner and native subcorpora: a normalised frequency per 1,000 words, and a relative frequency of the perfect verb phrases proportionate to all finite verb phrases. The first type of measurement has been used in the majority of the corpus-based studies (e.g. Biber et al. 1999; Mindt 2000; Schlüter 2002a etc.) and is therefore best suited for a direct comparison with previous research findings on the perfect; the second type of measurement allows for a more precise count of the perfect verb phrases in proportion to all finite verb phrases in a corpus, since it neglects possible bias effects that might result from one corpus being 'verbier' than the others despite the equal number of words. First, the normalised frequencies of the present and past perfects in the British and the American subcorpora of LOCNESS were calculated – the results for the two native subcorpora are presented in Table 2.

Table 2. Frequencies of the perfect in the British and American subcorpora of LOCNESS, with significance values indicating underuse[1] ($p < 0.01$)

Aspect	USSCU2	N/1,000	BRSUR3	N/1,000	LL
perfect	84	4.5	126	6.6	-7.61

The results reveal highly significant differences between the British and the American data, thus confirming previous corpus-based findings (cf. Biber et al.'s 1999; Mindt 2000, Schlüter 2000, 2002a) with respect to the preference of the perfect by British English, which in this case equals a ratio of 3:2 perfects for the British subcorpus.

Table 3 compares the frequencies of the present and past perfects in the learner subcorpora with those in the British and American subcorpora in turn. The normalised frequency for the perfect (present and past) in the Bulgarian learner subcorpus is the highest of all subcorpora, whereas the normalised frequency in the American subcorpus is the lowest. The statistical significance test shows that there are highly significant differences ($p < 0.001$) between learner and native use of the perfect in the case of the comparison of the Bulgarian learner subcorpus with the American subcorpus: Bulgarian EFL learners overuse the perfect significantly in comparison to American novice writers. On the other hand, German EFL learners underuse the perfect considerably in comparison to British novice writers ($p < 0.05$). There are no significant differences between the Bulgarian learner subcorpus and the British subcorpus, or between the German learner subcorpus and the American subcorpus.

Table 3. Frequencies of the perfect in the NNS and NS subcorpora with significance values indicating overuse and underuse ($p < 0.05$)

NNS corpora	N perfect	N/1,000	N perfect		N/1,000	LL
BUCLE-part	144	7.7	BRSUR3	126	6.6	+1.47
			USSCU2	**84**	**4.5**	**+15.59**
GICLE_part	95	5	**BRSUR3**	**126**	**6.6**	**-4.35**
			USSCU2	84	4.5	+0.47

The second type of frequency measurement relates the number of finite verb phrases marked for the present and past perfects to the total number of finite verb phrases across the learner and native subcorpora. The proportions of the tensed perfect verb phrases of all finite verb phrases in the four subcorpora are illustrated in Figure 2.

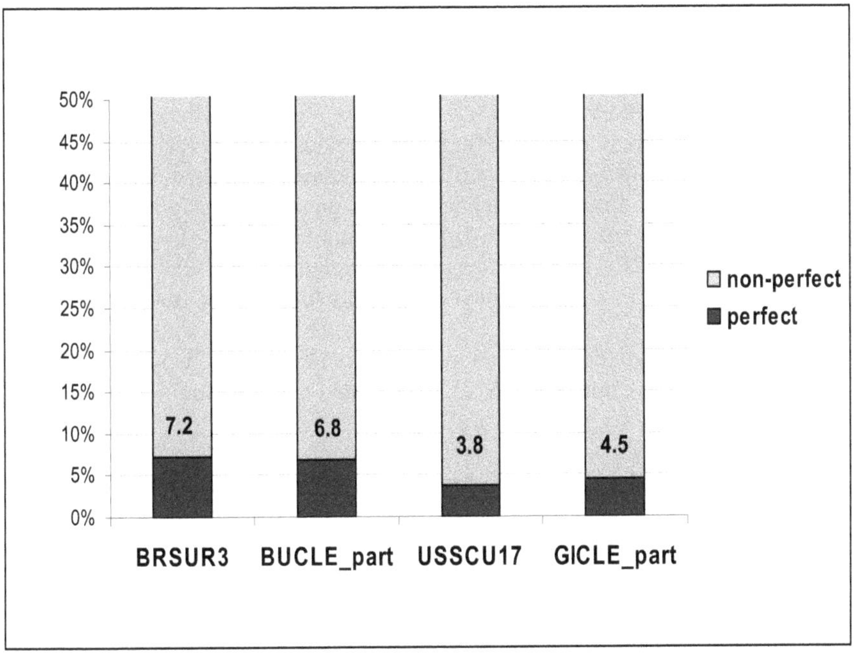

Figure 2. Proportions of the present and past perfect VPs in the NNS and NS subcorpora

The British subcorpus has the highest percentage of tensed perfect verb phrases (7.2%), while the American subcorpus has the lowest proportion – almost half as many tensed perfects as the British subcorpus (3.8%), the difference being highly significant. The proportions of the tensed perfect verb phrases of all finite verb phrases in the learner subcorpora lie in between the two native values, with the Bulgarian learner subcorpus showing the higher percentage of the two (6.8%). Again, there are significant differences between the Bulgarian learner subcorpus and the American native subcorpus in terms of Bulgarian EFL learners' overuse of the perfect verb phrases compared to American novice writers' use ($p < 0.0001$), and in terms of German EFL learners' significant underuse compared to British novice writers' use ($p < 0.001$).

4. Qualitative results: measuring learner misuse

In the qualitative part of the study, learner uses of the perfect were evaluated by the author and a native speaker of American English in terms of their acceptability within the temporal framework of each learner essay. The native informant was asked to judge all verb phrases in the learner subcorpora for their grammaticality, indicating the erroneous verb phrases with an error tag. This kind of problem-oriented error-tagging approach helps to determine the total number of obligatory contexts for the present and past perfects in the learner subcorpora, accounting for omissions of the perfect in obligatory contexts, substitutions of the perfect by other tense-aspect forms in obligatory contexts, and overuse of the perfect in non-obligatory contexts (cf. Pica 1983). The identification of ungrammatical perfect verb phrases oversupplied in non-obligatory contexts, and in particular ungrammatical present perfect verb phrases was fairly straightforward in the case of inappropriate combinations of the present perfect with definite past time adverbials. For instance, both Bulgarian and German EFL learners tend to misuse the perfect as a narrative tense which relates events that happened at a definite point in the past, as illustrated in the following three examples:

(1) *I've only found* the answer a few days *ago*. (ICLE-BG-SUN-0027.1)
(2) Our society is not as stable as it *has been* a generation *ago*. (ICLE-FR-ULG-0018.2)
(3) *Have you been yesterday* on the report on the growth of the rubbish-mountains? (ICLE-GE-AUG-0033.1)

These examples show that both learner populations have difficulty differentiating between the present perfect and the simple past and are equally insensitive to past-tense temporal contexts signalled by adverbials such as *ago* or *yesterday*. Example (3) could also be interpreted as direct transfer from German, where the perfect has almost supplanted the German preterite in all past-time contexts (cf. Löbner 2002). Other ungrammatical uses of the present perfect appear to indicate the inability of the learners to recognise the temporal framework of a given sentence and to use the perfect in a coherent sequence of tenses. Two such examples from the Bulgarian and the German learner subcorpora are presented in (4) and (5):

(4) Many eras *have passed* till man discovered simple truths as the fact that the earth is round, for instance, and those mentioned above. (ICLE-BG-SUN-0028.1)
(5) On the other hand it *has also been* one of the grey little boxes that broke the news about my sisters new born baby-boy. (ICLE-GE-AUG-0023.1)

The present perfect has been incorrectly supplied in both contexts, since the events the learners are referring to are clearly situated in the past, with an obvious gap between their completion and the present moment (cf. Quirk et al. 1985: 183). However, the learners here seem to have been looking for the past perfect in their desire to relate an event which happened prior to the time referred to by the simple past, failing to use the correct past perfect form.

Apart from evaluating learner misuse of the perfect aspect, learner non-use of the present and past perfects and their substitution by other verb forms in obligatory contexts were also investigated. The results are remarkable insofar as they show a difference in the underuse of the perfect in obligatory contexts between the two learner populations: twenty-two of the obligatory contexts for the present perfect in the German learner subcorpus have been incorrectly supplied with a different verb form, whereas only five of the obligatory perfect contexts in the Bulgarian learner subcorpus have been underused in this way. The majority of the obligatory contexts for the present perfect in the German learner subcorpus have been incorrectly supplied with simple past verb forms – the following two examples illustrate this:

(6) The telephone really *changed* our lives and we can be grateful about it. (ICLE-GE-AUG-0026.1)

(7) This phenomenon *became* clearly visible in the last two decades and has not reached its climax yet. (ICLE-FR-ULG-0001.2)

In both cases, the learners are referring to events which have happened at an indefinite point of time in the past with an obvious present result having current relevance. Unlike the more common substitution of the present perfect in obligatory contexts by simple past verb forms, there are only two substitutions of the present perfect by simple present verb forms in both learner subcorpora, which show learners' inability to relate the 'pastness' of the state leading up to the present:

(8) Rare plants, the Alpenveilchen and the Silberdistel, *are* laid to rest. (ICLE-GE-AUG-0018.1)

(9) The modern times could be regarded as times when imagination *fuses* to a great extent with the dry science. (ICLE-BG-SUN-0007.1)

A major advantage of the problem-oriented error tagging of all verb phrases in the learner subcorpora is that it allows for a quantification of the distribution of the perfect in obligatory contexts, its omission or replacement by other verb phrases, as well as its overuse in non-obligatory contexts. These distributional patterns can be quantified by two types of measurements: a suppliance-in-obligatory-context analysis (SOC) and a target-like-use analysis (TLU) (cf. Pica 1983). The SOC analysis includes both the incorrect use and the omissions of the perfect in obligatory contexts and is calculated after the following formula (Pica 1983: 474):

$$\text{SOC}=\frac{(\text{n correct suppliance in obligatory context x 2})\ (\text{n misformations in obligatory context})}{\text{total obligatory contexts x 2}}$$

Likewise, the TLU analysis calculates the frequency with which the perfect has been correctly supplied or omitted in obligatory contexts; in addition, it also calculates the instances of incorrect suppliance in non-obligatory contexts after the following formula (Pica 1983: 474):

$$\text{TLU} = \frac{\text{n correct suppliance in obligatory context}}{\text{(n obligatory contexts)} + \text{(n suppliance in non-obligatory contexts)}}$$

Both the SOC and the TLU scores can be used to measure learners' grammatical accuracy by counting the erroneous perfect verb phrases out of all verb phrases; however, the TLU analysis goes one step further, taking into account the overuse of the perfect in non-obligatory contexts too, thus ensuring greater accuracy of results. The SOC and the TLU scores for the perfect in the Bulgarian and German learner subcorpora are presented in Figure 3.

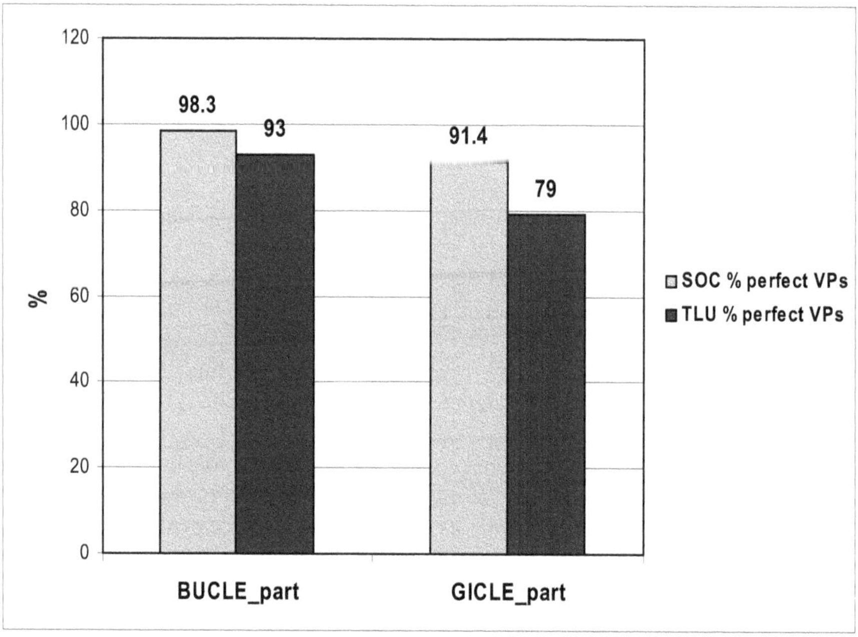

Figure 3. SOC and TLU scores for the perfect in the Bulgarian and German learner subcorpora

The TLU scores are lower than the SOC scores for both learner subcorpora; in addition, the German learners' accuracy scores for the perfect (both SOC and TLU) are lower than the Bulgarian ones. The TLU scores for the German learner subcorpus (79%) are the lowest, not least because of the higher rates of overuse of the perfect in simple past contexts in addition to its underuse in obligatory perfect contexts in the German learner subcorpus. Since the raw error frequencies in both subcorpora are fairly small, no statistical tests of comparison were computed for the present study; nevertheless, these two types of error rate quantification serve as good indicators of the accuracy rates of the perfect for the two learner populations, especially if one assumes that a complete form-to-function mapping of the perfect in learner language requires an accuracy rate of at least 90% (cf. Ellis and Barkhuizen 2006: 73-74).

5. Discussion

The preliminary findings on the use of the perfect aspect in academic writing produced by advanced Bulgarian and German EFL learners can be interpreted from two perspectives: on the one hand, they reveal significant quantitative and functional differences between non-native and native use of the perfect, and on the other, they reveal different error types and accuracy rates for the two learner subcorpora. Furthermore, they also confirm previous results concerning the differences in use of the perfect between British and American English (cf. Biber et al. 1999; Mindt 2000, Schlüter 2002a).

The quantitative data illustrate a certain tendency among EFL learners to follow either British or American patterns of use of the perfect aspect – both the normalised frequencies of use and the proportions of the perfect verb phrases of all finite verb phrases in the German learner subcorpus resemble the American normalised frequencies and proportions; on the other hand, the frequencies and proportions of perfect verb phrases in the Bulgarian learner subcorpus resemble the British normalised frequencies and proportions. A similar tendency based on the same learner subcorpora was discovered for the use of the progressive aspect (cf. Rogatcheva 2009), indicating possible differences in the target-language exposure for the two learner populations and a potential bias towards either an American or a British native-speaker norm. One possible explanation is the amount of target-language exposure: whereas over 50% of the German learners in GICLE have had at least one month of target-language exposure in an English-speaking country, less than 10% of the Bulgarian learners in BUCLE have been abroad (cf. Granger et al. 2002, 2009). Moreover, whereas the majority of the GICLE learners have had practical EFL courses taught by native speakers of English (Lorenz 2002: 102 in Granger et al. 2002), the BUCLE learners have had very few native speakers as teachers at school or university (Blagoeva 2002: 85 in Granger et al. 2002). This proves that Bulgarian EFL classrooms may be seen as "impoverished learning environments" (Kasper 1997 quoted in Gilquin and Paquot 2007: 6) in terms of the exposure to native-speaker input to a much greater extent than German EFL classrooms. At the same time, it also indicates that Bulgarian EFL classrooms may adhere more closely to a traditional British English native-speaker norm (as reflected by textbooks and grammars) than German EFL classrooms, again due to the limited authentic input. Unfortunately, neither the countries of target-language exposure, nor the origin of the EFL teachers in ICLE are specified in the learner profiles (cf. Granger et al. 2002, 2009).

In terms of the accuracy of use of the perfect aspect in argumentative writing, both Bulgarian and German EFL learners have difficulties differentiating between the functions of the present perfect and the simple past in English, since they both misuse the present perfect as a narrative tense, combining it freely with definite past-time adverbials. Moreover, both learner populations have problems maintaining a sequence of tenses within a coherent stretch of writing – this finding goes in line with the results obtained by other researchers such as Granger (1999) on French-speaking EFL learners or Eriksson (2008) on Swedish EFL learners. Like other EFL learners, Bulgarian and German EFL learners are prone to make unmotivated tense shifts which influence the overall accuracy rates of the perfect aspect, since they directly affect all other tense-aspect forms in the neighbouring discourse context of the essays.

One major difference in the accuracy rates of the perfect between the Bulgarian and the German learner subcorpus results from German learners' replacement of the present perfect by the simple past tense in obligatory perfect contexts. This type of underuse points towards German learners' insensitivity to some of the central meanings of the present perfect like the "past-with-current-relevance" meaning (e.g. Quirk et al., 1985: 192). At the same time, it resembles the use of the colloquial preterite in American English, thus contributing to the stronger narrative character and the slightly more colloquial overtone of the essays in the German learner subcorpus (cf. Axelsson and Hahn 2001: 22). Moreover, it also confirms the fact that German EFL learners must have been exposed to conversational English to a greater extent than Bulgarian EFL learners.

6. Concluding remarks

The results presented in this pilot study show that the use of the perfect aspect differs for the two learner corpora involved, both quantitatively and qualitatively. The frequency analysis revealed patterns of both overuse and underuse of the perfect in learner writing in comparison to native-speaker novice writing. Whereas Bulgarian EFL learners' frequencies and proportions of the perfect verb phrases are similar to British novice writers', German EFL learners' frequencies and proportions are similar to American novice writers'. A word of caution should be given here: comparing the perfect verb phrases as a proportion of all finite verb phrases in a corpus may be a more precise measure for overuse and underuse than comparing normalised frequencies per 1,000 words; yet, it is still influenced as a frequency value by the parts-of-speech frequency profiles of the corpora.

The qualitative analysis revealed that both Bulgarian and German EFL learners have difficulties using the perfect aspect in a target-like manner, and fail to employ it correctly within the temporal and discourse context of their essays, although to a different extent. The TLU analysis of the perfect measuring the (non)suppliance of the perfect in obligatory contexts proved as a good measurement of comparison between the error rates in the learner subcorpora in addition to the frequency counts traditionally used within the CIA framework; moreover, the TLU accuracy scores can be used as an alternative approach to error counts (cf. Dagneaux et al. 1998). To conclude, complete error statistics and a more detailed analysis based on the entire learner corpora are necessary in order to examine the difficulties Bulgarian and German EFL learners have with the perfect aspect and highlight those areas which require particular attention in the EFL classroom.

Notes

1 The LL value is always a positive number; '+' and '-' signs have been used here to indicate overuse or underuse in the learner corpora relative to the native corpora (cf. Rayson 2008).

References

Axelsson, M. and A. Hahn (2001), 'The use of the progressive in Swedish and German advanced learner English – a corpus-based study', *ICAME Journal,* 25: 5-30.

Biber, D., S. Johansson, G. Leech, S. Conrad and E. Finegan (1999), *Longman Grammar of Spoken and Written English*. Harlow: Longman.

Blagoeva, R. (2002). 'The Status of English in Bulgaria', in: S. Granger, E. Dagneaux and F. Meunier (eds.) *International Corpus of Learner English.* Louvain-la-Neuve, Belgium: Presses Univ. de Louvain. 81-86.

Comrie, B. (1976), *Aspect: An Introduction to the Study of Verbal Aspect and Related Problems*. Cambridge: Cambridge University Press.

Dagneaux, E., Dennes, S. and S. Granger (1998), 'Computer-aided error analysis', *System,* 26: 163-174.

Ellis, R. and G. Barkhuizen (2006), *Analysing Learner Language.* Oxford: Oxford University Press.

Eriksson, A. (2008), *Tense and Aspect in Advanced Swedish Learners' Written English,* Acta Universitatis Gothoburgensis, 92. Göteborg: Göteborgs Univ. Press.

Gilquin, G. and M. Paquot (2007), 'Spoken features in learner academic writing: Identification, explanation and solution', in: M. Davies, P. Rayson, S. Hunston and P. Danielsson (eds.) *Proceedings of the Corpus Linguistics Conference CL2007.* University of Birmingham, UK, 27-30 July 2007.

Granger, S. (1996), 'From CA to CIA and back: An integrated approach to computerized bilingual and learner corpora', in: K. Aijmer and B. Altenberg (eds.) *Languages in Contrast.* Lund: Lund University Press. 37-51.

Granger, S. (1999), 'Use of tenses by advanced EFL learners: Evidence from an error-tagged computer corpus', in: H. Hasselgård and S. Oksefjell (eds.) *Out of Corpora. Studies in honour of Stig Johansson.* Amsterdam: Rodopi, 191-202.

Granger, S., E. Dagneaux and F. Meunier (2002), *International Corpus of Learner English. Version 1.1.* Louvain-la-Neuve UCL Presses Univ. de Louvain.

Granger, S., E. Dagneaux, F. Meunier and M. Paquot (2009), *International Corpus of Learner English. Version 2.* Louvain-la-Neuve UCL Presses Univ. de Louvain.

Housen, A. (2002), 'The development of Tense-Aspect in English as a second language and the variable influence of inherent aspect', in: R. Salaberry and Y. Shirai (eds.) *The L2 Acquisition of Tense-Aspect Morphology*. Amsterdam: Benjamins. 155-197.

Kasper, G. (1997). *Can Pragmatic Competence be Taught?* (NetWork #6). Honolulu: University of Hawai'i, Second Language Teaching & Curriculum Center. <http://www.nflrc.hawaii.edu/NetWorks/NW06/> accessed: 18 June 2007.

Klein, W. and H. Vater (1998), 'The perfect in English and German', in: L. I. Kulikov and H. Vater (eds.) *Typology of Verbal Categories. Papers Presented to Vladimir Nedjalkov on the Occasion of his 70th Birthday*. Linguistische Arbeiten, 382. Tübingen: Niemeyer. 215-237.

Kortmann, B. (1995), 'Compositionality and the perfect', in: W. Riehle (ed.) *Proceedings of the Anglistentag 1994.* Tübingen: Niemeyer. 183-199.

König, E. and V. Gast (2009), *Understanding English-German Contrasts*. 2nd ed. Berlin: Schmidt.

Löbner, S. (2002), 'Is the German Perfekt a perfect perfect?', in: I. Kaufmann and B. Stiebels (eds.) *More Than Words*. Berlin: Akademie. 369-391.

Lorenz, G. (2002). 'Language corpora rock the base: On Standard English grammar, perfective aspect and seemingly adverse corpus evidence', in: B. Kettemann, G. Marko, and T. McEnery (eds.) *Teaching and Learning by Doing Corpus Analysis. Proceedings of the Fourth International Conference on Teaching and Language Corpora*, Graz 19-24 July 2000. Language and computers, 42. Amsterdam: Rodopi. 131-145.

Marshall, H. W. (1989), 'The colloquial preterit: Language variation in the ESL classroom', in: M. R. Eisenstein (ed.) *The Dynamic Interlanguage. Empirical Studies in Second Language Variation.* New York: Plenum Press. 297-315.

McEnery, T., Y. Tono and R. Xiao (2006), *Corpus-Based Language Studies: An Advanced Resource Book.* London: Routledge.

Mindt, D. (2000), *An Empirical Grammar of the English Verb System*. Berlin: Cornelsen.

Pica, T. (1983), 'Methods of morpheme quantification: Their effect on the interpretation of second language data', *Studies in Second Language Acquisition,* 6(1): 69-78.

Pravec, N. A. (2002), 'Survey of learner corpora', *ICAME Journal,* 26: 81-114.

Quirk, R., S. Greenbaum, G. Leech and J. Svartvik (1972), *A Grammar of Contemporary English*. London: Longman.

Quirk, R., S. Greenbaum, G. Leech and J. Svartvik (1985), *A Comprehensive Grammar of the English Language*. London: Longman.

Rayson, P. (2008), *Wmatrix: a Web-Based Corpus Processing Environment.* Lancaster University Computing Department. <http://ucrel.lancs.ac.uk/wmatrix/>

Rogatcheva, S. (2009), 'I've only found the answer a few days ago: Aspect use in Bulgarian and German EFL writing', in: C. Prado-Alonso, L. Gómez-García, I. Pastor-Gómez and D. Tizón-Couto (eds.) *New Trends and Methodologies in Applied English Language Research. Diachronic, Diatopic and Contrastive Studies.* Frankfurt: Peter Lang. 255-278.

Scatton, E. A. (1984), *A Reference Grammar of Modern Bulgarian.* Columbus, Ohio: Slavica Publ.

Schlüter, N. (2000), 'The Present Perfect in British and American English: Selected results of an empirical analysis', in: C. Mair and M. Hundt (eds.) *Corpus Linguistics and Linguistic Theory. Papers from the 20th International Conference on English Language Research on Computerized Corpora* (*ICAME 20*). Amsterdam: Rodopi. 313-320.

Schlüter, N. (2002a), *Present Perfect: eine Korpuslinguistische Analyse des Englischen Perfekts mit Vermittlungsvorschlägen für den Sprachunterricht.* Tübingen: Narr.

Schlüter, N. (2002b), 'Temporal specification of the Present Perfect: A corpus-based study', in: P. Peters, P. Collins and A. Smith (eds.) *New Frontiers of Corpus Research.* Amsterdam: Rodopi. 307-316.

Scott, M. (2004), *WordSmith Tools.* Version 4.0. Oxford: Oxford University Press.

Swan, M. and B. Smith (eds.) (1987), *Learner English: a Teacher's Guide to Interference and Other Problems.* Cambridge: Cambridge University Press.

Thematic progression in learner language

Sylvi Rørvik

Hedmark University College

Abstract

This study examines the use of thematic progression in material from the Norwegian component of the International Corpus of Learner English (*NICLE*). The Integrated Contrastive Model *is employed to investigate whether Norwegian advanced learners of English use the same thematic-progression strategies as native-speaker professional writers of English, or whether they are influenced by Norwegian discourse conventions. The influence of transfer is examined through comparison with Norwegian texts written by professional writers. In addition, a comparison with non-professional writers of English and Norwegian is included in order to identify potential similarities between novice writers, regardless of whether or not they are writing in their L1 or L2. The results indicate that there are differences in the use of thematic-progression strategies between the NICLE writers and professional writers of English, and that some of these differences are most probably due to transfer from Norwegian. In addition, novice writers seem to share certain characteristics in the way they structure their texts which are different from the strategies employed by professional writers.*

1. Introduction

This paper examines thematic progression (TP) in argumentative English texts written by Norwegian advanced learners of English. It has been shown that there are differences between Norwegian and English in terms of thematic structure (see e.g. Hasselgård 1997, 2004, and 2005). As learners might be expected to transfer thematic structures from their native language (L1) into the foreign language, (L2), it seems reasonable to hypothesize that the Norwegian learners will choose thematic structures that are more common in Norwegian than in English.

So far, little research has been carried out on thematic structure in English texts produced by Norwegian advanced learners. One exception is Hasselgård (2009: 137-138), where it is shown that Norwegian novice writers have problems adapting to English discourse conventions. In addition, Boström Aronsson (2003: 206-207), in a study of English produced by Swedish advanced learners, discusses learners' problems in choosing thematic structures that resemble those of native speakers of English. Swedish and Norwegian are closely related languages, so one might hypothesize that Norwegian advanced learners would have similar problems. In this paper I address the following two questions:

1. In terms of TP, how native-like are English texts produced by Norwegian advanced learners compared to texts written by professional writers of English?
2. Which tendencies emerge if one compares the TP patterns in the English output of Norwegian advanced learners with the TP patterns in texts written by novice (non-professional) English and Norwegian writers writing in their respective L1s?[1]

Section 2 discusses the material and method of the study; Section 3 focuses on the analytical framework, and Section 4 gives an overview and discussion of the results. Section 5 contains a summary and conclusion.

2. Material and method

When studying learner language, the choice of control corpus is perhaps more complicated than for other corpus-based studies. Gilquin and Paquot (2008: 45) observe that "[native-speaker] student writing is arguably a better type of comparable data to EFL learner writing if the objective of the comparison is to describe and evaluate interlanguage(s) as fairly as possible". For the present study, this would entail the use of LOCNESS as the only yardstick by which to measure whether the NICLE writers use thematic progression patterns in the same way that native speakers of English do. Gilquin and Paquot (2008: 45) also note, however, that "professional writing has a major role to play in learner corpus research as soon as pedagogical applications are considered". Ädel (2006: 207) concludes that "[t]he ideal case [...] would be to use both native-speaker student essays and professional texts as standards of comparison. [...] [A]s a result, we would get a broader picture of what the status of the learner essays is in relation to native-speaker texts". This study follows Ädel's recommendation, and uses both native-speaker student essays and professional texts as control corpora.

The analytical procedure employed is inspired by the Integrated Contrastive Model, as outlined and described by Granger (1996) and Gilquin (2000/2001). This method involves a combination of contrastive analysis of texts produced by native speakers and contrastive interlanguage (learner language) analysis. "[Contrastive analysis] data helps analysts to formulate predictions about interlanguage which can be checked against [interlanguage data]" (Granger 1996: 46). To enable the use of this model, material was selected from five categories, with 100 texts from each category. The first category comprises texts from the Norwegian component of the International Corpus of Learner English (NICLE),[2] the second and third consist of argumentative texts from Norwegian and English newspapers (editorials, etc.), and the fourth and fifth are argumentative essays by novice native speakers of English[3] and Norwegian writing in their respective L1s.[4]

The issue of representativeness is of course crucial here. Ideally, the category of novice Norwegian texts would have to be collected in co-operation with schools to ensure comparability with the NICLE material. The essays used here have been characterized as argumentative by their authors, but for practical reasons it was not possible in this case to examine the actual essay questions. The results should therefore be interpreted with a certain degree of caution.

When it comes to the native-speaker expert categories, i.e. the newspaper editorials, etc., these were chosen from what could be considered argumentative text types within newspapers. Most online newspapers have a comments section, where such material can easily be found. To a certain extent, the use of newspaper texts implies that this is considered to be the standard to which students aspire when they write argumentative texts. This is not necessarily the case, and one alternative might be to use published academic papers for the professional native-speaker category. It is my view, however, that although the students are being trained to write academic papers, it would be unfair to compare the NICLE texts with this text type, simply because the NICLE topics do *not* encourage academic discussions. Instead, they ask for the students' opinions. Thus, it was felt that argumentative newspaper texts would be the best choice.

The texts were divided into T-units[5] and analyzed manually for TP features (see Section 3 below), using the UAM Corpus Tool.[6] Table 1 gives an overview of the text categories, with the average number of words and T-units for the texts in each category. 'NICLE' is the English texts written by the Norwegian advanced learners. The native-speaker professional categories, i.e. the newspaper texts, have been labeled 'ENG NEWS' and 'NOR NEWS'. 'LOCNESS' is the native-speaker English novice category, and 'NOR ESSAYS' is the native-speaker Norwegian novice category.

Table 1. Average number of words and T-units in each text category

Text category	Average number of words	Average number of T-units	Total number of words
NICLE	684.9	44.1	68,490
NOR NEWS	643.4	41.2	64,340
ENG NEWS	872.9	48.8	87,290
LOCNESS	534.3	38.8	53,430
NOR ESSAYS	1,028.6	72.3	102,860

The integrated contrastive model was employed, and the procedure consisted of the following steps:

1. contrastive analysis of the English and Norwegian newspaper texts, to identify differences between English and Norwegian and formulate hypotheses about the interlanguage of the Norwegian advanced learners of English
2. comparison of NICLE texts with professional L1 texts, to test the hypotheses resulting from step 1

3. comparison of NICLE texts with novice native-speaker texts in English and Norwegian, to explore the possibility that novice writing shares characteristics independent of whether the writer is a native speaker or not (cf. Gilquin et al. 2007)

3. Analytical framework

The present study uses Halliday's definition of theme as "the point of departure for the message" (Halliday 2004: 58). In English, theme is typically realized by first position in the clause, and "ends with the first constituent that is either participant, circumstance or process. We refer to this constituent, in its textual function, as the **topical Theme**" (Halliday 2004: 79; original emphasis). The rest of the sentence is the rheme. There are two points where the framework used in the present study differs from Hallidays'. First, constructions that have a non-referential *it* or *there* in thematic position are analyzed as 'empty' theme, following Berry (1995) and Hasselgård (2009). Second, for a cross-linguistic study it is necessary to have a definition of theme that works for both languages involved. Because of the verb-second constraint in Norwegian, which dictates that the second element in any declarative sentence must be the finite verb, the theme in sentences with obligatory inversion is considered to include the first experiential element following the finite verb. The verb-second constraint causes problems only for sentences where the lexical verb is finite, since an auxiliary would not be considered referential in any case. One may compare *Derfor protesterte han* (lit: 'Therefore protested he') with *Derfor ville han protestere* (lit: 'Therefore would he protest'); the first sentence has a finite lexical verb which would be topical theme if one adhered strictly to Halliday's principles, while the second has the subject as its topical theme.

For an investigation of thematic progression, it is also important to know whether the theme contains given or new information. The analysis of the material for this study is based on the principles of Jones (1983) and Chafe (1987). Accordingly, 'given' is defined as either something mentioned before (however distant from the repetition) or inferable from the context.

In addition to the 'empty' and 'new' categories mentioned above, five patterns of thematic progression involving given themes have been used in the analysis: 'simple linear', 'simple continuous', 'complex linear', 'complex continuous', and 'extended reference'.[7] 'Simple linear progression' (Daneš 1974: 118) involves sentences where the theme of a sentence is taken from the rheme of the sentence immediately preceding it:[8]

(1) So why is it that <u>we</u> lock up our criminals?
We lock them up preferably to forget about them, [...] (ICLE-NO-HE-0003.1)

'Simple continuous' is the pattern found in consecutive sentences with the same theme (Daneš 1974: 118-119):

(2) I got much more than 8 hours of sleep each night.
I even had time to get bored! (ICLE-NO-BU-0003.1)

In cases where the theme is taken from the rheme of a sentence other than the immediately preceding one, we get 'complex linear progression' (Rørvik 2004: 153). Intervening T-units are in italics:

(3) In a way I feel sorry for people with no dreams.
I think they are missing out on something for what could possibly feel better than accomplishing your goals?
Dreams are forever, whether big or small! (ICLE-NO-AC-0011.1)

Similarly, where the theme was previously used as the theme of another sentence, but not the one immediately preceding, we get 'complex continuous progression' (Rørvik 2004: 153-154). Intervening are T-units in italics:

(4) The prisons system should help the prisoners to get a new start in life.
8 T-units
The jail system needs to be changed. (ICLE-NO-AC-0017.1)

Finally, the term 'extended reference' is taken from Halliday and Hasan (1976: 52-53), and refers to cases where the theme of a sentence does not refer to one easily identifiable part of a T-unit, but rather to an entire clause or stretch of clauses:

(5) Most university degrees are theoretical.
There is no practical exercise.
Is **that** a good thing? (ICLE-NO-AG-0018.1)

4. Results and discussion

Table 2 shows the results for the various TP patterns, including the category 'new', i.e. themes containing new information, in the native-speaker expert categories. The percentages are averages for each pattern in each text type. Thus, for instance, the average percentage of simple linear progression in NOR NEWS texts is 8.8%. From the figures in Table 2 one might infer that the only major difference between the two categories is in the proportion of 'new' themes, where ENG NEWS has 53.3% and NOR NEWS has 45.8%. However, a look at which differences are statistically significant reveals a more complex picture. Table 3 shows the distribution of differences between these two text categories.[9]

Table 2. Average figures in percent for the various TP patterns in native-speaker expert categories

	Simple linear	Simple continuous	Complex linear	Complex continuous	Extended reference	Empty	New
ENG NEWS	8.1%	9.6%	6.8%	6.4%	9.5%	6.3%	53.3%
NOR NEWS	8.8%	10%	8.1%	6.1%	12.7%	8.5%	45.8%

Table 3. Statistically significant/non-significant differences in use of TP patterns in ENG NEWS and NOR NEWS (cf. Table 2 for an overview of the proportional distribution of TP patterns in each text category)

	Significant	*p*-value	Non-significant	*p*-value
Simple linear			X	0.2412
Simple continuous			X	0.6190
Complex linear	X	0.0170		
Complex continuous			X	0.6039
Extended reference	X	0.0000		
Empty	X	0.0000		
New	X	0.0000		

As can be seen from Table 3, in four of the seven TP patterns there are statistically significant differences between ENG NEWS and NOR NEWS: 'complex linear', 'extended reference', 'empty', and 'new'. One might thus hypothesize that the NICLE writers will have problems with these categories, since they represent areas where English and Norwegian are different.

If we add the corresponding figures for NICLE to those in Table 2 (included below in Table 4, for convenience), we can check whether this hypothesis is valid.

Table 4. Average figures in percent for the various TP patterns in native-speaker expert categories and NICLE

	Simple linear	Simple continuous	Complex linear	Complex continuous	Extended reference	Empty	New
ENG NEWS	8.1%	9.6%	6.8%	6.4%	9.5%	6.3%	53.3%
NOR NEWS	8.8%	10%	8.1%	6.1%	12.7%	8.5%	45.8%
NICLE	11.4 %	13.1%	8.8%	8.3%	12.6%	7.5%	38.3%

The percentages in Table 4 indicate that the NICLE writers overuse all the TP patterns as compared to ENG NEWS, but underuse 'new' themes.[10] Within two of the patterns, 'extended reference' and 'empty', it is the NOR NEWS category that has the highest proportion. It would also seem from the figures in Table 4 that the NICLE texts are closer to the NOR NEWS texts in all categories except 'complex continuous', which could be taken as an indication that transfer from Norwegian is to blame for the NICLE writers' failure to use the same TP patterns as native speakers of English. But percentages can be misleading, as we can see when we examine these differences more closely to see whether they are statistically significant.

Table 5 shows that the differences between NICLE and ENG NEWS are statistically significant for all TP patterns, which confirms the impression given by Table 4 that the NICLE writers do not employ the same TP strategies as native speakers. What is also apparent from Table 5 is that the NICLE texts are indeed more similar to the NOR NEWS texts than they are to the texts in the ENG NEWS category, but to a smaller extent than Table 4 seemed to suggest. Nonetheless, for the categories 'complex linear', 'extended reference', and 'empty', the differences between NOR NEWS and NICLE are not statistically significant. This could again be taken as evidence of transfer from Norwegian in the NICLE texts, because as Table 3 shows, these are categories where the differences between ENG NEWS and NOR NEWS are statistically significant.

Table 5. Statistically significant/non-significant differences in use of TP patterns in NICLE vs. ENG NEWS and NOR NEWS (cf. Table 4 for an overview of the proportional distribution of TP patterns in each text category)

	NICLE vs. ENG NEWS		NICLE vs. NOR NEWS			
	Significant	*p*-value	Significant	*p*-value	Non-significant	*p*-value
Simple linear	X	0.0000	X	0.0000		
Simple continuous	X	0.0000	X	0.0000		
Complex linear	X	0.0004			X	0.2867
Complex continuous	X	0.0002	X	0.0000		
Extended reference	X	0.0000			X	0.9012
Empty	X	0.0267			X	0.770
New	X	0.0000	X	0.0000		

Finally, Table 5 tells us that there are four TP patterns which the NICLE writers use differently from both ENG NEWS and NOR NEWS: 'simple linear', 'simple continuous', 'complex continuous', and 'new'. Interestingly, with the exception of 'new', these are all patterns where we find no statistically significant differences between ENG NEWS and NOR NEWS (cf. Table 3). These patterns are therefore indicative of cases where the NICLE writers fail to use the appropriate English patterns, but where this failure is not due to transfer from Norwegian. In an attempt to explain this particular characteristic of the NICLE texts, we will now widen our discussion to include the two other novice-writer text categories, LOCNESS and NOR ESSAYS.

Previous studies have pointed out competence deficiencies in novice writing, e.g. Hannay (2007), on the use of patterns of multiple theme, and Gilquin and Paquot (2008), on learner academic writing and register variation. The next step in the present study is therefore a comparison of novice writing in an L2 (NICLE) with text produced by novice native speakers of English and Norwegian writing in their respective L1s. The aim is to identify possible features shared by novice writers regardless of mother-tongue background and regardless of whether or not they are writing in their L1 or L2. Table 6 expands upon Table 4 by the addition of the figures for the two other novice groups, LOCNESS and NOR ESSAYS. Here the figures have been arranged to show a scale from lowest to highest percentages in each category. We see that in four of the seven categories the novice writers are grouped at one end of the scale, and the expert writers at the other end:

Table 6. Average figures in percent for the various TP patterns in all text categories, low-high percentages

Simple linear	ENG NEWS (8.1%)	NOR NEWS (8.8%)	LOCNESS (10.7%)	NICLE (11.4 %)	NOR ESSAYS (12.2%)
Simple continuous	ENG NEWS (9.6%)	NOR NEWS (10%)	LOCNESS (10.2%)	NOR ESSAYS (10.9%)	NICLE (13.1%)
Complex linear	ENG NEWS (6.8%)	LOCNESS (7.2%)	NOR NEWS (8.1%)	NOR ESSAYS (8.1%)	NICLE (8.8%)
Complex continuous	NOR NEWS (6.1%)	ENG NEWS (6.4%)	LOCNESS (7.5%)	NOR ESSAYS (8.2%)	NICLE (8.3%)
Extended reference	ENG NEWS (9.5%)	LOCNESS (12%)	NICLE (12.6%)	NOR NEWS (12.7%)	NOR ESSAYS (12.8%)
Empty	ENG NEWS (6.3%)	NICLE (7.5%)	NOR NEWS (8.5%)	LOCNESS (8.8%)	NOR ESSAYS (10%)
New	NOR ESSAYS (37.8%)	NICLE (38.3%)	LOCNESS (43.6%)	NOR NEWS (45.8%)	ENG NEWS (53.3%)

In the categories ‘simple linear’, ‘simple continuous’, ‘complex continuous’, and ‘new’, the novice categories share either the high end of the scale (for the three TP patterns), or the low end of the scale (for new themes). For the other three categories, ‘complex linear’, ‘extended reference’, and ‘empty’, the novice categories do not, seemingly, display the same degree of similarity. This suggests that TP strategies used by the writers in the NICLE, LOCNESS, and NOR ESSAYS text categories do share some characteristics. In order to be able to draw any conclusions about this, it seems sensible to first compare the LOCNESS and NOR ESSAYS texts with the expert text categories in their respective L1s, i.e. ENG NEWS and NOR NEWS. Table 7 gives an overview of the relevant differences:

Table 7. Statistically significant/non-significant differences in use of TP patterns in LOCNESS vs. ENG NEWS and NOR ESSAYS vs. NOR NEWS (cf. Table 6 for an overview of the proportional distribution of TP patterns in each text category)

	LOCNESS vs. ENG NEWS				NOR ESSAYS vs. NOR NEWS			
	Sig.	*p*-value	Non-sig.	*p*-value	Sig.	*p*-value	Non-sig.	*p*-value
Simple linear	X	0.0000			X	0.0000		
Simple continuous			X	0.4425			X	0.1199
Complex linear			X	0.4934			X	0.9387
Complex continuous			X	0.0547	X	0.0000		
Extended reference	X	0.0003					X	0.7977
Empty	X	0.0000			X	0.0078		
New	X	0.0000			X	0.0000		

In Table 5 above, wc saw that NICLE was different from ENG NEWS with respect to all TP patterns. Table 7, in contrast, shows that both LOCNESS and NOR ESSAYS are different from texts by professional native-speaker writers of their respective L1s in only four of the seven categories. For LOCNESS as compared to ENG NEWS, the differences are in the use of the patterns 'simple linear', 'extended reference', 'empty', and 'new', whereas the writers in the NOR ESSAYS category use 'simple linear', 'complex continuous', 'empty', and 'new' differently from the NOR NEWS writers. It seems probable, therefore, that there are certain aspects of textual patterning that are common to novice writers, regardless of whether they are writing in their L1 or L2.

A further comparison, between NICLE and the two other novice categories, may shed more light on this apparent tendency for novice writers to use TP strategies differently from professional writers. Although all three novice categories in the present study exhibit differences from the professional-writer categories, it does not, of course, necessarily follow from this that themselves are similar. Indeed, as discussed above, there is evidence of transfer from Norwegian in NICLE, which would obviously not be a problem for novice writers writing in their L1, as is the case for both LOCNESS and NOR ESSAYS. In Table 8, we see the differences and similarities between NICLE and the two other novice categories, grouped according to statistical significance or non-significance.

It is evident from Table 8 that NICLE is more similar to NOR ESSAYS than it is to LOCNESS. On the one hand, this is surprising, because the NICLE texts are written in English, and one might hope they would be more similar to English texts written by novice native writers. On the other hand, one might expect this result, given the evidence of transfer that we saw in the comparison of the NICLE texts with the professional L1 categories of ENG NEWS and NOR NEWS.

Table 8. Statistically significant/non-significant differences in use of TP patterns in NICLE vs. LOCNESS and NOR ESSAYS (cf. Table 6 for an overview of the proportional distribution of TP patterns in each text category)

	NICLE vs. LOCNESS				NICLE vs. NOR ESSAYS			
	Sig.	*p*-value	Non-sig.	*p*-value	Sig.	*p*-value	Non-sig.	*p*-value
Simple linear			X	0.3385			X	0.1887
Simple continuous	X	0.0000			X	0.0002		
Complex linear	X	0.0148					X	0.1959
Complex continuous			X	0.1702			X	0.7871
Extended reference			X	0.4468			X	0.6874
Empty	X	0.0301			X	0.0000		
New	X	0.0000					X	0.5793

As a final element in the attempt to identify shared characteristics among the novice categories, one might compare LOCNESS, the novice L1 English category, with NOR ESSAYS, the novice L1 Norwegian category. There are only two statistically significant differences between these two categories: in the use of 'simple linear progression' ($p = 0.0283$), and in the use of 'new' themes ($p = 0.0000$). In contrast, the professional native-speaker categories of ENG NEWS and NOR NEWS were different in their use of four of the seven TP patterns (cf. Table 3). This seems to be a strong indication that novice writers fail to employ some of the same TP strategies as expert writers, and that they are instead more similar to other novice writers.

5. Conclusion

Two research questions formed the starting point for this investigation:

1. In terms of thematic progression, how native-like are English texts produced by Norwegian advanced learners?
2. Which tendencies emerge if one compares the TP patterns in the English output of Norwegian advanced learners with the TP patterns in texts written by novice (non-professional) English and Norwegian writers writing in their respective L1s?

As regards the first question, the results presented above indicate that English texts produced by Norwegian advanced learners differ from native-speaker English texts written by professional writers. The statistics show that the NICLE writers use all TP patterns differently from the writers in the ENG NEWS category (cf. Table 5). Some of these differences are most probably due to transfer from Norwegian, as for three of the TP patterns the differences between NICLE and NOR NEWS are not statistically significant (cf. Table 5). For a possible explanation for the other differences, however, we turn to research question 2.

The results presented above indicate that there are areas where the two native-speaker novice categories, LOCNESS and NOR ESSAYS, are different from their respective L1 professional-writer categories, i.e. ENG NEWS and NOR NEWS, which suggests that novice writers do not use the same TP strategies as professional writers, even when they write in their own language (cf. Table 7). At the same time, the NICLE writers have more in common with the LOCNESS writers than with the ENG NEWS writers, and more in common with the NOR ESSAYS writers than with the NOR NEWS writers (cf. Table 8). Finally, a comparison of LOCNESS with NOR ESSAYS showed that these categories exhibited statistically significant differences in the use of only two of the seven TP patterns. All these aspects seem to point in the same direction: novice writers do share some characteristics in the way they use the various TP patterns, regardless of whether they are writing in their L1 or L2, and these are, to a certain extent, different from the strategies employed by professional writers.

As was discussed in Section 2 above, the results of the present study should be interpreted with a certain amount of caution. However, despite these limitations, the results of the present study do point to some areas worthy of future investigation. Two aspects stand out as deserving of future research. It would be interesting to look at the influence of transfer in more detail, to examine which patterns or constructions the NICLE writers are reluctant to leave behind when they write English. Also, a more detailed comparison with the native-speaker novice categories could shed light on the reason why some TP strategies seem to be more difficult to master than others, even when writing in one's first language.

Notes

1 The term *novice writer* is used in this paper to refer to student writers, i.e. non-professionals.

2 I.e. texts written by non-native speakers (NNS) of English. For more information, see http://cecl.fltr.ucl.ac.be/Cecl-Projects/Icle/icle.htm.

3 From LOCNESS (the Louvain Corpus of Native English Essays), the native-speaker supplement to ICLE.

4 This last text category comprises essays downloaded from a website where Norwegian high school students can upload essays they have written (http://www.daria.no/skole/?kat=9).

5 A T-unit is "a clause complex which contains one main independent clause together with all the hypotactic clauses which are dependent on it" (Fries 1995:318).

6 See http://www.wagsoft.com/CorpusTool/index.html

7 *Empty* themes and themes containing new information cannot, obviously, be part of any thematic progression pattern, but for convenience they are mentioned in subsequent tables together with the TP figures.

8 All examples are from NICLE, and are reproduced as they occur in the corpus. Topical themes are in bold type, and theme origins have been underlined.

9 All statistical values are the results of chi-square calculations with one degree of freedom.

10 Obviously, overuse of one TP pattern necessarily means that another pattern must be underused. However, what is interesting in this case is whether the differences between NICLE and ENG NEWS are more pronounced than the differences between NICLE and NOR NEWS.

References

Ädel, A. (2006), *Metadiscourse in L1 and L2 English.* Amsterdam: John Benjamins.

Berry, M. (1995), 'Thematic options and success in writing', in: M. Ghadessy (ed.) *Thematic Development in English Texts.* London: Pinter. 55-84.

Boström Aronsson, M. (2003), 'On clefts and information structure in Swedish EFL writing', in: S. Granger and S. Petch-Tyson (eds.) *Extending the Scope of Corpus-based Research. New Applications, New Challenges.* Amsterdam and New York: Rodopi. 197-210.

Chafe, W. (1987), 'Cognitive constraints on information flow', in: R. Tomlin Russel (ed.), *Coherence and Grounding in Discourse.* Amsterdam: John Benjamins Publishing Company. 21–52.

Daneš, F. (1974), 'Functional sentence perspective and the organization of the text', in: F. Daneš (ed.) *Papers on Functional Sentence Perspective.* Prague: Academia. 106-128.

Fries, P. H. (1995), 'Themes, development and texts', in: R. Hasan and P. Fries (eds.) *On Subject and Theme.* Amsterdam: John Benjamins. 317-359.

Gilquin, G. (2000/2001), 'The integrated contrastive model. Spicing up your data', *Languages in Contrast*, 3(1): 95-123.

Gilquin, G., S. Granger and M. Paquot (2007), 'Learner corpora: The missing link in EAP pedagogy', *Journal of English for Academic Purposes*, 6: 319-335.

Gilquin, G. and M. Paquot (2008), 'Too chatty. Learner academic writing and register variation', *English Text Construction*, 1(1): 41-61.

Granger, S. (1996), 'From CA to CIA and back: An integrated approach to computerized bilingual and learner corpora', in: K. Aijmer, B. Altenberg and M. Johansson (eds.) *Languages in Contrast. Papers from a Symposium on Text-based Cross-linguistic Studies*. Lund: Lund University Press. 37-52.

Halliday, M. A. K. (2004), *An Introduction to Functional Grammar*. 3rd edition, revised by C. M. I. M. Matthiessen. London: Arnold.

Halliday, M. A. K and R. Hasan (1976), *Cohesion in English*. London: Longman.

Hannay, M. (2007), 'Patterns of multiple theme and their role in developing English writing skills', in: C. Butler (ed.) *Functional Perspectives on Grammar and Discourse: In Honour of Angela Downing*. Amsterdam: Benjamins. 257-278.

Hasselgård, H. (1997), 'Sentence openings in English and Norwegian', in: M. Ljung (ed.) *Corpus-based Studies in English. Papers from the Seventeenth International Conference on English Language Research on Computerized Corpora*. Amsterdam: Rodopi. 3-20.

Hasselgård, H. (2004), 'Thematic choice in English and Norwegian', *Functions of Language*, 11(2): 187-212.

Hasselgård, H. (2005), 'Theme in Norwegian', in: K. L. Berge and E. Maagerø (eds.) *Semiotics from the North: Nordic Approaches to Systemic Functional Linguistics*. Oslo: Novus. 35-48.

Hasselgård, H. (2009), 'Thematic choice and expressions of stance in English argumentative texts by Norwegian learners', in: K. Ajmer (ed.) *Corpora and Language Teaching*. Amsterdam: Benjamins. 121-139.

Jones, L. B. (1983), *Pragmatic Aspects of English Text Structure*. Chapter 3: 'Functions of first mention references in discourse'. Arlington: The Summer Institute of Linguistics. 49-75.

Rørvik, S. (2004), 'Thematic progression in translation of fiction from English into Norwegian', in: K. Aijmer and H. Hasselgård (eds.) *Translation and Corpora: Selected Papers from the Göteborg-Oslo Symposium 18-19 October 2003*. Gothenburg: Acta Universitatis Gothoburgensis, 89, 149-161.

The transitive *into -ing* construction in early twentieth-century American English, with evidence from the *TIME Corpus*

Juhani Rudanko

University of Tampere

Abstract

The study examines the transitive into -ing *pattern in American English in the 1920s, with data from the new* TIME Corpus. *The paper gives information about the frequency of the pattern, and also examines the nature of matrix verbs selecting the pattern, in order to establish semantic generalizations about the verbs in question. Particular attention is paid to usages involving matrix verbs that are not listed with the pattern in established works of reference, and to the analysis of such usages on the basis of the hypothesis that the pattern represents a type of the caused motion construction. The non-conventional use of matrix verbs with transitive* into -ing *complements, idiomatic in their contexts, emphasizes the potential of the pattern as a source of novel coinages, and the interpretation of such usages is argued to provide further motivation for the construction-based approach to explaining the syntax and semantics of the pattern.*

1. Introduction

Consider sentence (1):

(1) ...he can browbeat a girl into marrying him (TIME, 1924)

There are two verbs in sentence (1), the higher verb *browbeat* and the lower verb *marry*. It is assumed here that each has its own subject and that as a consequence, there are two clauses in (1), the lower one embedded in the higher one. This assumption has been made by traditional grammarians, including Jespersen ([1940] 1961: 140), and in more modern treatments, including Chomsky (1986: 114-131) and Huddleston and Pullum (2002: 1193). Apart from an appeal to tradition, the postulation of such an implicit or understood subject also has other motivations. For instance, it makes it possible to represent the argument structures of the two verbs in sentence (1) in a straightforward fashion.

Regarding the argument structure of the higher verb in the pattern of sentence (1), which is *browbeat*, it is observed that the verb assigns a semantic role to the NP *a girl*. This means that the pattern is one of control, rather than NP Movement or *Acc -ing*. Taking account of work on control, the lower subject is represented by PRO. The structure of sentence (1) may then be given as in (1′). (1′) also incorporates the traditional idea that the lower clause is a nominal clause, which may be taken to mean a sentence dominated by an NP node:

(1′) [[he]$_{NP1}$ can [browbeat]$_{Verb}$ [a girl]$_{NPO}$ [into]$_{Prep}$ [[[PRO]$_{NP2}$ marrying him]$_{S2}$]$_{NP}$]$_{S1}$

The pattern of (1′) is one of object control. That is, PRO is controlled by the higher object. The pattern of (1) is here called the transitive *into -ing* pattern.

In the transitive *into -ing* pattern the matrix verb selects three arguments. Typically, the first of them, realized by the NP *he* in (1), has the semantic role of Agent, the second, realized by the NP *a girl* in (1), that of Patient or Undergoer, and the third, realized by *into* PRO *marrying him,* that of Goal. Sag and Pollard (1991: 66) have the labels Influence, Influenced and SOA (State of Affairs) as labels for the three arguments. The more traditional labels of Agent, Patient and Goal are retained here, but it should also be recognized, even on the basis of sentence (1), that the notion of influencing is helpful in describing the semantics of the pattern in a general way.

Into -ing complements may also be found in an intransitive pattern, as in (2):

(2) ...four years, after which he would *graduate into being* an "Ancient,"... (TIME, 1926)

In (2) there is undoubtedly likewise a PRO, representing the lower subject, but this PRO is controlled by the higher subject, and the pattern is one of subject control. The present investigation focuses on the object control construction, leaving the subject control variant for a later treatment.

Another type of sentence worth a mention here is illustrated by (3):

(3) ...Boyd put everything he owned *into buying* up all possible rights to Hopalong Cassidy. (TIME, 1950)

In sentence (3) the sequence of constituents is NP-Verb-NP *into* Verb-*ing*, which is similar to the pattern of sentence (1). However, the direct object of the matrix sentence designates a resource at the disposal of the referent of the matrix subject, and it is the referent of the higher subject that controls the interpretation of the understood subject. A sentence of the type of sentence (3) is one of subject control, and is set aside here.

It may also be noted that many higher verbs of the type of *browbeat* that select the transitive *into -ing* pattern may also be found in the non-sentential pattern of NP Verb NP *into* NP, as in (4):

(4) ...she was a shrewish wife trying to *browbeat* her husband *into submission.* (TIME, 1967)

Gerundive *-ing* clauses, as in (1), are at the nominal end of sentential complements, and it is therefore not surprising that matrix verbs often select both types of complement. (See also de Smet 2008 on the alternation often found with matrix predicates with respect to the two patterns.)

While the non-sentential pattern deserves study, it is not the focus of this investigation. The present focus on the transitive *into -ing* pattern is in the tradition of earlier work on English grammar, including Poutsma (1905: 657; 1929: 959; n.d.) and Francis et al. (1996: 396-9). It is also motivated by a semantic consideration. Both the sentential and non-sentential patterns involve the idea of a transition from one state of affairs to another for the referent of the NP with the Patient role, but in the sentential pattern there is an entailment that the second state of affairs is actually reached, whereas in the non-sentential pattern this is not necessarily the case. For instance, consider *He urged her into the room.* This sentence does not necessarily entail that she entered the room, and this semantic property distinguishes the non-sentential pattern from the sentential one.

It may be added that the verb *urge* does not seem likely with the sentential pattern. For instance, a search in the approximately 400 million word *Corpus of Contemporary American English* (COCA) for the verb *urge* with *into* following within three words to the right produces over 50 tokens of *urge* NP *into* NP, for instance of the type *urge someone into action*, but not a single token of the transitive *into -ing* pattern. This suggests that while many verbs select both *into* patterns, the two sets of verbs selecting the two patterns may not be exactly the same, and this consideration further supports the separation of the patterns and the decision to focus on one of the patterns, the sentential one, here.

By contrast, the passive version of the transitive *into -ing* pattern is taken into account in this study. For instance, consider sentence (5):

(5) ...he allowed himself to be cajoled by friends *into accepting* a lift. (TIME, 1927)

To simplify sentence (5) a little, in a sentence such as *He was cajoled by friends into accepting a lift,* the argument structure of *cajole* is the same as in the active version *Friends cajoled him into accepting a lift.*

The purpose of this investigation is to study the grammatical properties of the transitive *into -ing* pattern in early twentieth-century American English. The data are taken from the new *TIME Magazine Corpus* (TIME), with the year indicated for each illustration. The text type examined is therefore American news-magazine English. For reasons of space this study is restricted to the first decade of the corpus. The corpus starts with the year 1923, and the part examined comprises the seven years from January 1, 1923 to December 31, 1929. The transitive *into -ing* pattern has been investigated on the basis of the *British National Corpus* and of the *Bank of English Corpus* in the literature (Francis et al. 1996, 396-9; Rudanko 2000, 79-87; Hunston and Francis 2000, 102-4), but the earlier history of the construction has been largely neglected so far.

This study aims to shed light on a number of research questions. One of them is to find out what matrix verbs selected the pattern in the 1920s. Another is to find out whether the association of the pattern with a negative semantic prosody that has been noted in current English (cf. Hunston and Francis 2000: 102-4; Rudanko 2000: 83-4; Wulff et al. 2007) also holds for the 1920s. A third is whether or not it is possible and appropriate to view the transitive *into -ing* pattern as a construction in the sense of Adele Goldberg's (1995; 2006) work in earlier English, as has been suggested for current English (Rudanko 2000, 88; 2002, 14-22; 2006, 315-7). A fourth is whether a corpus-based study of American newsmagazine English brings to light matrix verbs that are not featured with the pattern in the *OED*, Bridgeman et al. (1965), Francis et al. (1996), and Herbst et al. (2004). Of special interest here is Bridgeman et al. (1965), because their project was meant to provide an exhaustive list of relevant matrix verbs. Connected with the third question, it is also of interest to inquire into whether usages not recognized in standard works of reference can be explicated with the help of a construction grammar analysis.

2. The transitive *into -ing* pattern in the 1920s

The 1920s subcorpus comprises 7.6 million words. The search string used was into [v?g*] with the tag [vv*] within nine words to the left, thus allowing for zero to eight words between the matrix verb and the preposition *into*. The search string was chosen to achieve adequate recall and it retrieves 193 tokens from the corpus. Many of them are irrelevant, and there are many tokens for instance of *come into being, go into hiding*, or *go into mourning*. Of the 193 tokens 87 are relevant. This represents a frequency of 11.4 per million words.

Here is an alphabetical list of the matrix verbs retrieved, with information on their frequencies:

Table 1. Matrix verbs selecting the transitive *into -ing* pattern in the 1920s

7	*force, trick*
5	*bully, coerce, frighten, inveigle*
4	*cajole, terrorize*
3	*dupe, fool, mislead,*
2	*pique, prod, seduce, shame, tease, wheedle, worry*
1	*argue, beguile, bluff, browbeat, bulldoze, deceive, drag, guide, heckle, heffle, hornswoggle, hypnotize, kid, lift, lure, maneuver, misguide, rouse, stampede, talk, terrify, thumbscrew*

Table 1 indicates that there was no one verb that was much more frequent with the pattern than the rest. Here are illustrations of some of the verbs listed:

(6) a. No man was ever *argued* into being a Fundamentalist. (1923)
b. Dr. John Morris Arthur of Boyce Thompson Institute, New York tried to *fool* them into working all night as well as all day... (1928)

c. What other nation is in the frightful position that it is *forced* into prostituting its own womanhood at the behest of a foreign Power? (1924)
d. In February, 1921, he *terrorized* Persia into accepting him as her Minister of War;... (1925)
e. ... stories of naked hermits met in far, desert places, whose repeated word was the strange word which eventually *worried* Rome into believing it: (1929)

As noted above, the transitive *into -ing* pattern in current English has been analysed as a type of the caused motion construction in the sense of Goldberg's work. The structural configuration of the caused motion construction is as in (7):

(7) [SUBJ] [V OBJ OBL]

With respect to the symbols, the "V is a nonstative verb and OBL is a directional phrase" (Goldberg 1995: 152).

The caused motion construction, like other constructions, carries a meaning, and it is linked to a number of related senses. One of them is 'X causes Y to move Z', and I suggested in Rudanko (2000: chapter 5) that this sense is relevant to the transitive *into -ing* construction.

In order better to understand the proposal that the transitive *into -ing* pattern is a type of the caused motion construction, we should examine the nature of the verbs listed in Table 1 from a grammatical point of view. It is possible to identify three distinct types. The verb *force,* as in (6c), represents one type. Sentence (6c) may be simplified to *Something forced the nation into prostituting herself,* and it is clear that the verb occurs with three arguments. This verb is often found with three arguments in English, as in (8):

(8) ... his health *forced* him to resign his pastorship of Westminster Chapel. (1923)

The pattern of sentence (8) is that of NP Verb NP *to* Verb, that is, the transitive *to* infinitive pattern, but the subject and object arguments of *force* have much the same semantic roles in the transitive *to* infinitive and transitive *into -ing* patterns, and the sentential arguments likewise have the same role of Goal.

In Goldberg's framework, the semantic roles of the arguments of a verb are termed participant roles. Such roles are verb specific, and in the case of *force*, they would be Forcer, Forcee, and Forced action. As regards constructions, they have argument roles, which are of a more general nature. In the case of the caused motion construction, they are Agent, Patient and Goal. With *force,* and other verbs which independently select three arguments or participants in patterns similar to the transitive *into -ing* pattern, it is straightforward to match the participant roles of the verb with the argument roles of the construction.

A second type of verb may be illustrated by *fool.* Sentence (6b) may be simplified to (6b′).

(6b′) Dr. Morris tried to *fool* them into working all night.

The verb *fool* commonly occurs with two arguments, as in (9):

(9) They couldn't *fool* her. (1928)

The verb *fool* in (9) has its ordinary meaning of 'deceive', 'make a fool of', and the participant roles of *fool* are Fooler and Fooled/Foolee. The caused motion construction, by contrast, involves three argument roles, which are Agent or Instrument, Undergoer or Patient, and Goal. The Fooler participant role of the verb is matched with the Agent argument role of the construction, and the Foolee participant role of the verb is matched with the Undergoer argument role of the construction. Sentence (6b′), of course, has a third argument role, and a construction grammar analysis makes it possible to say that the third argument role is supplied by the construction.

The construction grammar approach becomes even more attractive when account is taken of the analysis of the more specific semantic interpretation of a caused motion construction as presented by Goldberg and Jackendoff (2004). Their discussion refers to resultatives but is relevant to the caused motion construction because this may be viewed as a type of resultative:

> ... the meaning of a resultative sentence contains two separable subevents. One of them, the VERBAL SUBEVENT, is determined by the verb of the sentence. The other subevent, the CONSTRUCTIONAL SUBEVENT, is determined by the construction. A resultative sentence means more than just the conjunction of the verbal subevent and the constructional subevent. ... That is, for the bulk of cases... the verbal subevent is the MEANS by which the constructional subevent takes place. (Goldberg and Jackendoff 2004: 538; emphasis in the original)

In other words, part of the meaning of a sentence such as (6b′) is 'Dr. Morris tried to cause them to work all night by means of fooling them'.

An alternative analysis of *fool* in (6b′) would be to postulate another distinct sense for the verb *fool* in it, a sense that would be causative, along the lines of 'cause someone to do something by means of deception'. Senses of this type have sometimes been given in dictionaries, and this procedure can be defended, especially when *into -ing* complements are frequent. However, in a theoretical treatment, it is possible to dispense with such senses and to specify that *fool*, for instance, selects the transitive *into -ing* construction and that the causative meaning, with the element of means included, follows as a consequence. The construction grammar account of the transitive *into -ing* pattern thus fleshes out the notion of influencing (Sag and Pollard 1991, 66) in so far as it relates to the pattern.

Quite a number of the verbs listed in Table 1 are of the syntactic type of *fool* in that they ordinarily select two arguments. For instance, *trick, frighten, dupe, tease, terrorize* may be cited as illustrations.

There is also a third syntactic type among the verbs listed. The verbs *argue* and *talk* do not commonly occur with two participant roles that could be matched with the argument roles of the caused motion construction. Unlike what was the case with *fool*, it is not possible to find relevant examples of *argue* with two participant roles. For instance, while sentence (9) is well formed, **They couldn't argue her* is ill formed. Although the matrix verb *argue* can readily select two arguments, as in *K reads on the average a book a day, argues politics with his father,....* (1934, TIME) or in *He argued his case*, but the semantic role of the object NP in such sentences designates the matter argued over, and is different from the Undergoer role of the typically + Human object NP of the transitive *into -ing* pattern.

With a construction grammar approach it is possible to say that *argue* in (6a) has only one participant role, Arguer, which is matched with the Agent role of the caused motion construction. The two other argument roles of the caused motion construction with *argue* in (6a) are supplied by the construction.

When the transitive *into -ing* pattern is viewed as a construction and account is taken of Goldberg and Jackendoff's point about the means interpretation of the verbal subevent, the task of the semantic characterization of matrix verbs selecting the pattern, in their relevant senses, reduces to that of specifying the means by which the causation takes place. Here are suggested semantic classes of verbs selecting the pattern, with the relevant senses of the verbs taken into account:

Table 2. Semantic Classes of Verbs Selecting the Transitive *into -ing* construction in the 1920s (NP_1 causes NP_O to perform S_2)

by means of deception or trickery	*beguile, bluff, dupe, deceive, fool, hornswoggle, hypnotize, inveigle, kid, lure, misguide, mislead, trick*	29 tokens
by means of force or pressure	*bulldoze, coerce, drag, force, maneuver, prod, stampede thumbscrew*	19 tokens
by means of bullying or arousing fear or terror	*browbeat, bully, frighten, terrify, terrorize*	16 tokens
by means of verbal persuasion	*argue, cajole, heckle, heffle, talk, wheedle*	10 tokens
by other means	*guide, lift, pique, rouse, seduce, shame, tease, worry*	13 tokens

Some verbs, in their relevant senses, are easier to classify than others. For instance, *talk* is more prototypical as a verb of causation by means of verbal persuasion than *cajole*. And one or two of the verbs that have been classed as verbs of verbal persuasion, such as *heckle*, come rather close to verbs of force or pressure, because of the intensity of the influencing that they express. However, the main lines of the semantic groups are clear enough.

The semantic classes are helpful in giving an overall picture of the relative prominence of different types of matrix verbs selecting the transitive *into -ing* construction. In the light of the *TIME Corpus*, it seems that the transitive *into -ing* pattern was especially associated with verbs expressing deception or trickery, force or pressure, or bullying or arousing fear or terror in the 1920s, and that verbs of deception or trickery were especially frequent with the construction. Verbs of such semantic groups typically carry a negative tinge in themselves, linking the whole pattern with a negative semantic prosody in the 1920s. By contrast, verbs that have a positive flavor are hard to find. *Talk* might potentially be such a verb, but it is noteworthy how rare the verb is in this material from the 1920s, and the one token that is found does not appear to have a positive flavour either:

(10) A respectable scion (Monte Blue) of a respectable New England family is *talked* into marrying a respectable young woman (Irene Rich) by his eminently respectable father. (1924)

The repetitiousness of (10) gives the sentence an ironic flavour.

From a lexico-grammatical point of view, the huge majority of the verbs listed in Table 1 are featured with the transitive *into -ing* pattern in the *OED*, in Bridgeman et al. (1965), in Francis et al. (1996) or in Herbst et al. (2004). They may be regarded as conventional or conventionalized usages since they are recorded in such standard works of reference. Such verbs include even *bulldoze*, *kid*, and *pique,* which one might have supposed to be less established with the pattern.

Further, we may recall the grammatical similarity of the transitive *into -ing* pattern to the transitive *into* NP pattern. If illustrations of the latter pattern in the *OED* are taken into account in cases where the notion of influencing is relevant and the semantic roles of the constituents are similar in the two patterns, a number of other verbs may be recognized as non-innovative in a causative use. These verbs include *hornswoggle*. Illustrations of the verb in the *OED* include ... *to hornswoggle us into increased insurance contributions* (1968, *The Guardian*). In order not to exaggerate the role of innovation or of non-conventionalized usages, it is prudent also to take into account the criterion of whether or not the verbs in question are recorded with causative *into* NP complements in the *OED*.

The 1920s corpus does bring to light some matrix verbs that are not featured with either the transitive *into -ing* pattern in the four standard works of reference or with the comparable transitive *into* NP pattern in the *OED*. In particular, the three verbs *terrorize*, *thumbscrew*, and *heffle* are of special interest here. Here are illustrations of these:

(11) a. Last week Senator Heflin tried, at length, to *heffle* the Senate into adopting a resolution condemning the nameless bottle-thrower and charging him, in effect, with attempted murder of a U.S. Senator. (1929)
b. Insatiable, he set sail from Japanese waters last spring with a privateering expedition, recaptured part of Shantung, *terrorized* banks and merchants into yielding him more gold, was finally driven out a second time. (1929)

c. Mr. Lewis repeated the miners' charge that railroads, notably the Pennsylvania, had *thumbscrewed* the mine operators into thumbscrewing the miners. (1928)

Terrorize and *thumbscrew* are found as verbs in the *OED*, of course. *Terrorize* is glossed 'to fill or inspire with terror, reduce to a state of terror; *esp.* to coerce or deter by terror' (*OED*) and *thumbscrew* is glossed 'to torture by screwing the thumbs; to torture with or as with thumbscrews' (*OED*). Both verbs readily select two arguments. As regards *terrorize*, here is an illustration from the *OED* ... *no crafty scheme to terrorize my mind* (*OED,* 1823, *Douglas, or Field, of Otterburn*) and as for *thumbscrew*, the lower sentence of (11c) may serve as an illustration. A construction grammar analysis accounts for the use of these verbs with the transitive *into -ing* pattern in a straightforward way. In the same way as with *fool*, the caused motion construction supplies the third argument role of the construction in (11c), for instance. Taking account of the Goldberg-Jackendoff analysis of the two subevents involved, it is possible to say that part of the meaning of sentence (11c) is then along the lines of 'had caused the mine operators to thumbscrew the miners by means of torturing them as if with a thumbscrew'.

Heffle, illustrated in (11a), is probably the most interesting matrix verb in the whole material. There is no verb *heffle* found in the *OED*, and in spite of having been used in the 1920s, it has not become a conventionalized lexical item. It is found with the transitive *into -ing* pattern only once in the *TIME Corpus*, but it is found in the corpus elsewhere, as in (12a). It is also found in a nominalization, related to the verb, as in (12b):

(12) a. "Alabama!" he *heffled* in conclusion. "I'd give my life to protect its good name and honor." (1932)
b. Most Senators thought they had heard the final *heffling* of James Thomas ("Tom-Tom") Heflin, their hulking colleague for a decade, when on March 4, 1931 the 71st Congress was silenced. (1932)

The verb is clearly derived, with some adjustment in the spelling, from the name of Thomas Heflin, who was a United States Senator in the 1920s. In (12a) the verb appears to have the sense 'to speak in the manner of Heflin', and the verb only takes the subject argument. When used with the transitive *into -ing* pattern, as in (11a), the caused motion construction supplies two of the three arguments, and part of the meaning of sentence (11a) is 'tried to cause the Senate to adopt a resolution ... by means of speaking in the manner of Senator Heflin'.

The verb *heffle* is unlikely now ever to be recorded in a work of reference, barring an unexpected revival of interest in the Senator. However, even though the verb and its selection of the transitive *into -ing* construction lack the status of a being recorded in a work of reference, the ease with which the combination is understood as a possible and idiomatic pattern in English by speakers who had never heard it before and the interpretation of the combination as predicted by the approach of

Goldberg and Jackendoff (2004) testify to the attraction of the construction grammar analysis of the transitive *into -ing* pattern in English.

It is also worth noting that the three verbs *terrorize*, *thumbscrew*, and *heffle*, which were not found in the four works of reference with the transitive *into -ing* construction, are all accommodated in the semantic classes established above. Further, it is observed that each of the three matrix verbs represents a different verb class, with the meaning of the verb class shedding light on the interpretation of the creative usage. In the study of creative and non-conventionalized usages it is therefore fruitful to make use of a level of semantically derived verb classes.

3. Concluding observations

The present study into the use of the transitive *into -ing* pattern in the text type of American newsmagazine English substantiates the use of the pattern with a number of matrix verbs in the 1920s. It also suggests that the pattern had a generally negative semantic prosody even in the 1920s.

It is also argued here that it is helpful to analyse the transitive *into -ing* pattern as a caused motion construction. Such an analysis is suitable for verbs such as *fool*, for it is possible to match the two participants roles of *fool*, Fooler and Fooled, derived from noncausative uses of the verb, with the Agent and Undergoer argument roles of the construction and to say that the third argument role, of Goal, is supplied by the construction.

Heffle, *terrorize*, and *thumbscrew* are not featured with the transitive *into -ing* pattern in standard works of reference, but tokens were encountered in the *TIME Corpus*. *Terrorize* and *thumbscrew* are of course established verbs, normally found with two arguments, and in their case, it is possible to say that when the verbs occur with *into -ing*, the caused motion construction again supplies the third argument. As for *heffle*, the verb is not recognized as a word in standard works of reference. However, it was found independently with one participant role in the *TIME* data, and when it occurs in the caused motion construction both the Undergoer and Goal argument roles are supplied by the construction. Even though the verb is hardly known today, let alone conventionalized, its use with the *into -ing* pattern is felt to be entirely natural and appropriate in the context of the *TIME* article. Further, the resulting pattern is interpreted without any difficulty. In its interpretation it is helpful, applying Goldberg and Jackendoff (2004), to refer to the subevent of the construction (along the lines of 'cause NP to perform an action or to move into a state'), and to the subevent of the verb (closely tied to the meaning of the verb), with the added proviso that the verbal subevent expresses the means by which the constructional subevent takes place.

Given the construction grammar analysis of the transitive *into -ing* pattern, the task of identifying semantic verb classes largely amounts to one of specifying types of different means that the verbal subevent involves. It is often possible to characterize heads selecting a certain pattern of complementation by postulating semantic classes, and in the present case, verbs that express deception, verbal persuasion, or force or pressure as the means by which the referent of the higher subject causes the referent of the higher object to undertake an action or move into a new state of affairs are prominent in early twentieth-century American English.

It was also argued that the semantic classes that were set up are relevant in explaining creative usages. It was observed that such usages are likely to be encountered of matrix verbs whose meanings accord with the semantic classes established, and, further, that creative usages were not restricted to any one particular semantic class. The three verbs *heffle*, *terrorize* and *thumbscrew* are cases in point, representing different semantic classes.

In later work it will be important to investigate the transitive *into -ing* construction in other decades of the *TIME Corpus* and in twentieth-century British English, and to extend the study of the *into -ing* construction to earlier stages of the language, in order to throw further light on the emergence of the pattern in English. It will also be of great interest to see if non-conventionalized usages identified in this study in the case of *heffle*, and in other cases in earlier work on present-day English (see Rudanko 2000, 82-3; Rudanko 2005), are encountered in earlier English. If so, it will be a further research task to examine whether or not the meaning of the matrix verbs in question is consistent with the ingredients of meaning underlying the verb classes established.

Acknowledgements

I am grateful to Ian Gurney, of the University of Tampere, for his comments on an earlier version of this article and for his help with some final revisions, and to Tiina Harjula and Veera Peteri, also of the University of Tampere, for their help in finalizing the article. I am responsible for any remaining shortcomings.

References

Bridgeman, L., D. Dillinger, C. Higgins, D. Seaman and F. Shank (1965), *More Classes of Verbs in English.* Bloomington, Indiana: Indiana University Linguistics Club.

Chomsky, N. (1986), *Knowledge of Language: Its Nature, Origin and Use.* New York: Praeger.

de Smet, H. (2008), *Diffusional Change in the System of Complementation. Gerunds, Participles, and* for…to-*Infinitives*. Doctoral Dissertation, Catholic University Leuven.

Francis, G., S. Hunston and E. Manning (1996), *Collins Cobuild Grammar Patterns 1: Verbs*. London: HarperCollins.

Goldberg, A. (1995), *Constructions. A Construction Grammar Approach to Argument Structure.* Chicago: Chicago University Press.

Goldberg, A. (2006), *Constructions at Work: the Nature of Generalization in Language.* Oxford: Oxford University Press.

Goldberg, A. and R. Jackendoff (2004), 'The English resultative as a family of constructions', *Language,* 80: 532-568.

Herbst, T., D. Heath, I. Roe and D. Götz (eds.) (2004), *A Valency Dictionary of English.* Berlin: Mouton de Gruyter.

Huddleston, R. and G. Pullum (2002), *The Cambridge Grammar of the English Language*. Cambridge: Cambridge University Press.

Hunston, F. and G. Francis (2000), *Pattern Grammar*. Amsterdam: John Benjamins.

Jespersen, O. [1940] (1961), *A Modern English Grammar on Historical Principles.* Part V: Syntax (Volume IV). London and Copenhagen: George Allen and Unwin LTD and Ejnar Munksgaard.

OED = The *Oxford English Dictionary*. Second edition. 1989. Prepared by J. Simpson and E. Weiner. Oxford: Clarendon Press.

Poutsma, H. (1905), *A Grammar of Late Modern English.* Part 1, the Sentence. 2nd edition 1929. Groningen: P. Noordhoff.

Poutsma, H. (n.d), *Dictionary of Constructions of Verbs, Adjectives, and Nouns*. Unpublished ms. Copyright: Oxford University Press.

Rudanko, J. (2000), *Corpora and Complementation.* Lanham, MD: University Press of America.

Rudanko, J. (2002), *Complements and Constructions*. Lanham, MD: University Press of America.

Rudanko, J. (2005), 'Lexico-grammatical innovation in current British and American English: A case study on the transitive *into -ing* pattern with evidence from the Bank of English Corpus', *Studia Neophilologica,* 77: 171-187.

Rudanko, J. (2006), 'Emergent alternation in complement selection: The spread of the transitive *into -ing* construction in British and American English', *Journal of English Linguistics,* 34: 312-331.

Sag, I. and C. Pollard (1991), 'An integrated theory of complement control', *Language,* 67: 63-113.

Wulff, S., A. Stefanowitsch and S. Th. Gries (2007), 'Brutal Brits and persuasive Americans', in: G. Radden, K. Köpcke, T. Berg and P. Siemund (eds.) *Aspects of Meaning Construction*. Amsterdam: John Benjamins. 265-81.

The secret life of the negative: An investigation of polarity and modality in a corpus of newsgroup texts

Anke Schulz and Elke Teich

University of Bremen and Saarland University

Abstract

The overall goal of our research is to uncover the linguistic options of expressing negative attitude and experience. To this end, a small corpus of English newsgroup texts about relationship problems and eating disorders, part of the Englische & Deutsche Newsgroup Texte – Annotiertes Korpus *(EDNA corpus), has been annotated manually, using Systemic Functional Grammar (Halliday 1994) as theoretical foundation. The EDNA corpus now contains information about Theme-Rheme structure, modality and negative polarity as well as process types, i.e. types of verbs such as action, relational, mental. In this paper, we focus on modality and negative polarity. We start by looking at syntactic negation, both at clause rank (*he didn't love me*) and at phrase rank (*I will leave, no second chances*). In addition, morphological negation will be considered, e.g.* That would be unfair. *In a second step, the use of epistemic modality (i.e. likelihood of a proposition) and root modality (expressing obligation, inclination or ability) in the EDNA corpus is studied. How do authors position themselves towards their audience and towards what they are saying by using modal auxiliaries (e.g.* can, could, may*) and modal adjuncts (e.g.* certainly, maybe*). Following that, we consider how modality and negative polarity combine. In our corpus, as many as 15% of all clauses carry a negative polarity marker, but as many 23% of clauses with a modality marker are also negated. Furthermore, clauses expressing root modality are more likely to be negated than clauses expressing epistemic modality (38% and 15% respectively). Our results suggest that modality markers and negative polarity markers attract each other.*

1. Introduction

This paper reports on an ongoing study of expressions of negative attitude and experience in English newsgroup texts: How do people express negative attitude and experience, and how is this instantiated in lexico-grammar?

In order to study these questions, we use a small corpus of 10,000 words of English newsgroup texts, collected in the *Englische & Deutsche Newsgroup Texte – Annotiertes Korpus* (EDNA corpus). This corpus has been manually annotated for features based on Systemic Functional Grammar (SFG, Halliday 1994) as a theoretical framework, with the assistance of a computer tool, the

UAM corpus tool (O'Donnell 2008). The annotations comprise three lexico-grammatical domains, instantiating the three metafunctions of SFG, i.e. theme-rheme structure (textual metafunction), modality and polarity (interpersonal metafunction) and process types, i.e. functional types of predicates such as *action*, *relational* or *mental* processes (experiential metafunction).

In this paper, we describe our research on syntactic negation in the service of the expression of negative attitude and experience, both at clause rank, e.g. *my friends won't understand,* and at phrase rank, e.g. *she has had no problem with this.* Furthermore, negative attitude and experience can be expressed by means of morphological negation of lexical word classes as well as prepositions, e.g. *to disagree, hopeless* and *without.* In addition, we investigate which types of modality are used in the context of negative attitude and experience, epistemic modality, e.g. *this will probably be the last resort*, and root modality, e.g. *two weeks ago I had to leave.* Finally, we analyse how negation and modality combine, and why they may be doing so.

2. Corpus design

For this study, we used the section of English texts collected in the *Englische & Deutsche Newsgroup Texte – Annotiertes Korpus* (EDNA corpus). The EDNA corpus consists entirely of asynchronous computer-mediated communication (CMC), i.e. newsgroup texts, where "users do not have to be online at the same time to communicate" (Beißwenger and Storrer 2009: 293). In this comparable corpus, there are 10,360 words of English text and another 10,425 words of German text, taken from the same genre. i.e. the newsgroup texts. The discourse fields covered in the EDNA corpus are relationship problems and eating disorders. All examples in this paper are taken from the English part of the EDNA corpus.

Here are two short extracts from the English newsgroup corpus to give the reader an idea of the kind of text we are dealing with, example (1) from a text on eating disorders and example (2) from a text on relationship problems:

(1) Hey... well I guess I will start out that I have depression. I started to read books about the afterlife and felt better about life and stuff. But then I stopped eating and it made me even happier. No-one noticed what was happening to me. I lost a total of 30 pounds. I then joined the swim team and all of a sudden I started gaining weight and I freaked out! I felt like I was losing control once again. But it wasn't that easy to hide my food like before. So I ate… and ate… and without thinking about it, I threw up my food.

(2) My wife of 5 years has a very bad temper. When she gets angry she yells and screams that she hates me, she wants a divorce, and throws her wedding rings at me, smashes wedding photos etc. This has happened some 50 times since we've been together. At first, I would be devastated, begging

> her to take back her comments. Rarely would she apologize. As it continued, I became more and more distant to the point where now I feel like letting it end but for some reason I always attempt to make peace with her. I still "love" my wife but I don't want this kind of relationship anymore.

The texts included in the corpus can be well described using Halliday's (1989) parameters of register description, i.e. *Field, Mode* and *Tenor*.

- *Field*: The experiential domain in half of the texts (i.e. 15 texts) is that of eating disorders; the second half of the texts (another 15 texts) deals with relationship problems. These two fields were chosen because one of the goals for building the corpus was to investigate how negative experience is expressed. These two fields lend themselves to such an investigation because the authors reveal their problems and experiences, most of them negative ones. The social activity from which the discourse emerges can probably best be described as "self-therapy by public display of experiences, thereby inviting feedback and support from others".
- *Mode*: The medium is written language, but the texts exhibit features of spoken language as well; therefore we describe it as written-as-if-spoken, informal language. The spatial distance is defined by the absence of the addressee (or addresser, respectively); there is no immediate feedback, no visual or aural contact.
- *Tenor*: Addresser and addressee have rare to regular contact; they are in an informal, equal power relationship which is non-hierarchical with minimal social distance. The participants in the discussion are "fellow sufferers": they display high affective involvement; they give away secrets, display weaknesses, possibly encouraged by the fact that the participants do not have to sit face to face, one way of "saving face". The spatial distance obviously helps to encourage the participants to open up and admit the existence of problems.

3. Theoretical framework

We employ Systemic Functional Grammar (SFG; Halliday 1994) as the theoretical framework for the description of the phenomena we investigate. In SFG, language is understood as a system of linguistic choices. Each choice is an option to express a certain meaning in a certain context. Whatever feature a speaker or writer chooses has a function in the situation where it is chosen. In SFG, the linguistic choices are described along the lines of three metafunctions. These three metafunctions are the ideational metafunction (divided into the experiential and the logical level), the interpersonal metafunction and the textual metafunction. In this paper the focus is on the interpersonal metafunction.

The interpersonal metafunction (Halliday 1994) describes the relationship of the participants involved in the discourse. Who is talking to whom? Are participants in an equal power relationship, and how big is the social distance between writer and reader, or speaker and listener? To describe how the interpersonal metafunction is instantiated in the English language in the present corpus, we analyse modality and different means to express negation. Modality in English is typically realised by modal auxiliaries, e.g. *can, could, will, have to, might*, and modal adverbs, e.g. *perhaps, really, honestly*. Occasionally we find a grammatical metaphor to express modality. A grammatical metaphor in our case is realised by a superordinate clause that has the function of modalising the subordinate clause, e.g. *I know these things take time* meaning the same as *these things probably take time*. In general, modal utterances "involve the speaker's comment on the necessity or possibility of the truth of a proposition or the actualization of a situation." (Depraetere and Reed 2006: 269). Two main types of modality are generally distinguished: epistemic and root modality. Quirk et al. (1985: 219) call these types extrinsic (human judgement of what is or is not likely to happen) and intrinsic modality (some kind of intrinsic human control over events).

Epistemic modality "reflects the speaker's judgement of the likelihood that the proposition underlying the utterance is true" (Depraetere and Reed 2006: 274). This type of modality is also used to express politeness. See examples (3) and (4), taken from the EDNA corpus, for epistemic modality.

(3) Epistemic, grammatical metaphor: *I guess* I will start out that I have depression.
(4) Epistemic, adverb: I am *certainly* obsessed with food and my weight.

The second type of modality, i.e. root modality, implies that some sort of authority (humans, social norms, general circumstances) controls the situation. Root modality in the present study has three subcategories: the first subcategory is obligation and permission, the second is inclination/volition and the third is ability (physical and mental abilities, skills), see examples (5), (6) and (7).

(5) Obligation, auxiliary: I *have to* restrict myself.
(6) Inclination, auxiliary: I just *need to* be alone.
(7) Ability, auxiliary: We *could* make it through anything together.

On the whole, any type of realisation, i.e. auxiliary, adverb or grammatical metaphor, can express any type of modality, i.e. epistemic or root modality. Figure 1 below shows the annotation scheme used for annotating the two types of modality and the three possible types of realization of modality. A curly bracket signifies that both systems are applicable at the same time, whereas a square brackets signifies an either/or relation.

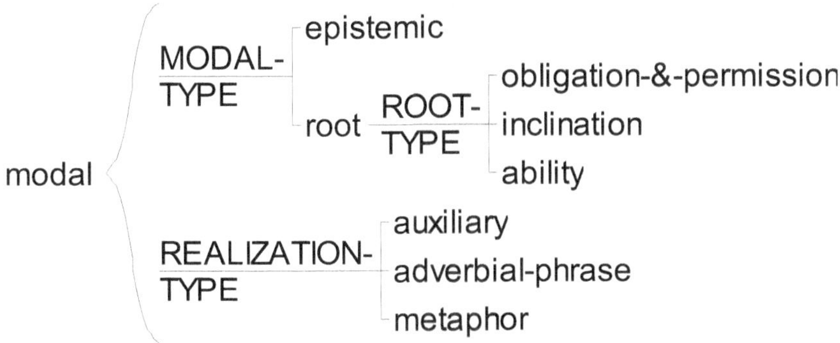

Figure 1. The annotation scheme for modality

The second feature used to describe the interpersonal metafunction is the way the authors negate their statements. To state that something is not the case, i.e. to express the opposite of a positive, there is first of all the well known syntactic negation with negation marker *not* or *no*. Syntactic negation can be found in the verbal group (example 8), in a nominal group – example (9) – or in an adverbial group – example (10).

(8) I *don't want* this kind of relationship anymore.
(9) *No-one* noticed what was happening to me.
(10) That is *no longer* the case.

In addition to syntactic negation shown above, prefixes or suffixes like *-less*, *un-*, *dis-* or *im-* are used in the English language to express the opposite of a positive. These affixes can be used with all lexical word classes, see examples (11) to (16) below.

(11) Verb: […] which I *disagreed* with.
(12) Predicative adjective: Is it *hopeless*?
(13) Adverb: It is *unfortunately* a bit unsettling at times.
(14) Attributive adjective: […] I am now at an extremely *uncomfortable* 160 pounds.
(15) Noun: e.g. *immortality* (no example of such noun found in the corpus)
(16) Preposition: My fears sprout *without* warning.

For the sake of convenience, the preposition *without*, as in example (16), has been cast into the category of morphological negation of lexical word class, although strictly speaking it is not a lexical but a function word. Figure 2 displays the annotation scheme used for negation.

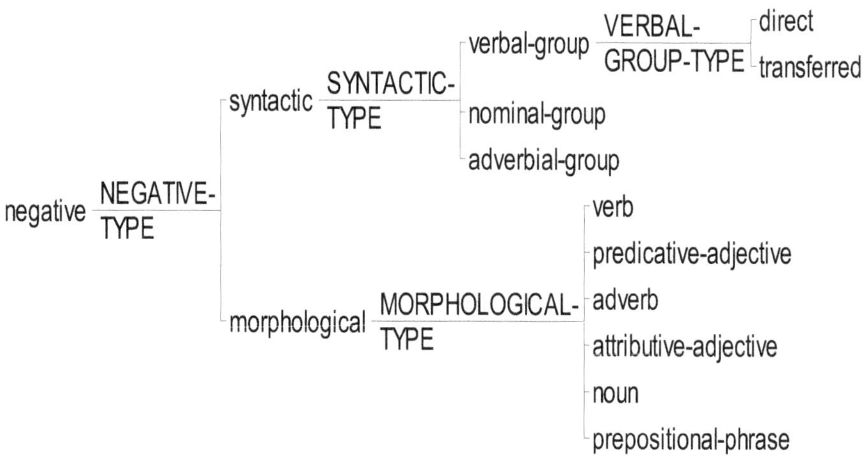

Figure 2. The annotation scheme for negation

4. Methodology

Following the descriptive account of the lexico-grammatical means that can potentially be used to express negative attitude and experience we embarked on the task of computer-assisted manual annotation of the English newsgroup corpus of 10,360 words. We annotated the corpus in terms of the lexico-grammatical features representing the three metafunctions of SFG. The tool we used for annotation as well as extraction of quantitative data is the UAM corpus tool (O'Donnell 2008). The UAM corpus tool allows the construction of individual annotation schemes that best suit the researcher's requirements. During the annotation process, the tool offers to the annotator all the options of the annotation scheme, going from left to right until there are no more delicate features to choose from. Our annotation schemes for the interpersonal metafunction can be seen in Figures 1 and 2 above. A clause is annotated for all three metafunctions in the end. The example in Table 1 shows an instantiation of the experiential, interpersonal and textual metafunction.

Table 1. Example of SFG annotation

I	*don't want*	*this kind of relationship*
Participant role: Emoter	Auxiliary + main verb, process: mental, emotional	Participant role: Phenomenon
	Negative, syntactic, verbal group, direct, non-modal	
Unmarked topical theme	Rheme	

Guidelines for the annotation of all three metafunctions have been written and used to guarantee inter- and intra-annotator agreement as far as possible (Schulz 2008). The texts have been annotated manually by two annotators, one of them one of the authors, the other a trained student. Note that each text has only been annotated by one of the annotators, hence we are not able to calculate inter-annotator agreement at the present stage. Finally, the annotated corpus has been revised once to improve consistency.

The annotated English newsgroup text corpus in its present state allows queries on individual features, but also on combinations of features. String-based queries are also possible on each layer. Table 2 shows the number of clauses, token and types for the English part of the EDNA corpus.

Table 2. Numbers for tokens, types and clauses in the English newsgroup texts, F = raw frequency

Feature	F
Token	10,360
Types	1,797
Types (lexical words only)	998
Clauses	1,542
Clauses with syntactic or morphological negation	236
Clauses containing modality	302

5. Some exploratory results

5.1 Syntactic and morphological negation

What exactly can the annotated corpus reveal about the linguistic construal of negativity? For a more detailed overview of the numerical results of negation see the tables below.

Table 3. Polarity in the corpus

Polarity	F	%
Positive clauses	1,304	85
Negative clauses	236	15
Clauses total	1,542	100

Table 3 demonstrates that even in these texts where people talk about nothing but negative experience, with a mere 15% of the total amount of clauses, negative clauses are rare compared to neutral or positive clauses. Our result is in accordance with the number given in Halliday and James (1993) who find that 13.25% of all finite clauses are negative (not counting morphological negation) in the COBUILD corpus of written texts (University of Birmingham, Dept. of Language and Literature 1987). Table 4 shows the two types of negation and Table 5 displays the location of the syntactic negation marker.

Table 4. Types of negation

Negation type	F	%
Syntactic negation	210	89
Morphological negation	26	11
Negative clauses total	236	100

Table 5. Types of syntactic negation

Syntactic negation	F	%
Verbal group	177	84
Nominal group	15	7
Adverbial group	18	9
Syntactic negation total	210	100

Syntactic negation with a negation marker is by far the most widespread type used for negating, i.e. to express the fact that something is not positive, with 210 out of 236 clauses. Syntactic negation markers can be used on clause rank, in a verbal group, or they can be downshifted to group rank, to a nominal group or an adverbial group. Of these options, the syntactic negation on clause rank has been found to be the most widely used one. In 177 out of 210 clauses we find the syntactic negation marker *not* in the verbal group. Here, there are two options; direct and transferred negation, see below.

Table 6. Syntactic negation in verbal group

Syntactic negation verbal group	F	%
Direct	169	95
Transferred	8	5
Verbal group total	177	100

Table 6 shows that most of the negation markers (169) are found in the verbal group in the clause where they logically belong, as for instance in examples (17) and (18).

(17) I am not just fat, but very obese.
(18) I don't want to be hurt again.

Some of the negation markers in a verbal group, however, are transferred from the subordinate clause where they logically belong to a superordinate clause, see examples (19) and (20). There are, however, only 8 instances in the 177 clauses. All of these instances except one are mental processes, where the superordinate clause expresses epistemic modality by way of a grammatical metaphor. Obviously this way of expressing epistemic modality is tied to this kind of process, or, to put it differently, the process in the superordinate clause does not have a function on the experiential, but on the interpersonal metafunction.

(19) I don't think I'm getting enough veggies, though.
~ I'm probably not getting enough veggies, though.
(20) I'm not sure if I am qualified as having an eating disorder.
~ Maybe I am not qualified as having an eating disorder.

At group rank, negation markers are more often found in adverbial groups, with 18 out of the 210 clauses: examples are shown in (21) and (22). Incidentally, example (22) is the only instance of a double negation found in the entire English newsgroup corpus.

(21) That is no longer the case.
(22) I have never not given him anything.

Less often, with 15 out of 210 clauses, the syntactic negation marker is down-shifted to the nominal group, where we find negation markers such as *no, nothing, no-one*, see examples (23) and (24).

(23) I do nothing.
(24) There was basically no physical relationship.

Turning our attention from syntactic to morphological negation, we find that only a mere 26 clauses contain negation by an affix (see Table 4 again), and that morphological negation is not distributed evenly across the lexical word classes – see Table 7.

Table 7. Types of morphological negation

Morphological negation	F	%
Verb	1	4
Predicative adjective	12	46
Adverb	1	4
Attributive adjective	2	8
Noun	0	0
Prepositional phrase	10	38
Morphological negation total	26	100

There is not a single noun in the 10,360 words with a negative affix, only one verb (*to disagree*), one adverb (*unfortunately*) and two attributive adjectives (*ruthless* and *uncomfortable*). The biggest role is played by predicative adjectives; there are 12 instances of 10 types: *needless* (2x), *impossible* (2x), *impatient, unsure, uncaring, unsettling, hopeless, uncomfortable, unfaithful*, and *unfair*, see (25) and (26) for examples.

(25) My spouse is being *unfaithful* to our relationship.
(26) I was *unsure* how he would react.

The second most frequently used word class in connection with a negative affix is that of prepositions, namely the preposition *without* which appears 10 times in the corpus; two instances are given in examples (27) and (28).

(27) She wants to do other things *without* me from time to time.
(28) I cannot shove one more crumb into my body *without* bursting.

These results suggest that in the English newsgroup text corpus, authors strongly favour the straight-forward syntactic negation at clause rank. If they use morphological negation, this is mostly done with predicative adjectives or the preposition *without*.

5.2 Modality

Apart from negation, modality is the second system of options to realise meaning on the interpersonal metafunction. Tables 8 and 9 below present the numbers from our corpus.

Table 8. Main types of modality

Modality type	F	%
Epistemic	201	67
Root	101	33
Modality type total	302	100

Table 9. Three types of root modality

Root modality type	F	%
Obligation & permission	48	48
Inclination	19	19
Ability	34	33
Root modality type total	101	100

Epistemic modality is expressed twice as many times as root modality in the newsgroup text corpus. Of the three types of root modality, almost half of all the instances express obligation and permission, followed by one third of all clauses expressing ability, and only every fifth instance involves inclination of some sort by the authors.

5.3 Modality and syntactic negation

Now that we have explored negation and modality separately, let us have a look at how the two combine. Table 10 below gives the total numbers of positive and negative as well as modal and non-modal clauses.

Table 10. Modal clauses with/without negation

	Clause, non-modal		Clause, modal		Clauses total
	F	%	F	%	
Positive clause	1,072	86	234	77	1,306
Negative clause	168	14	68	23	236
Clauses total	1,240	100	302	100	1,542

The table shows that of the 302 modal clauses, 68 are negated (23%), whereas of the non-modal clauses, only 14% are negated. Modal clauses thus seem to attract negation more than non-modal ones.

Our results in Table 11 below show that none of the clauses that contain morphological negation also contains modality. We can only speculate why that might be so. Is it because authors, although probably without realizing, feel that morphological negation is unobtrusive enough to not offend addressees and therefore does not need to be toned down?

Table 11. Negated clauses with/without modality

	Morphological		Syntactic		Clauses total
	F	%	F	%	
Clause, non-modal	26	100	142	68	168
Clause, modal	0	0	68	32	68
Clauses total	26	100	210	100	236

Now, if we consider negative clauses, then of the 210 syntactically negated clauses, 68 additionally carry modality (32%). In other words, if we have a syntactically negated clause, there is a chance that one out of three is also modalized. Authors either tone down a negative statement in that way, to take the edge off it – see examples (29 and (30) – or they intensify a negative statement with modality, see examples (31) and (32).

(29) [...] that may make having kids impossible.
(30) I haven't really binged though.
(31) I am certainly not having trouble eating.
(32) I sure as hell don't want to be fat, too.

We can also look at the combination of modality and negation from the perspective of modality. For clauses carrying modality, there is the chance that roughly one out of four clauses (23%) is also syntactically negated (see again Table 10).

Furthermore, we can ask which type of modality is negated more often. See Table 12 for results.

Table 12. Main types of modality with/without negation

	Epistemic modality		Root modality		Clauses total
	F	%	F	%	
Positive clauses	171	85	63	62	234
Negative clauses	30	15	38	38	68
Clauses total	201	100	101	100	302

As mentioned before, 68 clauses out of the total of 302 clauses containing modality are negated. There are twice as many clauses displaying epistemic modality as root modality; however, of the former, only 15% are negated. It is much more probable for an author to give a judgement on how likely something is, than on how unlikely it is. Of the 101 clauses displaying some kind of root modality, as many as 38% are negated. It is quite probable for an author to state that something should not be done or cannot be done. If we focus on the clauses containing root modality, Table 13 gives us some further insights.

Table 13. Three types of root modality with/without negation

	Obligation & permission		Ability		Inclination		Clauses total
	F	%	F	%	F	%	
Positive clauses	37	77	13	38	13	68	63
Negative clauses	11	23	21	62	6	32	38
Clauses total	48	100	34	100	19	100	101

From the results in the table above, it can be seen that two thirds of the clauses expressing ability are syntactically negated. In other words, it is more probable for the authors to state that something cannot be done than it is to say it can be done – the authors tend to admit inability rather than ability. When authors express inclination, i.e. when they state that they want to do something, syntactic negation of the clause still occurs fairly frequently. In as many as one out of three clauses they prefer to say they have no inclination to do something. When it comes to expressing obligation or permission, i.e. when stating what should be done, however, the authors seem to prefer to make themselves clear by using positive statements. Negated obligation or permission only occurs in less than one out of four clauses.

6. Summary

Summing up the results from our exploratory study, we now can say that only 15% of all clauses in the English newsgroup text corpus are syntactically or morphologically negated, thereby making negation more the exception than the rule, even in these texts that deal with negative experiences.

To express the opposite of something positive, authors strongly favour syntactic negation of the verbal group over syntactic negation in nominal or adverbial groups. Morphological negation is not used frequently, and almost exclusively with predicative adjectives or the preposition *without*.

Of the negated clauses, 32% do also contain modality. Of all the clauses in the corpus containing modality, epistemic modality is less likely to be negated with only 15% of the clauses carrying epistemic modality, compared to 38% of the clauses containing root modality. Authors thus express likelihood in positive terms, but root modality much less so. When it comes to expressing ability, with 62% negated clauses the authors express inability rather than ability.

Clearly wc must not forget that to express negative attitude and experience, syntactic or morphological negation is not sufficient. There are of course words which carry negative connotations as for example *to suffer*, *violent* or *trouble*. Lexical items may also express some synonymic relationship with a negative word (*lack* = *not have*) or antonymic relationship with positive words (*fail* and *succeed*). In addition, words with a negative suffix may have positive connotations, e.g. *blameless*, *priceless*. Martin and White (2005) offer a detailed framework within appraisal theory to take account of the lexical expression of negative attitude and experience. Due to space restrictions, however, we cannot explore these relationships in the present paper.

Our future work will involve analyses of how features from the other two metafunctions, i.e. the theme-rheme structure and process types, interact with the two features from the interpersonal metafunction, i.e. modality and negation. A thorough analysis of these linguistic features and their function in expressing negativity will not only shed some light on how people convey negative meaning, but can be of good use to practical applications such as opinion mining or sentiment analysis (see e.g., Annett and Kondrak 2008, Pang and Lee 2008).

Furthermore, we need to compare our results to a reference corpus to verify whether the proportions found in this corpus are not just characteristic of this type of discourse, the newsgroup texts, but also of a more general corpus. One small obstacle in doing this is the fact that no other corpus is annotated for SFG features the way the EDNA corpus texts are. We can therefore only analyse similarities based on grammatical patterns, rather than functions in the discourse, but it is a start. Developments in corpus linguistics seem to call for specific annotations to further the possibilities of research - not only to reveal the secret life of the negative.

Acknowledgement

We gratefully acknowledge the support of Dr. Kerstin Fischer and Dr. Anatol Stefanowitsch in making the EDNA corpus possible.

References

Annett, M. and G. Kondrak (2008), 'A comparison of sentiment analysis techniques: Polarizing movie blogs', in: S. Bergler (ed.) *Lecture Notes in Computer Science* Vol. 5032. Berlin and Heidelberg: Springer. 25-35. <http://www.springerlink.com>, accessed 15 January 2010.

Beißwenger, M. and A. Storrer (2009), 'Corpora of computer-mediated communication', in: A. Lüdeling and M. Kytö (eds.) *Corpus Linguistics. An International Handbook.* Series: Handbücher zur Sprach- und Kommunikationswissenschaft/Handbooks of Linguistics and Communication Science. Berlin: Mouton de Gruyter. 292-308.

Depraetere, I. and S. Reed (2006), 'Mood and modality in English', in: B. Aarts and A. McMahon (eds.) *The Handbook of English Linguistics.* Malden, Mass.: Blackwell. 269-90.

Halliday, M. A. K. (1989). *Spoken and written language.* 2nd ed. Oxford: Oxford University Press.

Halliday, M. A. K. and Z. L. James (1993/2005), 'A quantitative study of polarity and primary tense in the English finite clause', in: M. A. K. Halliday (ed.) *Computational and Quantative Studies.* London and New York: Continuum. 93-129.

Halliday, M. A. K. (1994), *An Introduction to Functional Grammar.* 2nd ed. London: Arnold.

Martin, J. R. and P. R. R. White (2005), *The Language of Evaluation: Appraisal in English.* Houndsmill; New York: Palgrave Macmillan.

O'Donnell, M. (2008), 'Demonstration of the UAM Corpus Tool for text and image annotation', in: *Proceedings of the ACL-08: HLT Demo Session (Companion Volume)*, Columbus, Ohio, June 2008. Association for Computational Linguistics. 13-16.

Pang, B. and L. Lee (2008), *Opinion Mining and Sentiment Analysis.* Hanover, Mass.: Now.

Quirk, R., J. Svartvik, G. Leech and S. Greenbaum (1985), *A Comprehensive Grammar of the English Language.* London: Longman.

Schulz, A. (2008), *Guidelines for Annotating the EDNA Corpus – English.* Technische Universität Darmstadt, unpublished. Available from the author.

University of Birmingham, Dept. of English Language and Literature (1987). *Collins COBUILD (Collins Birmingham University International Language Database) English Language Dictionary.* London: Collins.

Variation in the progressive in World Englishes: Some preliminary findings[1]

Paula Suoniemi

University of Tampere

Abstract

This paper introduces a study on variation in the progressive in World Englishes. The main purpose of the study is to shed light on how the progressive is used in varieties other than British or American English, which have been the main focus of previous studies on the progressive. The present data consists of approximately 800,000 words of spontaneous dialogues in a number of comparative corpora, and the data is scrutinized from both syntactic and semantic points of view. This paper focuses on a methodological issue related to the study of the progressive, i.e. whether the number of progressives should be related to the number of words in a corpus or to some other figure available to the researcher. Towards the end of the paper, some preliminary results on the frequency of the progressive are discussed in the light of the previous section on methodology. The results show that there is considerable variation in the frequency of the progressive in World Englishes, and that these results are largely consistent regardless of the method employed. Although some explanations for the differences in the frequency of the progressive are attempted, it is evident that there is a multitude of possible explanations available. The ongoing doctorate study is expected to shed more light on the use of the progressive as regards its frequency, and selected syntactic and semantic elements related to it, as well as the reasons behind the differences found in the present data on World Englishes.

1. Introduction

The progressive (auxiliary *to be* + present participle) has been studied quite extensively and from a number of different viewpoints. Previous research include, for instance, Leech et al. (2009) on the progressive in written British and American English, Smitterberg (2005) on historical aspects of the progressive, Römer (2005) on pedagogical aspects, and Nesselhauf (2007) on the futurate use of the progressive. Although the range of research focused on the progressive is vast and varied, little attention has been directed at the use of the progressive in World Englishes. Studies of individual varieties, such as South African English (Van Rooy 2006), have been conducted, but a comparative approach of more than a few varieties has only been taken up by Peter Collins in his 2008 and 2009 articles. Thus, there is a need for a study aiming at a large-scale comparison of the use of the progressive form. My ongoing doctorate study seeks to provide such a comparison. The present paper discusses some methodological issues related to the study and reports on some preliminary findings on the frequency of the progressive in World Englishes.

2. Work in progress: a corpus-based study on the progressive in World Englishes

2.1 Aims and research questions

My ongoing doctorate study is a comparative corpus-based study into the use of the progressive in eight varieties of English throughout the world. Both syntactic and semantic features of the progressive are taken into consideration, as well as possible reasons for the differences between varieties. The data represents varieties of English that range from Europe to the Asian continent, and arise from different historical and social backgrounds. The status of English varies from native to non-native, and from official to non-official. This diversity of varieties can be expected to bring out considerable variation in the use of the progressive. The varieties studied are British English (BrE), American English (AmE), Irish English (IrE), Jamaican English (JamE), Indian English (IndE), Philippino English (PhiE), Singapore English (SinE), and Hong Kong English (HKE).

In the course of the doctorate study, answers are sought to a number of research questions, including:

- What is the frequency of the progressive in different varieties of English?
- What kind of functions is the progressive used in?
- Are stative verbs used in the progressive in all the varieties studied?
- What kind of grammatical environments does the progressive occur in?
- How can the differences between varieties be explained?

The first three questions are commonly discussed in studies on the progressive. The functions are of great interest, since, to this day, there does not seem to be any clear-cut consensus on what the primary, let alone special, uses of the progressive are. In connection to the question on functions, the question of stative verbs is essential in any study focusing on the progressive. A number of previous studies (e.g. Meshtrie 2008) report on "the extension of *to be + -ing* to stative contexts." Other semantic features are also of interest – see the section on data and methods for further information. The study of grammatical environments includes looking into the forms of the progressive (e.g. present and past tense forms, the progressive passive, and so forth), as well as focusing on the clause types the progressive occurs in and the presence of temporal adverbials. Additionally, I investigate the differences found in the data and attempt to find explanations for them by looking into language contact situations, principles of second language acquisition and the possibility of features being shared by varieties and languages.

2.2 Data

The data used in the study come from the *International Corpus of English* and from the *Santa Barbara Corpus of Spoken American English.* Altogether seven components of the ICE are used, and together with the Santa Barbara Corpus they offer a representative view over the use of English throughout the world. The focus of the study lies on spoken language, and especially on spontaneous dialogue. The focus on spoken language is motivated by the fact that the progressive occurs more often in spoken rather than written language, and in casual speech in particular (Arnaud 1998: 128). Therefore, to focus the study on the essential part of language and also to restrict the amount of data, the selection of subcorpora was limited to a section labeled 'Direct conversations' or 'Face-to-face conversations' (in ICE-Ireland), and further to 100,000 words per corpus. Confining the data to 100,000 words per corpus not only limits the amount of data, but also diminishes the slight differences in the size of the corpora, thus making the analysis of the results more straightforward.

Extraction of data was performed with the help of WordSmith 4.0 Concordance software. First of all, a search for any word ending in the string *-ing* with any form of *to be* occurring within five words to the left was launched for each of the eight corpora. Although ICE-GB is tagged for part of speech and is also annotated with syntactic information, it was decided that it, too, should be checked manually rather than with the help of the search program supplied with the CD-ROM. This ensured that all eight corpora were handled in a similar manner. Searching manually for any word ending in the string *-ing* produces a number of irrelevant hits, such as adjectives and nouns ending in *-ing*. These were cleared from the data manually along with unclear or repeated tokens. At this point, *to be going to* and non-finite constructions were removed from the retrieved tokens. The *to be going to* construction was omitted because it has been argued that it is no longer a proper progressive form, but has evolved into something that expresses intention and futurity (Mair 2006: 95-100). Non-finite constructions were removed since there were rather few of them all in all, and because their semantic analysis might lead to difficulties. Once the progressive tokens were successfully extracted from the data they were placed in Excel spreadsheets for morphosyntactic and semantic analysis.

2.3 Methods

The three main components of the study, the grammatical environment, the semantic features, and finding explanations for the differing use of the progressive in the eight varieties, each require their own method. Exploring the grammatical environment that the progressive occurs in calls for a systematic categorization of the data surrounding the progressive form, whereas when looking into the semantics of the progressive one needs to focus more closely on the progressive element itself. The third component, in turn, requires yet another way of looking at the data – it is necessary to step outside the corpus data and inside the sociolinguistic domain in discussing the possible effect of both local languages, e.g. Malay,

Hindi or Jamaican Creole, and features of aspect shared by the varieties of English and the local languages.

A number of previous studies have discussed the grammatical environment of the progressive, including Collins (2008), Smitterberg (2005), and Römer (2005). Based on these studies, a number of grammatical features were selected for investigation in the present study. These features are verb patterns (including tense, voice, perfect progressive, and presence of modal auxiliaries), contraction, clause types (main/subordinate), and the co-occurrence of adverbials of time.

The second component of the study involves semantic analysis of the data in order to bring out the meanings and uses in which the progressive is found in each variety. This is achieved by subjecting the data to a series of analyses, including situation type analysis (e.g. Brinton 1988), and categorisation of verbs (Biber et al. 1999). These two types of analysis offer information on the types of situations that the progressive is used in (Activity, Accomplishment, etc.), or on the types of verbs used in the progressive (Active, Mental, etc.). With the help of these analyses, and by examining the contexts that the progressive occurs in, it is possible to determine the function of the progressive forms used. Naturally, this task is not only arduous, but susceptible to errors as it might be difficult to judge what meaning the speaker intended. However, with careful analysis the functions can be revealed. Of special interest in the course of the study are stative verbs, as it has been argued (e.g. Aitchison 2001: 109) that the increase in the use of stative verbs in combination with the progressive has acted as a catalyst in the increasing use of the progressive overall.

Additionally, possible reasons affecting the differences between the varieties will be briefly discussed. Finding the *exhaustive* explanations is nearly impossible as there are a number of possible factors - language contact, universal features, or aspects of second-language acquisition are all possible.

3. Some findings on the frequency of the progressive

3.1 Linguistic variable: Progressive vs. non-progressive

On more than one occasion, it has been brought to my attention that it is not sufficient to investigate the progressive alone and compare the number of progressive tokens to the number of words in the corpus. Instead, one should take into account the fact that the progressive form can only occur with verbs: a noun cannot take the progressive aspect, nor can an adverb. Thus, the comparison of the number of progressives should be made to the number of verbs in the corpus. Smitterberg (2005: 37-53) discusses this methodological issue in detail. In brief, Smitterberg summarises the benefits and drawbacks of the three most common ways of measuring the frequency of the progressive, and goes on to suggest a new solution to the matter, the S-coefficient (Smitterberg 2005: 45). The most common way of measuring the frequency of the progressive is the so-called M-coefficient (named M after Mossé), where the number of progressives is related to the number of words in a text, i.e.

$$M = N_{PROG} / N_{WORD} \times 100{,}000.$$

According to Smitterberg (2005: 40-42), the M-coefficient has certain advantages that make it a powerful tool: it is easy to calculate, it is objective, and it compares easily to results from other research. However, the M-coefficient fails to take into account the fact that the progressive can not occur in any slot in a text, which may lead to problems when comparing different genres, for instance. Furthermore, problems may arise when variation between texts is being tested for statistical significance. Nevertheless, the M-coefficient remains the most common device for measuring the frequency of the progressive.

A coefficient that takes into account the restrictions on the use of the progressive is the K-coefficient, i.e.

$$K = N_{PROG} / (N_{VERB} - N_{NOPROG}) \times 10{,}000.$$

Verb phrases where the progressive cannot occur are excluded altogether. In other words, "the K-coefficient gives the researcher an indication of the probability of a progressive occurring in a text" (Smitterberg 2005: 43). Calculating the K-coefficient requires the researcher to judge whether or not a verb phrase could appear in the progressive, which makes it a subjective method, as well as arduous.

Smitterberg reports on a third coefficient which, according to him, has the advantages of the K-coefficient, but lacks some problems related to both the M- and the K-coefficients. The V-coefficient simply relates the number of progressives to the number of finite verb phrases in a given text, i.e.

$$V = N_{PROG} / N_{VERB} \times 10{,}000.$$

The V-coefficient is fairly easy to calculate, even if one is working with a non-tagged corpus of moderate size. There are no subjective elements to it, and furthermore, it neutralizes the differences between the ratios of the number of verb phrases to the number of words (which may lead to problems in statistical testing). As Smitterberg (2005: 45) points out, the use of the V-coefficient implies that the researcher adopts a variationist approach to the data: the progressive and the non-progressive are considered variants of the verb phrase.

Finally, Smitterberg goes on to suggest a fourth coefficient, specially designed for the study of late Modern English (Smitterberg 2005: 45-48). The idea is to exclude from the calculation all such contexts where the progressive does not occur. For instance, the formula Smitterberg devises for the late Modern English excludes imperative verb phrases and *be going to* + infinitive constructions with future reference. With modifications that take into account contexts where the progressive does not occur, the so-called S-coefficient could be used for other periods of time, as well. However, this would require a great deal of work as there are no clear answers to where exactly the progressive is possible or not in the varieties studied here.

3.2 Methodology adopted for the present study

For the present study, two of the coefficients discussed above were chosen, the M-coefficient and the V-coefficient. The M-coefficient is used for comparisons to previous research, while the V-coefficient is used for the comparison between the varieties included in the study.

Calculating the M-coefficient presents no problems as all one needs to know is the number of progressives and the total number of words in a text. The number of words in a text, in this context, refers to the number of words in each corpus sample, i.e. approximately 100,000 words per corpus. The number of progressives was calculated with the help of a concordancer (see Section 2.2 above).

The V-coefficient, in turn, required considerably more work, as the corpora used for the present study are not tagged (except for ICE-GB, but it was decided that it should be handled similarly to the other corpora, i.e. as if it was not tagged, see Section 2.2. above). This meant that the verb phrases were located manually in the corpora, tagged, and then searched for with WordSmith Tools 4.0 Concordancer. The verb phrases were tagged for four parameters - progressive / non-progressive (P/V), present/past tense (R/A), occurrence of modal auxiliaries (M where relevant), and future reference (F where relevant). For instance, consider example (1):

(1) Here I think_VR this is_VR really weird <#> Was I telling_PA somebody this last night in the pub <#> (ICE-Ireland, S1A-006)

In this example, *_VR* refers to a present non-progressive verb phrase, and *_PA* to a past progressive verb phrase. Tagging the verb phrases enables a number of comparisons between the progressive and the non-progressive. For instance, it is possible to compare the use of present tense in these two variants of the verb phrase.

To sum up, the data in the present study were subjected to two kinds of calculations for measuring the frequency of the progressive. The M-coefficient

$$M = N_{PROG} / N_{WORD} \times 100{,}000$$

is used for comparison with previous research, and the V-coefficient

$$V = N_{PROG} / N_{VERB} \times 10{,}000$$

for comparison between the varieties included in the study, as well as for comparison of the progressive and the non-progressive. Section 3.3 presents the results for these calculations.

3.3 Frequency of the progressive in eight World English varieties

3.3.1 M-coefficient

In the present study, the M-coefficient does not differ much from the raw frequency of the progressive as the number of words in each corpus is approximately 100,000 which is also the normalization co-efficient in the formula. See Table 1 below for the exact M-coefficients:

Table 1. $M = N_{PROG} / N_{WORD} \times 100{,}000$

	Raw freq.	Words	M-coefficient
ICE-Ireland	1,074	100,028	1,074
ICE-India	891	101,066	882
ICE-Jamaica	859	100,511	855
ICE-Great Britain	847	100,410	844
ICE-Philippines	803	100,876	796
SBC (American English)	772	100,008	772
ICE-Singapore	733	100,812	727
ICE-Hong Kong	394	100,512	392

Note: The results are statistically significant at level $p < 0.001$, df=7.

The data shows that the progressive is most frequently used in Irish English, and least frequently in Hong Kong English. On the basis of the M-coefficient, it also seems that the other six varieties form two clusters, one consisting of Philippine English, American English and Singapore English, the other of Indian English, Jamaican English, and British English.

3.3.2 V-coefficient

As mentioned above, preparations for calculating the V-coefficient were more laborious, requiring considerable manual handling of the data. Once the verb phrases have been located, making the actual calculations is not difficult, however. See Table 2 below.

When the V-coefficient is compared to the M-coefficient we find that only a few rather insignificant changes have taken place. PhiE and BrE have exchanged their places on the list of most frequent use of the progressive, as have SinE and AmE. All in all, the differences between varieties have diminished considerably. The effective factor is the number of verb phrases, which is different for each variety. As a side-note, it is rather interesting that the number of verb phrases is highest in the native varieties, especially BrE and AmE.

Table 2. $V = N_{PROG} / N_{VERB} \times 10{,}000$

	Raw freq.	Verb phrases	V-coefficient
ICE-Ireland	1,074	12,480	861
ICE-India	891	11,348	785
ICE-Jamaica	859	11,811	727
ICE-Philippines	803	12,237	656
ICE-Great Britain	847	13,728	617
ICE-Singapore	733	12,422	590
SBC (AmE)	772	13,577	569
ICE-Hong Kong	394	10,022	393

Note: The results are statistically significant at level $p < 0.001$, df=7.

The ordering of the varieties as regards the frequency of the progressive does not show clear differences between native and non-native varieties – indeed they are dispersed very evenly. Greater differences are expected from the semantic analysis of the data. As Kortmann (2004: 1090) states, the progressive is used with a wider range of verbs and functions in many nonstandard varieties. However, it must be noted that the ICE corpora represent the standard within each variety rather than the nonstandard, which might lead to more subtle differences between the varieties even as regards the semantic features studied.

3.3.3 Discussion of results

The frequent use of the progressive in Irish English can be explained by the fact that it may be used relatively freely (Filppula 2008: 332). According to Filppula (ibid.), the progressive form may be used to mark progressivity, as in other varieties, but also for a number of other uses. These include the use of the progressive with stative verbs, with dynamic verbs or *would/'d/used (to)* to denote habitual activities (where standard English would use the simple present or the simple infinitive), with auxiliaries such as *do/does* and *will/'ll,* and finally, with verbs of saying and telling (this seems to be true for other varieties, as well). The fact that Welsh English and Scottish English share at least some of these features with Irish English lends support to the 'substratum' hypothesis, i.e. influence from Celtic languages (Filppula 2008: 334). The Irish English data from the present study seems to include a considerable number of instances on Filppula's list.

The least frequent usage of the progressive is found in the two varieties with considerable Chinese input, Singapore and Hong Kong English, and on the other hand, the two traditional varieties, British and American English. However, this does not suggest that the factors affecting these two groups are the same. Rather, it seems that the traditional varieties are low on the scale due to increased use of the progressive in the more recent varieties. In the case of HKE and SinE, it seems more likely that the Sinitic substrate languages have influenced the use of the progressive. According to Ansaldo (2004), tense and aspect marking are optional in Colloquial Singapore English. Ansaldo further argues that in SinE the progressive aspect can be marked with the adverbial *still* instead of the progressive form. The use of *still* as an aspectual marker can be explained as arising from contact situations with local languages which lack tense and aspect marking, but also as a result of "a 'universal' innovation process" that reanalyses time adverbials into aspect markers (Ansaldo 2004: 137-138). What this implies is that ICE-Singapore probably contains more progressive elements than merely the progressive form. However, the focus of the present study is on the use of the progressive aspect marked by *be* + *-ing*, thus the other possibly progressive elements are not included here.

Rather surprisingly, the data suggests that the progressive is used less often in American than in British English, contrary to most previous studies (e.g. Biber et al. 1999: 462). It must be noted however, that many of the previous studies focus on written rather than spoken language. One possible factor influencing these figures might be the content of the corpora, i.e. the types of text included in the sample, although the content of the corpora used in the present study seem relatively similar. In the light of the present data, it seems that, in spontaneous dialogues, the progressive is more frequent in BrE than in AmE, contrary to the situation in written language.[2]

At this point, it is rather difficult to further discuss the factors affecting the frequency of the progressive in any separate variety. More detailed analysis of both morphosyntactic and semantic variation is needed before the use of the progressive in the present corpora can be discussed any further.

4. Conclusion

This paper reported on an ongoing doctorate study into variation in the progressive in altogether eight World English varieties, focusing on some methodological issues related to it. Additionally, preliminary results on the frequency of the progressive were presented. The doctorate study seeks to fill a gap in research on the progressive – only a handful of recent papers have discussed the World English perspective related to the progressive. Based on reports by Kortmann (2004), for instance, it is evident that attention needs to be directed at the 'new' varieties, where the progressive is claimed to be used differently from the more traditional varieties.

The methodological discussion focused on using proper methods of measuring the frequency of the progressive. The fact that the progressive cannot occur in any slot of the language, but only occurs in verb phrases must be taken into account. Based on a study by Smitterberg (2005), two measurement types were chosen for the present study, the M-coefficient which is used for comparison to previous research, and the V-coefficient which is used to compare the data from the different varieties included in the present study. Results obtained using these coefficients are surprisingly similar – differences between the varieties are diminished, although the ordering of the varieties from most frequent use of the progressive to the least frequent changes slightly.

The preliminary findings on the frequency of the progressive presented in this paper bring out interesting results. It seems that native and non-native varieties do not group together with their own kind, but are dispersed rather evenly throughout the whole scale. The traditional varieties (BrE, AmE) are indeed found on the less frequent end, as are the Chinese-influenced varieties of English included in the study (HKE, SinE). More detailed analysis on the morphosyntactic and semantic elements is needed before the discussion on possible factors affecting the use of the progressive can be continued.

Notes

1 I am grateful to Geoffrey Leech and Paul Rayson for comments on earlier drafts of the paper. Any remaining shortcomings are my own responsibility.

2 One of the reviewers points out that one of the most likely reasons for this result is that the Santa Barbara Corpus is, in some way, incomparable to the ICE corpora. However, as the Santa Barbara Corpus is frequently used as a supplement for the American English component of the ICE corpora, I will continue to use it, albeit with the reviewer's comment in mind.

Corpora

The *International Corpus of English: Great Britain* (1998). The Survey of English Usage. University College London.

The *International Corpus of English: Hong Kong* (2006). Department of English, The University of Hong Kong and The Chinese University of Hong Kong, PRC.

The *International Corpus of English: India* (2002). Department of English, Shivaji University, Kolhapur and Freie Universität, Berlin.

The *International Corpus of English: Ireland* (2008). School of English, The Queen's University Belfast and Centre for Language and Communication Studies, Trinity College Dublin.

The *International Corpus of English: Jamaica* (2009). Englisches Seminar, Albert-Ludwigs-Universität Freiburg and Department of Language, Linguistics, & Philosophy, University of the West Indies.

The *International Corpus of English: the Philippines* (2004). Department of English and Applied Linguistics, De La Salle University, Manila.

The *International Corpus of English: Singapore* (2002). Department of English Language & Literature, The National University of Singapore.

The *Santa Barbara Corpus of Spoken American English* (2002-2005). Santa Barbara Center for the Study of Discourse, University of California, Santa Barbara.

References

Aitchison, J. (2001), *Language Change: Progress or Decay*? 3rd edition. Cambridge: Cambridge University Press.

Ansaldo, U. (2004), 'The evolution of Singapore English', in: L. Lim (ed.) *Singapore English: A Grammatical Description*. Amsterdam: John Benjamins Publishing Company. 127-149.

Arnaud, R. (1998), 'The development of the progressive in 19th century English: A quantitative survey', *Language Variation and Change*, 10: 123-152.

Biber, D., S. Johansson, G. Leech, S. Conrad and E. Finegan (1999), *Longman Grammar of Spoken and Written English*. London: Longman.

Brinton, L. J. (1988), *The Development of English Aspectual Systems*. Cambridge: Cambridge University Press.

Collins, P. (2008), 'The progressive aspect in World Englishes: A corpus-based study', *Australian Journal of Linguistics*, 28(2): 225-249.

Collins, P. (2009), 'The progressive', in: P. Peters, P. Collins and A. Smith (eds.) *Comparative Studies in Australian and New Zealand English: Grammar and Beyond*. Amsterdam: John Benjamins Publishing Company. 115-123.

Filppula, M. (2008), 'Irish English: morphology and syntax', in: B. Kortmann and C. Upton (eds.) *Varieties of English 1: The British Isles*. Berlin: Mouton de Gruyter. 328-359.

Kortmann, B. (2004), 'Synopsis: Morphological and syntactic variation in the British Isles', in: B. Kortmann, K. Burridge, R. Mesthrie, E. W. Schneider and C. Upton (eds.) *Handbook of Varieties of English. Volume 2: Morphology and Syntax*. Berlin: Mouton de Gruyter. 1089-1103.

Leech, G., M. Hundt, C. Mair and N. Smith (2009), *Change in Contemporary English: A Grammatical Study*. Cambridge: Cambridge University Press.

Mair, C. (2006), *Twentieth-Century English*. Cambridge: Cambridge University Press.

Meshtrie, R. (2008), 'Synopsis: Morphological and syntactic variation in Africa and South and Southeast Asia', in: R. Meshtrie (ed.) *Varieties of English: Africa South and Southeast Asia*. Berlin: Mouton de Gruyter. 624-635.

Nesselhauf, N. (2007), 'The spread of the progressive and its "future" use', *English Language and Linguistics*, 11(1): 191-207.

Römer, U. (2005), *Progressives, Patterns, Pedagogy: A Corpus-driven Approach to English Progressive Forms, Functions, Context and Dialects*. Amsterdam: John Benjamins Publishing Company.

Smitterberg, E. (2005), *The Progressive in 19th Century English. A Process of Integration*. Amsterdam: Rodopi.

Van Rooy, B. (2006), 'The extension of the progressive aspect in Black South African English', *World Englishes*, 25(1): 37-64.

Telicity and the premodifying *ing*-participle in English

Turo Vartiainen

University of Helsinki

Abstract

The topic of this paper is a specific class of premodifiers in English, prenominal ing-*participles. The participle category and its semantics and syntax will be discussed in detail in the course of the paper, and after considering the relevant data, I will suggest that the category of verbal participles should be kept separate from adjectival participles, and also that the use of verbal participles is best explained by semantic underdeterminacy with a strong preference to interpret the participles' meaning as atelic descriptions.*

1. Introduction

Participles have always been regarded as a somewhat special class, and their peculiar nature was noted by the very first linguists of the Western world. In his *Tekhnē Grammatikē*[1], Dionysius Thrax states that:

> A participle is a word which participates in the characteristics of both the verbs and the nouns. It has the same attributes as the noun and the verb, except for person and moods. (Kemp 1987: 182)

We can see from this that the description Thrax offers is surprisingly modern. Thrax does not discuss adjectives as a separate class in his *Tekhnē* (many subclasses of adjectives are included in nouns, however), but basically, the idea of participles as a fuzzy category that is simultaneously participating in nominal and verbal grammar is already present in Thrax's work. This is quite astonishing, considering that according to the Aristotelian idea of categorization, all categories were sharply and clearly divided from one another. Such a notion should have left no room for vague or overlapping word classes (see e.g. Lakoff 1987; Seuren 1998).

Modern linguists have offered several solutions to the problematic dual nature of participles. Some have lumped all premodifying participles together with adjectives (e.g. Borer 1990; Haspelmath 1994; Bresnan 1996; Pullum and Zwicky 1999; Biber et al. 1999), while others have noted the special characteristics of participles and acknowledged their "verbhood" or "verbal force", or at least their different qualities from adjectives (e.g. Bache 1978; Quirk et al. 1985; Brekke 1988; Bennis and Wehrmann 1990; Laczkó 2001; Aarts 2007; Meltzer

2007). Yet others have suggested that verbal *ing*-participles and gerunds have merged in Present-Day English and should be regarded as a single class, even if their historical forms have been different (Huddleston 1985; Pullum 1991; Huddleston and Pullum 2002; Blevins 2005). The underlying idea here is that the *ing*-morpheme is underspecified in the lexicon, which allows it to be realized as a participle, gerund or part of the progressive construction (see e.g. Blevins 2005: 28; also Chomsky 1970: 21-22). Indeed, the status of the *ing*-form has been discussed quite extensively, especially in the generative framework, although research has mostly concentrated on deverbal nouns and gerunds and constraints concerning the co-occurrence of multiple *ing*-forms (see e.g. Milsark 1988; Pullum and Zwicky 1999; Lee 2007). Insofar as premodifying *ing*-forms have been studied, the focus has been more on the semantics of the *ing*-forms that behave like adjectives, not on the more verb-like *ing*-forms (e.g. Brekke 1988; Meltzer 2007; but see Laczkó 2001).

Interestingly, the widely read comprehensive grammars of the English language (Quirk et al. 1985; Biber et al. 1999; Huddleston and Pullum 2002) all analyse premodifying *ing*-participles differently. In this paper, I will focus more on the verbal *ing*-participles, so I will now turn to the description offered in *A Comprehensive Grammar of the English Language* (Quirk et al. 1985; henceforth the *CGEL*), the grammar that supports the idea that *ing*-participles may exhibit verbal force.[2]

The *CGEL* clearly regards *ing*-participles as a gradient category where the participles may retain some of their verbal properties (their *verbal force*) even when functioning as premodifiers. The authors also note that there are many adjectives with a similar ending (Quirk et al. 1985: 413), but what they exactly mean by this is left unclear. The question about the relationship of *ing*-adjectives (e.g. *charming*, *fascinating*) and verbal *ing*-participles is not elaborated upon, so it is not clear whether Quirk et al. consider words like *interesting* or *charming* to be participles or adjectives, or possibly an intersection of both.

While the term *verbal force* in itself implies some kind of gradience inside the participle class, this gradience is curiously played down in the *CGEL*'s analysis of the *ing*-participles (1985: 1325). Here, as well as in the earlier grammar by Quirk et al. (*the Grammar of Contemporary English*, 1972) the authors propose that a crucial property of the premodifying participle is its potential to "indicate a permanent or characteristic feature" (Quirk et al. 1972: 908; Quirk et al. 1985: 1325). According to Quirk et al. (1972: 909) this interpretation will lead us to regard *a wandering minstrel* as a minstrel "habitually given to wandering", and also to consider a question such as *who is the wandering man* strange if we are describing a scene where a man is wandering down the street at the time of description. This, in the authors' opinion, is because the information described by the premodifying *ing*-participle makes us interpret the eventuality as somehow permanent or characteristic to the modified referent.[3] The authors therefore suggest that the *ing*-participle cannot be used in descriptions of temporary and current events. So, *a drinking man* is, according to the *CGEL*, a man habitually given to drinking, not someone who is having a drink at the moment, while *a working man* is a man who goes to work regularly, not a man at work at the time of speaking (see Haspelmath 1994: 164 for related arguments).

While this analysis arguably has some appeal, it is problematic for several reasons. Let us first consider *a drinking man* in more detail and then expand the discussion to include further examples.

First of all, as is also apparent from the re-phrasing in the *CGEL*, the participle in *a drinking man* ('a man who drinks regularly') actually includes more information than is expressed by the form of the word (the fact that the man drinks regularly, i.e. a habitual interpretation of the event). This in itself is not a problem: language users are certainly sensitive to aspectual differences that are not grammatically encoded in the word forms. However, *a drinking man* not only implies that the man is drinking regularly (which is what Quirk et al. suggest), but also the fact that the man is drinking a specific substance, i.e. alcohol. This means that *a drinking man* includes specific, lexicalized information. This in turn suggests that the habitual reading of *a drinking man* is not a result of a regular grammatical process (the use of the *ing*-participle in a premodifying position) but rather a use of a polysemous sense of the verb *to drink*. The same effect emerges from other constructions as well. For example, the simple present tense has a habitual reading with activity verbs: *My dad didn't drink when I was young*; *I drink*. In fact, even in the *CGEL* the authors have included the example *Bill drinks heavily* in their discussion of the habitual present (Quirk et al. 1985: 179).

The above argument gains further support from the fact that the "habitual drinking" described in *a drinking man* does not readily allow other than human agents. For example, while *a drinking woman* (and also *a drinking girl/boy*) can refer to the (regular) consumption of alcohol, *a drinking horse/cat/dog/antelope* or any other animate being cannot.[4] Therefore, the antelope in (1) is not 'an antelope that drinks regularly', much less 'an antelope who drinks alcohol', but simply 'an antelope that is drinking (water)'.

(1) During the TV nature show, we were all afraid to look as the crocodile stealthily swam toward *the drinking antelope.*[5]

Therefore, the inference we usually make when processing *a drinking man* cannot be explained only with reference to the syntactic position of the *ing*-participle; instead it requires an explanation that takes into account the entire construction, the restrictions on the thematic role of the head noun, and possibly other considerations as well. World knowledge certainly plays a part; as children rarely drink alcohol as frequently as adults, the referent in *a drinking girl* with the meaning 'a girl who drinks alcohol regularly' is probably interpreted as a young adult or a teenager, not a young child.

In addition to the above problems, it soon becomes clear that Quirk et al.'s claim that "everything here [in their description of premodifying *ing*-participles] depends on the potentiality of the participle to indicate a permanent or a characteristic feature" (Quirk et al. 1985: 1325) is too strong in other ways as well. It is not at all difficult to find examples in the present-day corpora where the participle describes a feature which is not permanent or characteristic to the referent. Consider the following examples from the F-LOB corpus:

(2) He kept his salutations to a "thank you" before an audience of *three goose-stepping platoons*... (A A05:58)
(3) Premier John Major was drowned out by *a screaming mob* last night... (A A06:65)
(4) The British team, sponsored by the Horse Trials Support Group, were drawn first of *the 10 competing countries*... (A A08:51)
(5) As the 60-year-old Archdeacon left the nave of York's famous Minster, *one fuming worshipper* accused him of "misusing the pulpit". (A A12:4)
(6) Hundreds of soldiers, volunteers, hoteliers and fishermen worked frantically to scoop up oily slime from beaches after a sudden weather change pushed *floating crude* landwards, blackening pebbly shores. (A A14:56)
(7) But Willie Carson, *the winning jockey*, stressed that this colt was "potentially" a very nice type of horse... (A A08:10)
(8) Companies as diverse as BAT Industries and BTR, George Wimpey and T&N, all reporting this week, will demonstrate this as they report *plummeting profits*, or even losses. (A A16:4)
(9) "David Who? Never heard of him," said *sun-bathing Sam Blumberg* from Wisconsin on Miami Beach. (A A19:26)

All the above participles describe events that are taking place at the time of description, but which nevertheless are temporary and by no means characteristic to the referent they are modifying. For example, in (2), the platoons are goose-stepping, but certainly goose-stepping is not a characteristic feature attached to a group of soldiers, but rather something they only do in certain situations, parades. The screaming mob in (3) is screaming only in response to John Major's speech, and again we find the description to be about the current state of affairs, not permanent characteristics of the mob. In (4), the countries are competing in horseracing, but other than that, their more general or characteristic competitive nature is not implied. Similar to (3), the worshipper in (5) may be enraged, fuming, at the time of the description, but again no lasting characteristic is implied. Similar arguments can be presented for all examples from (6) to (9): we are clearly dealing with descriptions of current events that have nothing to do with permanent or characteristic qualities of the referents they are modifying. Rather, the participles are used much like relative clauses would, and they describe the situation at hand in a manner similar to other forms of expression, although in a more compact way.

It may be that the idea of permanence in the *CGEL* (and the earlier *Grammar of Contemporary English*) is derived from a notion the authors discuss in conjunction with participles: definiteness. Quirk et al. point out that "the indefinite article favours the habitual or permanent [whereas] the definite article the specific or temporary" (1985: 1326; see also Section 3.2 below). To illustrate this idea, they argue that especially speakers of British English may find the following sentence strange because the temporary reading is preferred for the definite article, whereas the premodifying participle requires a permanent reading:

(10) *The approaching train* is from Liverpool.

Although not a native-speaker myself, I concur with Quirk et al. in that example (10) does seem a little odd. However, I do not find anything strange about the following sentence taken from the BNC:

(11) In fact, *the approaching train* was already audible. (CE9 666)

The authors of the CGEL also claim that the sentence in (12) is also strange:

(12) *The barking dog* is my neighbour's.

Again, it is easy to find examples where the definite noun phrase *the barking dog* is used in a more natural way. For example:

(13) I tried to dodge *the barking dog*.

It therefore seems that examples (10) and (12) are odd for other reasons than a clash between the temporary reading of the definite article and the permanent reading of the participle. Perhaps the oddness arises because a definite NP is seldom used as a subject in these kinds of identifying clauses or simply because sentences out of context often seem less acceptable than sentences in context. To illustrate this, I do not find the sentence in (14) to sound any more idiomatic or natural out of context than (12), although the participle is removed, and therefore, no semantic clash should occur:

(14) The dog is my neighbour's.

To summarize, the aspectual analysis of the *ing*-participles in the *CGEL* must be abandoned as too strong and inaccurate. Although permanent and characteristic attributes may explain phrases like *a drinking man*, this explanation cannot account for examples (2) to (9) above, nor can it explain other similar examples that abound in different corpora. In Section 3 I will introduce an alternative analysis, which is also based on verbal aspect. In my analysis, however, permanence (or temporal stability or a characteristic feature) is not the relevant aspectual property; atelicity is.

2. Adjectival and verbal participles

Before going into the analysis of verbal participles, I would like to return to the question of the nature of the participle category – the question whether or not we should keep adjectival and verbal participles separate or simply consider all prenominal *ing*-forms to be adjectives. The ideas developed in Hengeveld (1992; see also e.g. Rijkhoff 2002; Hengeveld et al. 2004) serve as a useful starting point for the distinction between adjectival and verbal participles. In Hengeveld's functional model, the major word classes (nouns, verbs, adjectives and adverbs) each have their prototypical syntactic functions. For example, nouns function prototypically as terms of predicates, while adjectives function as modifiers of terms. Hengeveld's key idea is that the word classes may potentially appear in these functions without any morphological or syntactic operations (i.e. "without further measures" = WFM). Therefore, verbs (which may function as predicates of the clause WFM) cannot function as modifiers to terms WFM. However, *with further measures*, verbs can function as modifiers to terms: both *ing*-participles and *ed*-participles readily occur prenominally as modifiers in English. In my opinion, there are no grounds for calling these participles "adjectives" just because uninflected verbs cannot function as modifiers to terms. Although the prenominal (attributive) position is typical to adjectives, not verbs, one would expect all *ing*-participles to show adjectival behaviour in other ways than their syntactic position if they truly were adjectives.

To see whether this is the case, let us take a look at some word class tests that are usually used to determine whether a word belongs to the adjective class or not[6] (see e.g. Quirk et al. 1985; Laczkó 2001). Each criterion is followed by two *ing*-participles, which both can be used in the prenominal position[7]; the first of these, *interesting*, passes all the tests, while the second one, *playing*, fails in all but the last one:

1. Modification with *very* (very interesting/*very playing)
2. Gradability (more/most interesting/*more/most playing)
3. Ability to occur in the attributive and the predicative position (The interesting girl/the girl is interesting; the playing girl/*the girl is playing[8])
4. Prefixation with *un-* (uninteresting/*unplaying)
5. Suffixation with *–ly* (interestingly/?*playingly[9])

These tests clearly illustrate that *interesting* and *playing* exhibit very different behaviour; *interesting* truly seems to fulfil the necessary criteria for an adjective much better than *playing*. We can also consider another criterion that can be used to identify verbal *ing*-participles. This provides even more support to the idea that *playing* is a verb, not an adjective:

6. Verbal participles may retain their verbal argument structure whereas adjectival participles may not.[10] (e.g. *two men played cards* vs. *two card-playing men*;[11] *the play interested me* vs. **the me interesting play*)

Based on the above discussion, I argue that there are strong empirical grounds for establishing two classes of *ing*-participles: adjectival *ing*-participles (e.g. *interesting*) and verbal *ing*-participles (e.g. *playing*). This division is reflected in the syntax of the noun phrase as well: verbal *ing*-participles tend to occur closer to the head word than adjectival *ing*-participles (see also Bache 1978).[12] Therefore, we could predict that a phrase like *the charming playing children* would be used more frequently than *the playing charming children.*

To see whether this indeed is the case, let us take a look at some corpus data. There are only 27 NPs in the BNC with both an adjectival and a verbal premodifying participle. Of these NPs, 26 conform to the adjective+verb ordering, and only one follows the opposite order. Consider the following examples, where example (18) is the only counterexample to the adjective+verb ordering in the entire BNC:

(15) Well, to start with, you are quite likely to meet *some fascinating flying men and women before you even get into the aircraft.* (CAU 1159)
(16) SUPERSTAR Michael Jackson has a rival in a new series of Pepsi adverts … *the terrifying man-eating monster from the Alien films.* (CH6 5750)
(17) It seems that people with a history of schizophrenia may also have some difficulty in ignoring irrelevant stimuli (such as *other distracting flashing lights*)… (J14 633)
(18) Very few vehicles pass, but when they do, they bear down from nowhere full of *gun-toting unsmiling men…* (HH0 2531)

The difference between the two types of participles is also evident in coordination: different types are usually not coordinated. While there is nothing strange in *an interesting and illuminating exercise* (BNC, CN6 295), where two adjectival participles are coordinated, the coordination of an adjectival and a verbal participle produces an odd result: ?*an interesting and sun-bathing man.*

3. Verbal participles

In this section I will concentrate on verbal participles and their aspectual properties. Verbal aspect has played a prominent role in some recent studies on prenominal *ed*-participles (e.g. Haspelmath 1994) and *ing*-participles (Bresnan 1996; Meltzer 2009). However, the study of *ing*-participles has focused on adjectival participles, and the major issue has often been about the problems in the categorization of the participle class mentioned above.

In Section 2 I discussed (and rejected) Quirk et al.'s suggestion that the semantics of premodifying *ing*-participles may be explained by permanence or a characteristic feature (e.g. *a wandering minstrel, a drinking man*). Examples (2) - (9) all described a current event, which means that another explanation must be sought. The explanation I am offering is that while the participles in (2) - (9) do not describe a permanent or a characteristic feature of their referents, they do describe a situation whose endpoint is not specified, i.e. *an atelic situation.* Atelicity, in turn, *may* give rise to a habitual reading of the verb phrase.

3.1 Telicity

Telicity is a term that is defined in various ways by different linguists (see e.g. Comrie 1976; Dowty 1979; Bach 1986; Krifka 1989; Rothstein 2004). The exact definition of telicity lies outside the scope of this paper, so to simplify a little, a telic description includes an inherent endpoint (telic point) to the eventuality, which can be either potential or already realized (see e.g. Dahl 1981), whereas an atelic description includes no such endpoint. Telicity is a key feature in the division of verbs into aspectual classes. Usually, verbs are divided into four (sometimes five) aspectual classes, and these classes serve as a good starting point for the telicity-based analysis of the *ing*-participles (see e.g. Ryle 1949; Vendler 1957; Kenny 1963; Dowty 1979).

The four commonly acknowledged (lexical) aspectual classes are (a) states, (b) activities, (c) accomplishments, and (d) achievements. Examples include:

a. Love someone (state; non-durative, atelic)
b. Play the piano (activity; durative, atelic)
c. Build a house (accomplishment; durative, telic)
d. Win a prize (achievement; non-durative, telic)

The four aspectual classes can be distinguished using two binary features (Rothstein 2004: 12): [±stage] and [±telic]. The durative classes include stages and hence are [+stage] (activities and accomplishments), whereas the non-durative classes are [-stage] (states and achievements). States are [-stage] because they describe eventualities that do not have distinguishable parts. If we say *she loves you,* then the eventuality expressed by the clause is perceived to be stable, with no beginning, middle, or end (even though the loving of course starts and may stop in the real world). Achievements are [-stage] because they are perceived to happen instantaneously (i.e. they are punctual): *reach the summit* includes two states, one before the summit is reached and another after it has been reached; there is no in-between state. Activities and accomplishments, on the other hand, are [+stage]. For example, in the event of *playing the piano* (activity) or *building a house* (accomplishment), there are clearly identifiable stages in the described events.

The [±telic] feature, on the other hand, groups states together with activities, and accomplishments together with achievements. This means that the descriptions *love someone* (state) and *play the piano* (activity) do not express a set terminal point, whereas *build a house* (accomplishment) and *win a prize* (achievement) do.

As states are atelic by default, I will start with activities and accomplishments and conclude with a discussion of achievements.

3.2 Activities and accomplishments

In 3.1 we saw that the four classes of lexical aspect can be classified according to two parameters: [±stage] and [±telic]. It must be pointed out, however, that many verbs can be *used* in different ways. For example, the verb *sing*, which is typically an accomplishment verb, is used as part of an activity VP in (19), and an accomplishment VP in (20).

(19) The woman is singing opera. (activity; atelic)
(20) The woman is singing a song. (accomplishment; telic)

Similarly in (21), *build* describes an accomplishment, whereas (22) is a description of an activity:

(21) Jack is building a house. (accomplishment; telic)
(22) Jack is building houses. (activity; atelic)

Finally, in (23) we find *land* used as a punctual achievement with no stages, and in (24) as an accomplishment with clearly identified stages described in a sequence (see also Rothstein 2004: 51):

(23) Despite their prayers, *the director's plane landed safely*, claimed the raconteur. (BNC B78 2180). (achievement)
(24) Dutch Safety Board chairman Pieter van Vollenhoven said *the plane was landing on automatic pilot and the problem with the altimeter led to a loss of speed.* (http://news.bbc.co.uk/2/hi/7910215.stm) (accomplishment)

The above examples clearly indicate that the aspectual properties of the event may change when the type (count/mass) or the number of the object is changed (19 to 22), or when the grammatical aspect of the clause is altered (23 and 24). In other words, lexical aspect interacts with other grammatical properties of the clause.

The interesting thing about premodifying *ing*-participles is that while they readily allow descriptions of all kinds of atelic eventualities, it may not be possible to express the corresponding telic descriptions. For example, many verbs of motion (which are atelic activity verbs) cannot be used to express telic accomplishments. Consider:

(25) The man is running. (activity; atelic)
(26) The man is running a mile. (accomplishment; telic)
(27) the running man (activity; atelic)
(28) ?the mile-running man (accomplishment; telic)

It also seems that direction is not readily expressed with a premodifying participle construction with a verb of motion:

(29) ?a/the home-running man (accomplishment; telic)

One could try to argue that the restrictions that explain the unacceptability of (28) and (29) are syntactic, not semantic, as premodifying participles tend to be syntactically simple. This is not so, however. For example, we can express the direct object in (30) with a corresponding *ing*-participle, but not in (32). Clearly, the relevant constraint is about telicity, not transitivity:

(30) The mouse is singing opera. (activity; atelic)
(31) the opera-singing mouse[13]
(32) The mouse is singing a song. (accomplishment; telic)
(33) ?the song-singing mouse

To sum up the discussion so far, I would like to claim that these examples suggest that there is a general, strong tendency, by which premodifying *ing*-participle constructions are not used to express telic eventualities.

Interestingly, when we find a verb that can be used to describe both activities and accomplishments, the activity reading seems to be the preferred one with the premodifying *ing*-participle construction. Let us take an example of what may be the most classical example of an accomplishment: *build a house.* As noted above, *build a house* describes a telic eventuality (accomplishment), while *build houses* describes an atelic eventuality (activity). The following examples seem common enough:

(34) …work undertaken by *house-building firms*… (BNC, A69 108)
(35) the existing danger of *skilled house-building teams* being broken up and not replaced will be avoided. (BNC, A69 137)

Here the inference is that *the firms/teams build houses* (possibly including a house being built at the moment), and not that *the firms/teams have built a house.* For example, one would not call a firm *a house-building firm*, if it was not in the business of building houses (and therefore building houses on a regular basis). Hence, although the aspect is not overtly encoded in the *ing*-form, the inference leads us to regard the event as atelic.

The difference between the unacceptable ?*the mile-running man* and, for example, *a house-building firm* should be made clear, however. The bounding of atelic activities seems to be a hard constraint (or a strong tendency) whereas the preference for the activity reading of *a house-building firm* is a softer constraint (or a weaker tendency).[14] In other words, *ing*-participles with an accomplishment verb tend to describe atelic activities, not telic accomplishments, but this should not be understood as a deterministic grammatical rule.

The preference for the atelic reading for accomplishment verbs may be a result of the non-referentiality of the object of the participle. Non-referentiality allows the participle construction to be interpreted in many ways, but it does not readily allow some readings. In fact, it is not possible to express a quantized/individuated referent as the object of the *ing*-participle, which in turn has implications for the aspect of the event described by the participle and its object (for the relationship between the direct object and the aspect of the clause, see e.g. Verkuyl 1972; Van Voorst 1992: 72). Therefore, example (36) below cannot mean *the man who drinks/drank/is drinking a beer* (telic), but only *the man who drinks/drank/is drinking beer* (atelic).

(36) the beer-drinking man (object non-referential; necessarily atelic)

Thus, what we can say at this point is that naturally atelic eventualities (activities) cannot be made telic in the prenominal *ing*-construction. Furthermore, accomplishment verbs (like *build*) that can be used to express both telic accomplishments and atelic activities strongly favour the atelic reading.

I would like to suggest that it is precisely atelicity that gives rise to potential habitual readings both in the simple tenses (*I drank quite a lot, but now I don't drink*) and in the *ing*-participles. In other words, there is a strong tendency for *ing*-participles to express atelic eventualities, and this tendency may or may not result in habitual interpretations. Habitual readings may then further be lexicalized, especially with specific headwords (e.g. *a drinking man*).

3.3 Achievements

As seen above, achievements are descriptions of telic and non-durative (punctual) eventualities. Like achievements and accomplishments, they can be used in other ways as well (as a description of extended action). Therefore, from the achievement *win a race*, we get:

(37) We won the race. (achievement)
(38) We were winning the race. (progressive achievement or accomplishment)

The *ing*-participles with achievement verbs behave somewhat differently from those with activity verbs. While the participle in a phrase like *the reading girl* can be paraphrased using either the present or the past tense, the participle in the definite NP *the winning team* only rarely refers to ongoing action.[15] It usually either implies completed (past) action (39) or future action (40), while *a winning team* typically describes an extended achievement (41). Compare:

(39) *The winning team* came from Parmiter's School of Garston in Hertfordshire. (BNC: ALW 3018)
(40) *The winning team* will receive the City Monopoly Trophy… (BNC: CBX 651)
(41) The old adage about not changing *a winning team* is not true… (BNC: J1F 642)

Like all achievements, *winning something* includes an initial state, where the denotation of the VP does not hold, and a changed state, where the denotation of the VP holds. In other words, achievements are minimal changes from a non-state to a state (e.g. from a state of not winning to the state of winning). Rothstein (2004: 155) points out that an achievement is "the shortest possible non-stative eventuality", which means that the change from one state to another state happens in "next to no time" (id.: 23). Therefore, as ter Meulen suggests (1995:7; see also Rothstein 2004: 23), "none of its [i.e. the achievement's] internal structure is accessible for description".

If we consider examples (39) - (41), then in (41), *the winning team* describes the end-state of winning, and can only be paraphrased as 'the team that (had) won X'. In (40), on the other hand, *the winning team* has a future reading, but again the focus is on the end-state, although perhaps not as obviously. For the City Monopoly Trophy to be awarded to a team, the end-state must hold, so the condition for the awarding of the trophy concerns the end-state, not the entire achievement. In (41) on the other hand, the reading is iterative: "the team that wins (regularly)", i.e. an atelic reading.

The atelicity-based analysis can also be applied to examples (39) and (40). Above we saw that according to the binary feature system, achievements are [-stage] and [+telic]. If we change the telicity value, the achievement becomes [-stage] [-telic], i.e. similar to states (i.e. the end-state of the achievement is emphasized). It is important to point out that the end-state need not be realised (see Dahl 1981). Calling a team *the winning team* reflects the way the speaker construes the situation, and this construal may not correspond to the actual state of affairs in the real world. For example, the statement "the team is winning" does not necessarily entail that the team in question will become "the winning team". Consider example (42):

(42) *We were winning the race*, but screwed up the last beat and he got by us for his 6th race win in a row. Ouch.[16]

In (42) the referents are described as in the process of winning the race; for a while they could perhaps be called *the winning team*, but ultimately they did not become *the winning team*.

To summarize, premodifying *ing*-participles do not describe the punctual change-of-state that is inherent in achievements, but they rather focus on the end-state of the achievement or express extended actions (e.g. don't change *a winning team*). As states are always atelic, this can be taken as further support for the atelicity-based explanation offered in this paper.

4. Concluding remarks

In this paper I have discussed the premodifying *ing*-participles in the English language. First, based on the different morphosyntactic behaviour of *ing*-forms like *interesting* and *playing*, I suggested that it makes sense to keep adjectival participles separate from verbal participles. Then, after considering different types of lexical aspect, I suggested that there is a strong tendency for the verbal participles to express atelic eventualities. This claim was backed up by observations from different aspectual categories. For example, naturally atelic descriptions (activities) cannot be made telic in the participle construction (*the mile-running man). Moreover, accomplishment verbs (that can be used to express either accomplishments or activities) tend to favour the atelic reading. For example, no occurrences of *the house-building man* (meaning 'the man is building a house'; telic) can be found in corpora, or even the Internet, whereas *the house-building firm* (meaning 'the firm that builds houses'; atelic) is rather common.

One final word regarding the suggestions made in this paper is in order. All observations are intended to provide support for strong tendencies (like the one on the bounding of activities) or weaker tendencies (like the tendency for accomplishment verbs to be used in descriptions of activities). I find myself in agreement with Rosenbach (2002) and Hundt (2004), who point out that at least some semantic features that are relevant for grammar (such as animacy for the genitive or the progressive constructions, respectively) are "manifested in terms of preferences rather than in grammaticalised distinctions" (Rosenbach 2002: 43). For the corpus linguist, this could mean that certain readings are more frequent for some constructions than others. For the neurolinguist and the psycholinguist, this could imply that constructions with certain meanings are processed more easily than others and they are also evaluated to be "better" by language users. For example, Wagner (2009) found that speakers exhibited prototype effects for different tense/aspect combinations in an experimental setting. In future, it would be very interesting to see whether the atelic prototype suggested here could be further supported using psycholinguistic and neurolinguistic methods.

Notes

1 The origin and authenticity of *Tekhnē Grammatikē* has been subject to debate. Some say that the text is an example of the 2nd century BC Alexandrian thought, while others think that at least parts of the text are later additions (see e.g. Householder 1994).

2 Biber et al. (1999) consider all *ing*-participles adjectives, whereas Huddleston and Pullum (2002) conflate different *ing*-forms into a single category based on their synchronic morphological similarities: the *gerund-participle*.

3 The idea of pre- and postmodifying positions reflecting characteristic and temporary features, respectively, was discussed in detail already by Bolinger (1967).

4 There are certain contexts, such as animal testing, where *drinking* may imply that animals are drinking alcohol, but I think that this needs to be established in prior discourse, as in: *Blood alcohol levels in the drinking monkeys reached around 0.1 to 0.3l.* (http://www.physorg.com/news 194674023.html).

5 Mark Phillips: *The Wizard of Oz Vocabulary Builder*, p. 57. New York: A.J. Cornell Publications (2003).

6 These distributional tests are not foolproof, and words conform to them to a greater or lesser extent; see also e.g. Croft (2007) for a critical discussion of the use of distributional tests.

7 For example: *It's an interesting idea* (BNC: A0U 105); *The playing bondholders were also asked to pay the new extra, voluntary subscription…* (BNC: AMY 909).

8 The asterisk indicates that *playing* here is part of the verb phrase and does not form an independent AP.

9 It seems that *playingly* is somewhat more acceptable than, say, *unplaying*. However, it is a lexicalized adverb and not a result of a regular word-formation process. The relationship between word-pairs *interesting* ~ *interestingly* and *playing* ~ *playingly* is different: *interestingly* ~ 'in an interesting manner'; *playingly* ~ 'in a play*ful* manner'.

10 There are a few exceptions to this; namely participles that are somehow ambiguous between states and achievements (e.g. *awe-inspiring*, *hate-enticing*).

11 An anonymous reviewer pointed out that *two card-playing men* seems more acceptable than *two playing men* and that this could imply that the verb *has to* be accompanied by its verbal argument structure. While I agree with the acceptability judgement, there are instances of prenominal *playing* that occur without verbal complements (see e.g. note 7), which is why I would prefer a more careful wording regarding the occurrence of verbal arguments. In any case, the difference to adjectival participles is clear.

12 There is also a functional class of participles which I discuss in another article (see Vartiainen, in press) that occurs even further to the left in the NPs premodification, i.e. directional participles, such as *coming*, *ensuing*, *following*, forthcoming, *foregoing* etc.

13 From a review by the British author Martin Amis published in the *Guardian* (June 2, 2002): I remember thinking that I was like Josephine, *the opera-singing mouse* in the Kafka story: Sing? "She can't even squeak." http://www.guardian.co.uk/books/2002/jun/01/philosophy.society

14 See e.g. Bod, Hay and Jannedy 2003. *Probabilistic Linguistics*.

15 A sports broadcast where the action is portrayed live may provide a special context for using, say, *the winning team* to describe ongoing action. I thank an anonymous reviewer for this observation.

16 From the blog written by Tim Wadlow and Chris Rast: http://www.search4sailing.com/PNews.php?berichtid=22&spr=deu&Titel=Wadlow/Rast+Olympic+Campaign+Update:+Olympic+Trials+Story.

Corpora

The *Freiburg-LOB Corpus* ('F-LOB') (original version) compiled by Christian Mair, Albert-Ludwigs-Universität Freiburg.

The *British National Corpus*, version 3 (BNC XML Edition). 2007. Distributed by Oxford University Computing Services on behalf of the BNC Consortium. URL: <http://www.natcorp.ox.ac.uk/>

References

Aarts, B. (2007), *Syntactic Gradience. The Nature of Grammatical Indeterminacy*. Oxford: Oxford University Press.

Bach, E. (1986), 'The algebra of events', *Linguistics and Philosophy,* 9: 5-16.

Bache, C. (1978), *The Order of Premodifying Adjectives in Present-day English.* Odense: Odense University Press.

Bennis, H. and P. Wehrmann (1990), 'On the categorial status of present participles', in: R. Bok-Bennema and P. Coopmans (eds.) *Linguistics in the Nederlands 1990*. Dordrecht: Foris. 1-11.

Biber, D., S. Johansson, G. Leech, S. Conrad and E. Finegan (1999), *The Longman Grammar of Spoken and Written English.* London: Longman.

Blevins, J. P. (2005), 'Remarks on gerunds', in: C. O. Orgun and P. Sells (eds.) *Morphology and the Web of Grammar: Essays in Memory of Steven G. Lapointe*. Stanford: CSLI Publications. 25-47.

Bod, R., J. Hay and S. Jannedy (2003), *Probabilistic Linguistics*. Cambridge (Mass.): MIT Press.

Bolinger, D. (1967), 'Adjectives in English: Attribution and predication', *Lingua,* 18: 1-34.

Borer, H. (1990), 'V + *ing*: It walks like an adjective, it talks like an adjective', *Linguistic Inquiry*, 21: 95-103.

Brekke, M. (1988), 'The experiencer constraint', *Linguistic Inquiry*, 19: 169-180.

Bresnan, J. (1996), 'Lexicality and Argument Structure'. Invited paper given at the *Paris Syntax and Semantics Conference*. <http://www.stanford.edu/~bresnan/paris.pdf> Accessed November 30, 2009.

Chomsky, N. (1970), 'Remarks on nominalization', in R. A. Jacobs and P. S. Rosenbaum (eds.) *Readings in English Transformational Grammar*. Waltham: Ginn and Company. 232–286. [Reprinted in *Studies on Semantics in Generative Grammar*, The Hague, Mouton. 1-61.]

Comrie, B. (1976), *Aspect*. Cambridge: Cambridge University Press.

Croft, W. (2007), 'Beyond Aristotle and gradience. A reply to Aarts', *Studies in Language*, 31(2): 409-430.

Dahl, Ö. (1981), 'On the definition of the telic-atelic (bounded-nonbounded) distinction', in: P. J. Tedeschi and A. Zaenen (eds.) *Syntax and Semantics 14: Tense and Aspect*. New York and London: Academic Press. 79-90.

Dowty, D. (1979), *Word Meaning and Montague Grammar. The Semantics of Verbs and Times in Generative Semantics and in Montague's PTQ*. Dordrecht: Reidel.

Haspelmath, M. (1994), 'Passive Participles Across Languages', in: B. Fox and P. J. Hopper (eds.), *Voice: Form and Function*. Typological Studies in Language, 27. Amsterdam: Benjamins. 151-177.

Hengeveld, K. (1992). 'Parts of speech', in: M. Fortescue, P. Harder and L. Kristoffersen (eds.) *Layered Structure and Reference in a Functional Perspective*. Pragmatics and Beyond New Series, 23. Amsterdam: Benjamins. 29-55.

Hengeveld, K., J. Rijkhoff and A. Siewierska (2004), 'Parts-of-speech systems and word order', *Journal of Linguistics*, 40: 527-570.

Householder, F. W. (1994), 'Dionysius Thrax, the Technai, and Sextus Empiricus', in: R. E. Asher and J. M. Y. Simpson (eds.) *The Encyclopedia of Language and Linguistics*. Oxford: Pergamon Press. 931-935.

Huddleston, R. (1985), *Introduction to the Grammar of English*. Cambridge: Cambridge University Press.

Huddleston, R. and G. Pullum (2002), *The Cambridge Grammar of the English Language*. Cambridge: Cambridge University Press.

Hundt, M. (2004), 'Animacy, agentivity, and the spread of the progressive in Modern English', *English Language and Linguistics*, 8(1): 47-69.

Kemp, A. (1987), 'The *Tekhnē Grammatikē* of Dionysius Thrax: English translation with introduction and notes', in: D. J. Taylor (ed.) *The History of Linguistics in the Classical Period*. Studies in the History of the Language Sciences 46. Amsterdam: John Benjamins. 169-190.

Kenny, A. (1963), *Actions, Emotions and Will*. New York: Humanities Press.

Krifka, M. (1989), 'Nominal reference, temporal constitution and quantification in event semantics', in: R. Barsch, J. van Bentham and P. van Emde Boas (eds.) *Semantics and Contextual Expressions*. Dordrecht: Foris. 75-115.

Laczkó, T. (2001), 'Another look at participles and adjectives in the English DP', in: M. Butt and T. Holloway King (eds.) *Proceedings of the LFG01 Conference*. Standord: CSLI Publications. 201-220.

Lakoff, G. (1987), *Women, Fire, and Dangerous Things: What Categories Reveal about the Mind*. Chicago, IL: Chicago University Press.

Lee, S.-A. (2007), '*Ing* forms and the progressive puzzle: A construction-based approach to English progressives', *Journal of Linguistics*, 43: 153-195.

Meltzer, A. (2007), 'The experiencer constraint revisited', in: N. Hilton, R. Arscott, K. Barden, A. Krishna, S. Shah and M. Zellen (eds.) *CamLing 2007*. Cambridge: Cambridge Institute of Language Research. 177-184.

Meltzer, A. (2009), 'Present participles: Categorial classification and derivation', *Lingua*, 120(9): 2095-2318.

Milsark, G. (1988), 'Singl-*ing*', *Linguistic Inquiry*, 19(4): 611-634.

Pullum, G. (1991), 'English nominal gerund phrases as noun phrases with verb-phrase heads', *Linguistics*, 29(5): 763-799.

Pullum, G. and A. Zwicky (1999), 'Gerund participles and head-complement inflection conditions', in: P. Collins and D. Lee (eds.) *The Clause in English. In Honour of Rodney Huddleston*. Amsterdam and Philadelphia: John Benjamins Publishing Company. 251-272.

Quirk, R., S. Greenbaum, G. Leech and J. Svartvik (1972), *A Grammar of Contemporary English*. Harlow: Longman.

Quirk, R., S. Greenbaum, G. Leech and J. Svartvik (1985), *A Comprehensive Grammar of the English Language*. London: Longman.

Rijkhoff, J. (2002), *The Noun Phrase*. Oxford Studies of in Typology and Linguistic Theory. Oxford: Oxford University Press.

Rosenbach, A. (2002), *Genitive Variation in English. Conceptual Factors in Synchronic and Diachronic Studies*. Berlin and New York: Mouton de Gruyter.

Rothstein, S. (2004), *Structuring Events: A Study in the Semantics of Lexical Aspect*. Oxford: Blackwell.

Ryle, G. (1949), *The Concept of Mind*. London: Hutchinson.

Seuren, P. A. M. (1998), *Western Linguistics: An Historical Introduction*. Oxford: Blackwell.

ter Meulen, A. (1995), *Representing Time in Natural Language: The Dynamic Interpretation of Tense and Aspect*. Cambridge, MA: MIT Press.

Van Voorst, J. (1992), 'The aspectual semantics of psychological verbs', *Linguistics and Philosophy*, 15: 65-92.

Vartiainen, T. (in press), 'The proximal and distal perspectives in relation to the position of directional modifiers in the English noun phrase', in: A. Meurman-Solin, M. J. López-Couso and B. Los (eds.) *Information Structure and Syntactic Change in the History of English*. Oxford Studies in the History of English. Oxford: Oxford University Press.

Vendler, Z. (1957), 'Verbs and times', *The Philosophical Review*, 66: 143-160.

Verkuyl, H. J. (1972), *On the Compositional Nature of the Aspects*. Dordrecht: D. Reidel.

Wagner, L. (2009), 'I'll never grow up: Continuity in aspect representations', *Linguistics*, 47(5): 1051-74.

Corpus, coursebook and psycholinguistic evidence on use and concept: The case of category ambiguity

Elaine W. Vine and Paul Warren

Victoria University of Wellington

Abstract

We report on interdisciplinary research which draws on both corpus linguistics and psycholinguistics, using three sorts of data on the use and concept of five high frequency multifunctional words: like, up, down, can *and* will. *First, we present corpus frequency data on the uses of these words in spoken and written English from the British National Corpus and corpora of spoken and written New Zealand English. Second, we present data on how the five words are used in two coursebooks for adult learners of English as a second language.*

*Although the five words differ from each other in their frequency within each corpus, the patterns of occurrence for each word are similar between the British and New Zealand corpora. Furthermore, for four of the words (*up, down, can *and* will*), the category forms which occur more frequently in the corpus data also occur more frequently in the coursebook data. For* like, *however, the corpus data show a clear preference for prepositional usage over verb usage, while the coursebook data indicate that* like *is first introduced to learners as a verb with no discussion of its prepositional usage.*

Third, we present data from a psycholinguistic experiment which gives an insight into naïve native-speaking English users' processing of the five words. The self-paced reading experiment focuses on category ambiguity: verb and preposition uses of like, up *and* down, *and modal and lexical verb uses of* can *and* will. *We found that for* up, down, can *and* will, *the processing preferences are compatible with the corpus and coursebook data. However, for* like, *the preferences are consistent with the corpus data rather than with the coursebook data.*

We argue that, while corpus frequency data and native speaker processing preferences need not be pedagogically prescriptive, they should inform pedagogy.

1. Introduction

Corpus linguistics focuses on how people use language through analysis of large collections of texts, which can be both spoken and written (e.g. Ädel and Reppen 2008; Biber et al. 1998; Connor and Upton 2004; Halliday et al. 2004; Kennedy 1998; Sinclair 2004). Findings from corpus linguistic studies of English language use currently have a certain popularity in English language teaching contexts. A common assumption is that patterns of frequency of use revealed by such studies should be reflected in pedagogical decisions about which language items should be taught and in what order (e.g., Kennedy 2003; Gardner and Davies 2007). We set out in this paper to explore some aspects of how corpus linguistic findings relate to pedagogical uses and to psycholinguistic processing. We conclude by reflecting on the relevance that corpus data on patterns of language use and psycholinguistic data on language processing preferences might have for language coursebook writers and language teachers.

It has been estimated that one in four words of ordinary English text are ambiguous (Whitney 1998: 209). Native speakers of English are rarely aware of this level of ambiguity, which indicates that their processing of ambiguous words is usually efficient and effective. Three main types of lexical ambiguity are between-category homonymy (one word-form occurs with different grammatical uses, e.g. *drill* as a noun or as a verb), within-category homonymy (unrelated words share the same word-form, e.g. *bat* as a flying mammal and as a piece of sports equipment), and polysemy (related senses of a single word, such as *point* as the tip of a blade or as a promontory). Our focus is on the first of these types, which we refer to as category ambiguity. This type of ambiguity allows us to explore the interaction of lexical and sentential information in language processing.

Category-ambiguous words are a key area for the examination of language processing because their comprehension in sentence contexts has implications for both lexical and grammatical knowledge, e.g. frequencies of use of different category exemplars of the homonym as part of lexical knowledge and parsing preferences as part of grammatical knowledge. This is because the interpretation of category-ambiguous words by definition involves grammatical distinctions between their multiple uses, placing them at the intersection between word- and sentence-level processing. The strategies used by native speakers in understanding sentences containing a category-ambiguous word include the rapid and effective assessment of the possible uses of the word against their developing interpretation of the sentence. It is the bringing together of lexical and grammatical knowledge and processing that contributes to successful and efficient sentence comprehension.

In this paper, we report on interdisciplinary research which draws on both corpus linguistics and psycholinguistics. We explore three sorts of data on English speakers' use and processing of five high frequency category-ambiguous words: *like*, *up*, *down*, *can* and *will*.

First, we present corpus frequency data on the uses of these words in spoken and written English from the *British National Corpus* (BNC), the *Wellington Corpus of Spoken New Zealand English* (WCSNZE) and the *Wellington Corpus of Written New Zealand English* (WCWNZE). Data from these native speaker corpora provide baseline information about patterns of use in general English (cf. Biber et al. 1999). Second, we present data on how the five words are used in two coursebooks for teenage and adult learners of English as a second language at beginner and elementary levels (L. Soars and J. Soars 2002, 2006). Data from the two coursebooks provide some indication of the uses of target words that English learners are likely to have met. We examine whether the coursebook patterns of use match those found in the corpora. Third, we present data from a psycholinguistic experiment which gives an insight into naïve English users' processing of the five words. The potentially different patterns of use evidenced in the first and second sources of data contribute to the design and interpretation of our psycholinguistic experiment, and we consider whether people's processing preferences match corpus and coursebook patterns of use for these words. The category ambiguities which the experiment focuses on are: verb and preposition uses of *like*, *up* and *down*, and modal and lexical verb uses of *can* and *will*. The corpus analyses will include further category uses for each of these words as appropriate.

2. Corpus frequencies

Because we are based in New Zealand and use New Zealand English speakers as our native speaker participants in our experimental work, we began with a comparison of frequencies of our focus words (as lemmas) in the WCSNZE, the WCWNZE and the BNC. Very similar patterns of occurrence are evident in the BNC (see Table 1) and the NZE corpora (see Table 2), though the corpora are different in other respects. The BNC has 100 million words (90% written and 10% spoken) and was completed in 1994, while there are one million words in each of the WCSNZE and the WCWNZE, with the spoken corpus collected in 1988-1994 and the written corpus from writings published 1986-1990.

Table 1. BNC* – Spoken and Written (per 10,000 words)

Lemma	*will*	*can*	*like*	*up*	*down*
Spoken	52	37	39	32	17
Written	31	22	14	17	9
Average of Spoken and Written	42	30	27	25	13

* Calculated from Kilgarriff (1995-6)

Table 2. WCSNZE and WCWNZE – (per 10,000 words)

Lemma	*will*	*can*	*like*	*up*	*down*
Spoken	42	39	53	44	19
Written	26	23	17	24	10
Average of Spoken and Written	34	31	35	34	15

Since the patterns of usage in the BNC and NZE corpora are somewhat similar, in the following analysis we will present data only from the BNC to simplify the reporting. As the larger corpus, the BNC is more likely to be representative of general patterns. We will also report data from the BNC as a whole (i.e. the whole BNC, 90% written and 10% spoken, not the average of the two), because although there are differences between the spoken and written parts of the BNC, we are going to compare with data from English language teaching coursebooks, which include both spoken and written texts.

In the BNC, modal uses of *can* and *will* occur far more frequently than noun and verb uses, as shown in Table 3. We address the category ambiguity between modal and verb uses in our psycholinguistic experiment.

Table 3. Frequency of *can* and *will* in the BNC (per 10,000 words)

	modal	noun	verb
can	23	0.16	0.08
will	32	0.88	0.14

Preposition uses of *down, up* and *like* occur far more frequently than verb uses. We have highlighted these uses in Table 4, because we address the category ambiguity between preposition and verb in our experiment. It should be noted, though, that for *up* and *down*, adverbial uses (which account for most of the 'other' category) occur more frequently than either preposition or verb uses. A more diverse range of uses is included in the 'other' category for *like*.

Table 4. Frequency of *down, up* and *like* in the BNC (per 10,000 words)

	preposition	verb	other
down	1	0.02	8
up	2	0.02	17
like	11	4	1

3. Coursebook frequencies

We have also identified all uses of the five focus words in two ESL coursebooks: the Beginner (NHB) and Elementary (NHE) student's books (L. Soars & J. Soars 2002, 2006) in the *New Headway* series. We chose this series because, while it is published in England, it is widely used in New Zealand. The total number of words in NHB is 33,773 and in NHE the total is 57,443. All sections of the books have been included in the total counts. The five focus words are listed in Table 5 in order of their overall frequencies in the BNC.

Table 5. Frequency of *can, will, down, up* and *like* in BNC and NHB and NHE (per 10,000 words)

	BNC	NHB	NHE
will	33	0	4
can	24	66	52
up	19	21	10
like	16	75	50
down	10	2	3

The frequencies (see Table 5) are similar in the two coursebooks: *can* and *like* occur most frequently, followed by *up* and then by *will* and *down*. However, the frequency order in the BNC is different from in the coursebooks: *will* occurs most frequently, followed by *can*, *up*, *like* and *down*. Also, the frequencies for *can* and *like* in the coursebooks are very much higher than in the BNC.

We have analysed how each occurrence of each word is used grammatically in its context. We have seen above that the coursebooks are inconsistent with corpus frequencies in that they use *can* much more frequently than *will*, whereas in the BNC the reverse is the case. However, as shown in Table 6, the coursebooks show greater consistency with corpus frequencies in the relative category frequencies of *can* and *will*. Both occur overwhelmingly more frequently in both corpora as modals than as nouns or lexical verbs.

Table 6. Grammatical uses of *can* and *will* in NHB, NHE and BNC

	modal	noun	verb
can NHB+NHE	100%	-	-
can BNC	99%	0.7%	0.3%
will NHE	100%	-	-
will BNC	97%	3%	0.4%

By contrast, in the case of *down* and *up*, the coursebooks are consistent with corpus frequencies in that they use *up* more frequently than *down*, and they use both *up* and *down* more often as an adverb than as a preposition, except that NHB uses *down* only as a preposition (see Table 7). All six instances are in the context of giving directions: *Go down ... Road.* Also in NHB most uses of *up* are in the phrasal verb *get up* and the other few are *stand up*.

Table 7. Grammatical uses of *down* and *up* in NHB, NHE and BNC

		preposition	verb	adverb
down	NHB	100%	-	-
	NHE	33%	-	67%
	BNC	10%	0.2%	87%
up	NHB	-	-	100%
	NHE	15%	-	85%
	BNC	8%	0.1%	91%

The case of *like* is different again (see Table 8). The coursebooks are inconsistent with BNC frequencies in that they use *like* exclusively (NHB) or much more frequently (NHE) as a verb than as a preposition. Interestingly, although *like* is sometimes used as a preposition in the NHE units, it is only presented as a verb in the word list and grammar reference sections of the book.

Table 8. Grammatical uses of *like* in NHB, NHE and BNC

	preposition	verb	other
NHB	-	100%	-
NHE	7%	92%	1%
BNC	67%	26%	7%

For four of the words we have studied (*up, down, can* and *will*), the category forms which occur more frequently in the corpus data also occur more frequently in the coursebook data. For *like*, however, the corpus data show a clear preference for prepositional usage ("I'm very interested that words *like* gestapo are suddenly coming into this business", WCSNZE, Recording dgi070) over verb usage ("that's one of the reasons that I *like* them yeah", WCSNZE, Recording dpc265), and yet the coursebook data – along with anecdotal evidence from language teachers – indicate that *like* is first introduced to learners as a verb with no discussion of its prepositional usage.

Our claim is not necessarily that coursebook usage patterns, or indeed pedagogical practice, should follow corpus frequency patterns, but it is interesting to notice that sometimes they do (at least to some extent) and sometimes they do not.

4. Psycholinguistic experiment

As noted above, analyses of corpora and of coursebook material show both similarities and differences in the category distributions of category-ambiguous words. Our concern in this section is whether native speaker processing preferences will be likely to reflect the frequencies of use found in general corpora, rather than those found in coursebooks or favoured by teachers. The comparison of *like* with the other words in our small set of category-ambiguous words allows us to test this hypothesis, since the corpus and coursebook analyses differed most strongly for this item. To test this hypothesis we designed a psycholinguistic experiment that reveals native English users' preferred category interpretation for each of the five words in ambiguous contexts.

Much research in psycholinguistics focuses on how people process language through experiments that aim to reveal their cognitive processes. Experiments using psycholinguistic techniques allow controlled study of the knowledge and processes being applied to language comprehension. Previous psycholinguistic research has shown that native-speaker listeners and readers achieve efficiency in processing category-ambiguous words through the rapid assessment of how well the different uses of the words fit the sentence context, leading to the selection of the most appropriate candidate category. Relevant lexical information that contributes to this selection process includes the range of the different uses of category-ambiguous words (e.g. *lift* as a noun or verb), as well as the frequencies with which these uses are encountered by language users (e.g. according to one corpus analysis (Kilgarriff 1995-1996), *lift* occurs almost three times more frequently as a verb than as a noun) (Elston-Güttler and Friederici 2005; Gibson 2006; Tanenhaus et al. 1979). However, views differ over whether this selection is immediate (Schwaneveldt et al. 1976; Simpson 1994) or delayed (Seidenberg et al. 1982; Swinney 1979), and over the precise role played in this process by differences in the frequency of the uses of category-ambiguous words (Duffy et al. 1988; Tabossi and Zardon 1993).

To examine what preferences native speakers of English have for the use of our five focus category-ambiguous words, we ran a self-paced reading experiment in which participants read word-by-word presentations of sentences containing a focus word. The words in the sentence were presented one at a time on a computer screen. At the onset of each sentence presentation, the sentence was presented as sets of dashes, one set for each word, with as many dashes as there were letters in the word and with spaces between each set of dashes. Each word was then presented in turn in its appropriate position, replacing the dashes for that word. As each new word was presented the preceding one was replaced again by a set of dashes. The task was self-paced because participants pressed a response time button to trigger the presentation of the next word. The time taken to press the key was recorded, and is interpreted as a measure of the reading time required for processing the word presented immediately before that key press. Preferences for how the category-ambiguous words are processed in the context of the sentences are reflected in the reading times – the dispreferred interpretation of the words results in garden path or misanalysis experiences, revealed by increases in reading time for words following the category-ambiguous word, once the intended meaning becomes clear. A comprehension question was presented at the end of each sentence to ensure that participants did actually process the sentences.

The participants in the self-paced reading experiment were 40 young adult native speakers of New Zealand English. The experimental materials for the experiment included 25 sentence sets with category-ambiguous words. There were five sentence sets for each of the category ambiguities comparing preposition and verb uses of *like*, *down* and *up*, and five for each of the ambiguities comparing modal and lexical verb uses of *can* and *will*. Within each set the crucial comparison is of a pair of sentences where either category is compatible with the sentence up to and including the category-ambiguous word. The appropriate category is then revealed by subsequent words in the sentence. The examples in (1a) and (1b) illustrate such sentences for *like*, as a preposition and verb respectively, and in (2a) and (2b) for *can*, as modal and lexical verb respectively:

(1a) Jack said that people *like* Marty take such good photographs
(1b) Jack said that people *like* Marty taking such good photographs
(2a) I want to find out whether they *can* work in that factory
(2b) I want to find out whether they *can* beans in that factory

Note that the focus words are presented in italics in the above examples, but they were not in italics in the experiment presentation. Also, in the experiment, the conditions were rotated across item lists, so that participants saw any one item in one condition only.

For analysis, each participant's reading times were normalised for word length, using a regression analysis of reading time against word lengths across all materials (including a large set of filler materials with different syntactic properties from the test materials). So, for instance, the actual reading time for an example of 'people' would be adjusted relative to the predicted reading time for all 6-letter words for that participant across all materials. The predicted time comes from a best-fit regression of reading time against word lengths for that participant, and the adjusted time is the residual reading time, i.e. the difference between the predicted and the actual reading times.

We compared participants' preferences for the interpretation of category-ambiguous words as revealed by the experiment with the interpretations expected on the basis of the corpus data reported above and with the coursebook data reported above. Figure 1 shows the results for *can* and *will* from the self-paced reading experiment. It reveals a significant difference between residual reading times for the modal and lexical verb versions of the sentences at all word positions **after** the ambiguous word. The difference shows up most strongly two words after the ambiguous word, and it indicates that the main verb reading is dispreferred. This finding is in accordance with the corpus and coursebook frequency findings reported above.

Note though that the main impact of this difference occurs not immediately after the category-ambiguous word (i.e. on *work* vs. *beans* in the example given in the figure) but at the point marked as amb + 2, i.e. two words after the ambiguous word. We believe that this intriguing result can be explained as follows. Sentence comprehension involves two sets of processes: bottom-up processes used in recognising words on the basis of their form (in this case the letter string), and top-down processes involved in integrating words into the sentence structure being developed as part of the interpretation of the sentence. During fast and efficient reading the recognition of a word can run ahead of its integration into the sentence context. It is only after a certain delay, then, that any comprehension difficulty arises. This shows up in the greater increase in reading times in the dispreferred lexical verb interpretation of the *can* and *will* sentences at point amb + 2 than at point amb + 1, though the separation of the standard error bars at both points in Figure 1 (as well as at later points in the sentence) reflects the fact that the difference is significant from immediately after the ambiguous word.

The results for *up* and *down* (see Figure 2) are similar to those for *can* and *will*, with a significant increase in reading times at the first two word positions <u>after</u> the ambiguous region for sentences in which the verb use of the ambiguous word is intended compared to those in which the preposition use is intended. The difference again shows up most strongly two words after the ambiguous region. The finding that the verb reading is dispreferred is also in accordance with the corpus and coursebook frequency findings reported above.

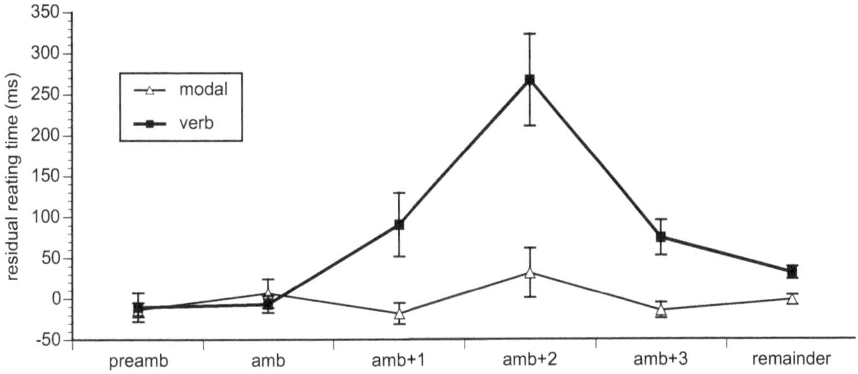

e.g.						
modal	… they	can	work	in	that	factory
verb	… they	can	beans	in	that	factory

Figure 1. Residual reading times (in milliseconds, with standard error bars) at key points during self-paced reading of sentences containing the category-ambiguous words *can* and *will*, involving modal vs. lexical verb ambiguity (as in the examples below the figure).

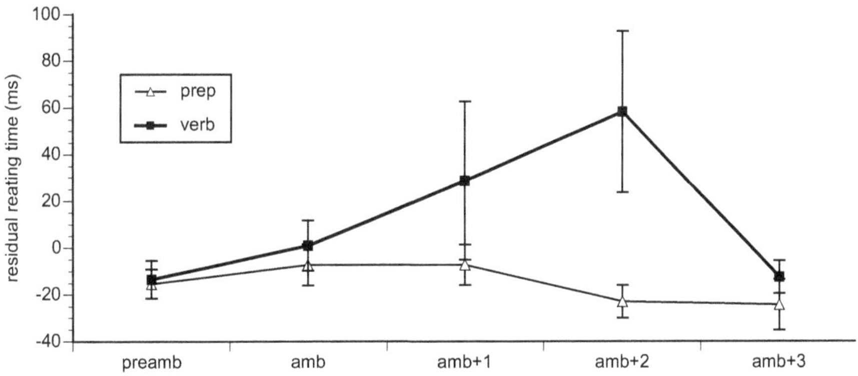

e.g.					
prep	… saw John	down the	road	and	called ….
verb	… saw John	down the	beer	and	called ….

Figure 2. Residual reading times (in milliseconds, with standard error bars) at key points during self-paced reading of sentences containing the category-ambiguous words *down* and *up*, involving preposition vs. verb ambiguity (as in the examples below the figure).

The results for *like* (Figure 3) are similar, in that one reading is dispreferred, in this case, the verb reading. However, unlike the other four words, the increase in reading times only occurs two words after the ambiguous region, i.e. there is no effect at position amb + 1. Also unlike the other four words, the finding is in accordance with the corpus frequency findings but not the coursebook findings.

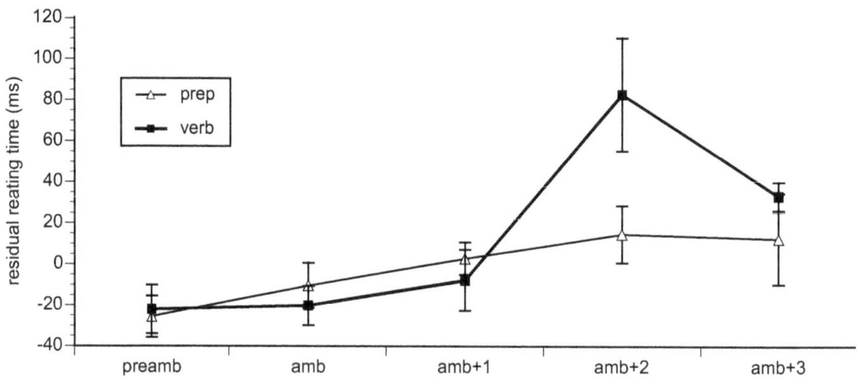

e.g.					
prep	… people	like Marty	take	such	good …
verb	… people	like Marty	taking	such	good …

Figure 3. Residual reading times (in milliseconds, with standard error bars) at key points during self-paced reading of sentences containing the category-ambiguous word *like*, involving preposition vs. verb ambiguity (as in the examples below the figure).

To sum up, for *up*, *down*, *can* and *will*, the results are clear and participants' processing preferences are compatible with both corpus and coursebook data. For *like*, the results are less clear-cut. The difference between frequencies of the preposition and verb uses in general English corpora is smaller than for the other words. However, the coursebook data show a much higher frequency for the verb use than the preposition use, which is in the opposite direction to the general corpus data. Furthermore, in temporarily ambiguous contexts such as "John said that people *like* Marty {take/taking} such good photographs", native speakers' preferences are consistent with the general corpus data rather than with the coursebook data.

5. Concluding comments

Corpus frequency data and native speaker processing preferences need not be pedagogically prescriptive, but we would argue that they should inform pedagogy. Coursebook writers and language teachers should be informed about the issues raised by the findings we have presented, so that if they choose not to be guided by corpus frequency data or language processing preferences, they do so in a principled way, not out of ignorance.

The NHB coursebook directly teaches and gives learners extensive practice of verb structures such as (3a), (3b), (3c) and (4a), (4b):

(3a) I *like* pizza (p. 33)
(3b) I don't *like* football (p. 33)
(3c) Do you *like* dogs? (p. 51)
(4a) I'd *like* a cup of coffee (p. 89)
(4b) I'd *like* to go to Turkey. (p. 91)

The NHE coursebook provides further practice of these verb structures. The target learners for the New Headway series are adults, and the books are also used in secondary schools, yet the sentence contexts for these verb uses of *like* do not, in our view, represent intellectually engaging material.

In NHE reading passages, learners also encounter sentences with preposition uses of *like*, such as (5) - (8).

(5) There are more houses *like* this in the south of France. (p. 41)
(6) The windows are *like* eyes. (p. 41)
(7) They try to move *like* cats. (p. 95)
(8) *Like* many big cities, London has problems with traffic and pollution. (p. 121)

However, these prepositional structures are not directly taught. These are not very complex structures, but they do present content that is more adult than food and other preferences. Why not teach *like* as a preposition early? *Like* as a preposition occurs very frequently in corpus data because people make all sorts of interesting comparisons when they talk and write. Language learners could too.

Our results have shown that for native speakers of English, relative frequency of occurrence (as indicated by general English corpus findings) predicts processing preferences for our focus words. However, we would not want to argue that relative frequency of occurrence is the only factor that contributes to processing preferences for native speakers, or for non-native speakers.

We are currently extending our research to include a wider range of category-ambiguous words, to explore whether our findings for these five focus words occur more widely. We are also extending our research to include non-native speakers of English, to explore whether native and non-native speakers of English process such words in the same way, and whether non-native speakers process them in the same way at different levels of proficiency in English. We predict that the familiarity that learners of English have with category-ambiguous words and with the possible sentence structures containing these words will influence the extent to which they process sentences effectively in the ways that native speakers do. If for example a learner has only encountered a word such as *like* in contexts where it is used as a verb, then this learner will have difficulty interpreting a sentence such as *People like John are very helpful.* If, however, they are familiar with *like* as both a verb and as a preposition, then we might expect to find an impact on their interpretation of this word from the likely structural interpretation at the point at which this word is encountered. There is evidence that, at least for native speakers, the interpretation of a category ambiguous word is dependent on a complex interplay of the frequency of use of that word in its particular categories and its likelihood in each category at a particular point in a sentence (e.g. Gibson 2006). We might therefore expect that if a learner is familiar with both the verb and preposition uses of *like*, but their immediate grammatical expectation, based on their experience of relevant structures, is that a word in the second position in a sentence will be a verb, then they will also fail to interpret the sentence *People like John are very helpful* efficiently, but for a different reason. Our extended research should shed some light on these issues.

Note

1 We thank Victoria University of Wellington for financial support, Anna Piasecki for her assistance in running our psycholinguistic experiment, and audiences in the School of Linguistics and Applied Language Studies seminar series, the Linguistic Society of New Zealand, and ICAME 2009 for their feedback on our research.

Corpora

British National Corpus (BNC XML Edition) (2007), Oxford University Computing Services.

Wellington Corpus of Spoken New Zealand English (1998), Victoria University of Wellington

Wellington Corpus of Written New Zealand English (1993), Victoria University of Wellington.

References

Ädel, A. and R. Reppen (2008), *Corpora and Discourse: The Challenges of Different Settings*. Amsterdam and Philadelphia: John Benjamins.

Biber, D., S. Conrad and R. Reppen (1998), *Corpus Linguistics: Investigating Language Structure and Use*. Cambridge: Cambridge University Press.

Biber, D., S. Johanssson, G. Leech, S. Conrad and E. Finegan (1999), *Longman Grammar of Spoken and Written English*. New York: Longman.

Connor, U. and T. A. Upton (2004). *Applied Corpus Linguistics. A Multidimensional Perspective*. Amsterdam: Rodopi.

Duffy, S. A., R. K. Morris and K. Rayner (1988), 'Lexical ambiguity and fixation times in reading', *Journal of Memory and Language,* 27: 429-446.

Elston-Güttler, K. E. and A. D. Friederici (2005), 'Native and L2 processing of homonyms in sentential context', *Journal of Memory and Language,* 52(2): 256-283.

Gardner, D. and M. Davies (2007), 'Pointing out frequent phrasal verbs: A Corpus-based analysis', *TESOL Quarterly,* 41(2): 339-359.

Gibson, E. (2006), 'The interaction of top-down and bottom-up statistics in the resolution of syntactic category ambiguity', *Journal of Memory and Language,* 54: 363-388.

Halliday, M. A. K., W. Teubert, C. Yallop and A. Cermakova (2004), *Lexicology and Corpus Linguistics: An Introduction.* London and New York: Continuum.

Kennedy, G. (1998), *An Introduction to Corpus Linguistics*. London; New York: Longman.

Kennedy, G. (2003), *Structure and Meaning in English: A Guide for Teachers.* Harlow: Pearson/Longman.

Kilgarriff, A. (1995-1996), *BNC Database and Word Frequency Lists.* <http://www.kilgarriff.co.uk/bnc-readme.html>, accessed 18th May 2009.

Schwaneveldt, R. W., D. E. Meyer and C. A. Becker (1976), 'Lexical ambiguity, semantic context, and visual word recognition', *Journal of Experimental Psychology,* 2: 243-256.

Seidenberg, M., M. K. Tanenhaus, J. M. Leiman and M. Bienkowski (1982), 'Automatic access of the meanings of ambiguous words in context: Some limitations of knowledge-based processing', *Cognitive Psychology,* 14: 489-537.

Simpson, G. B. (1994), 'Context and the processing of ambiguous words', in: M. A. Gernsbacher (ed.) *Handbook of Psycholinguistics.* New York: Academic Press. 359-374.

Sinclair, J. (2004), *Trust the Text: Language Corpus and Discourse*. London and New York: Routledge.

Soars, L. and Soars, J. (2002), *New Headway Beginner Student's Book.* Oxford: Oxford University Press.

Soars, L. and Soars, J. (2006), *New Headway Elementary Student's Book* (3rd edition). Oxford: Oxford University Press.

Swinney, D.A. (1979), 'Lexical access during sentence comprehension: (Re)consideration of context effects', *Journal of Verbal Learning and Verbal Behavior,* 18: 645-659.

Tabossi, P. and F. Zardon (1993), 'Processing ambiguous words in context', *Journal of Memory and Language,* 32: 359-372.

Tanenhaus, M. K., J. M. Leiman and M. S. Seidenberg (1979), 'Evidence for multiple stages in the processing of ambiguous words in syntactic contexts', *Journal of Verbal Learning and Verbal Behavior,* 18: 427-440.

Whitney, P. (1998), *The Psychology of Language*. Boston: Houghton Mifflin.

Highly polysemous verbs in New Englishes: A corpus-based pilot study of Sri Lankan and Indian English

Janina Werner and Joybrato Mukherjee

Justus Liebig University, Giessen

Abstract

The analysis of New Englishes has spawned a vast amount of literature over the past few decades. Linguistic research into new postcolonial Englishes extends to aspects of both structural nativization at all linguistic levels (i.e. the emergence of local forms and structures of English) and language functions as well as speaker attitudes. Within the area of structural nativization, processes of semantic acculturations of the English language to new socio-cultural contexts have also been described, including, for example, meaning shifts of individual lexical items (cf. Nihalani et al. 2004) and the emergence of culturally motivated collocational patterns (cf. e.g. Ooi 2000). What has so far been neglected, however, is a corpus-based and quantitative approach to gradual changes in meaning preferences of polysemous lexical items. Inspired by Gilquin's (2008) innovative approach to highly polysemous high-frequency verbs in American English, the present paper reports on the results of a comparative corpus-based pilot study of the two verbs give *and* take *in two New Englishes, i.e. Indian English and Sri Lankan English, and their historical input variety, i.e. British English.*

1. Introduction

Corpus linguistics has shown on the basis of a wide range of authentic language data that lexical items are variable in meaning and that much of their meaning depends on the actual context and the routinized patterns in which they are used. This converges with the cognitive-linguistic assumption that polysemy of lexical items is central rather than peripheral to the description of meaning. As Langacker (2008) puts it:

> A lexical item used with any frequency is almost invariably polysemous: it has multiple, related meanings that have all been conventionalized to some degree. Among these related senses, some are more central, or prototypical, than others [...]. (Langacker 2008: 37)

A particularly suitable framework for the description of polysemy, also in the sense of relations between more central and more peripheral meanings of a given lexical item, is provided by prototype theory. Inspired, for example, by the seminal work by Rosch and Mervis (1975), there have been various attempts at modelling the prototypicality of linguistic categories over the past decades.

Generally speaking, when the prototypicality of polysemous words is described, the word as such is the cognitive category and the various meanings can be seen as its semantic members. The concept of prototypicality has often been applied to account for the categorization of the various meanings of one and the same word in different contexts. Goldberg (1995: 75), for example, posits polysemy links between "a particular sense of a construction and any extension from this sense". Geeraerts (1989 [2006]) describes the overall advantage of prototypicality-driven models for the analysis of polysemous words as follows:

> [L]inguists developed a valid model for the polysemy of lexical items. This is perhaps the single most appealing characteristic of prototype theory: here at last is a descriptive approach to lexical meaning in which our pretheoretical intuitions about gradedness, fuzziness, flexibility, clustering of senses etc. receive due attention. (Geeraerts 1989 [2006]: 144)

In the present paper, the intention is to establish a link between a prototype-theoretical categorization of the various meanings of high-frequency verbs and the corpus-based description of the frequencies of the individual meanings in actual language use: our overall focus is thus on the relationship between the cognitive salience and the frequency of the meanings of polysemous verbs. The term 'prototype' has been applied both to highly salient exemplars of a category and to very frequent items in language use. Our interest is in the description of quantitative differences between varieties of English. In fact, in the description of lexico-semantic differences between Old and New Englishes, the focus so far has been on processes of semantic widening, narrowing and shift (e.g. the use of *boy* for 'male servant' in South Asian Englishes), whereas the analysis of differences in the use of polysemous words has so far been widely neglected. In this paper, we will present findings from a comparative analysis of the high-frequency verbs *give* and *take* in comparable corpora of South Asian Englishes, i.e. ICE-India and ICE-Sri Lanka, and their historical input variety, i.e. ICE-GB.

In what follows, the descriptive apparatus for our analysis and the corpus data will be described in more detail (Section 2). Thereafter, the findings will be presented and the extent to which the varieties under scrutiny display similar patternings and to what extent they are different will be discussed (Section 3). Finally, some concluding remarks and avenues for future research into polysemy in varieties of English will be offered (Section 4).

2. Descriptive apparatus and corpus data

In a very innovative paper, Gilquin (2008) analyses the use of *give* and *take* in two datasets:

- online sentence production experiments, which were intended to shed light on the cognitive salience of individual meanings (indicating cognitive prototypicality);
- corpus analyses of American English data, which were conducted in order to establish which meanings of the two verbs are more frequent and which are less (referring to frequency-based prototypicality).

Gilquin's (2008) study provides new insights into the relation – and discrepancies – between salience and frequency as two different kinds of prototypicality. She writes:

> While salience and frequency are different in nature [...], very often the unspoken assumption is that these two definitions of prototypicality coincide with one another, in other words, that the most salient exemplar in the mind is also the most frequent one in language [...]. Yet, several recent studies have demonstrated that the link between salience and frequency is not so obvious and that the two do not necessarily point in the same direction when it comes to language. (Gilquin 2008: 238)

Gilquin's (2008) own study adds to the growing body of evidence against a simple and straight-forward correlation between cognitive salience and frequency in language use. In her study, Gilquin (2008) distinguishes between 14 senses of *give*, which are listed and exemplified in Table 1. Additionally, there is a 15th category named OTHER, which contains the meanings that could not be suitably assigned to any of the other categories.

Table 1. Semantic classification of *give* (cf. Gilquin 2008: 243)

	Sense	Example
1	HAND	*He pulled a handkerchief from his pocket and **gave** it to him.*
2	PROVIDE	*Please **give** your seat to an elderly or disabled.*
3	COMMUNICATE	*Would you like to **give** me your name?*
4	CAUSE	*All that drinking has **given** me a headache.*
5	DO (DELEXICAL SENSE)	*He turned to us and **gave** a big smile.*
6	USE	***Give** your time to the community.*
7	ADMINISTER	*Can't you **give** her anything for the pain?*
8	ALLOW	*The draft would **give** him the power to appoint the bank's chairman.*
9	JOB	*My algebra teacher always **gives** us a lot of homework.*
10	ORGANIZE	*The ambassador is **giving** a banquet for the visiting president.*

Table 1 (cont.). Semantic classification of *give* (cf. Gilquin 2008: 243)

	Sense	Example
11	NO LONGER RESIST PRESSURE	*The branch suddenly **gave** beneath him.*
12	DECIDE	*The judge **gave** him a nine-month suspended sentence.*
13	IDIOMS	*You have to **give** way to traffic coming from the right.*
14	PHRASAL VERBS	*We're going to **give** up our sports club membership after this year.*
15	OTHER	

Table 2 shows the 17 senses of *take* that Gilquin (2008) distinguishes and gives examples for each category. Again, there are some cases that have to be subsumed under OTHER.

Table 2. Semantic classification of *take* (cf. Gilquin 2008: 243)

	Sense	Example
1	GRAB	*Let me **take** your coats.*
2	MOVE	*Our guide **took** us around the cathedral.*
3	BUY	*What newspaper do you **take**?*
4	INGEST	***Take** two aspirins and go to bed.*
5	REQUIRE	*It **takes** strength and stamina to be a long-distance runner.*
6	DO (DELEXICAL SENSE)	*Let's **take** a walk down the river.*
7	RECORD	*A nurse **took** his temperature every hour.*
8	ENGAGE IN	*Shelley is **taking** economics at university.*
9	CONSIDER	*She **took** his remarks as a compliment.*
10	ACCEPT	*Do they **take** credit cards in this shop?*
11	ASSUME	*I did all the work, but Gill **took** all the credit.*
12	EXPERIENCE	*The school **took** the full force of the explosion.*
13	USE	*It's more interesting to **take** the coast road.*
14	CAPTURE	*The rebels succeeded in **taking** the town.*
15	WORK	*If the cortisone doesn't **take**, I may have to have surgery.*
16	IDIOMS	*The Olympics **take** place every four years.*
17	PHRASAL VERBS	*The plane should **take** off on time.*
18	OTHER	

Tables 1 and 2 are in line with Gilquin's (2008) attempt at systematizing the prototypicality of the meanings of *give* and *take*. The semantic classification of the two verbs was based on five learner's dictionaries: *Oxford Advanced Learner's Dictionary* (Wehmeier 2000), *Collins Cobuild English Dictionary for Advanced Learners* (Sinclair 2001), *Longman Dictionary of Contemporary English* (Summers 2001), *Macmillan English Dictionary for Advanced Learners* (Rundell 2002) and *Cambridge Advanced Learner's Dictionary* (Gillard 2003). The order of senses reflects the decreasing degree of prototypicality, that is, the sense HAND is the most prototypical sense of the verb *give*, whereas the sense DECIDE is the least prototypical.

While Gilquin's (2008) focus is on the comparison of experimental data and corpus findings, the primary interest of the present paper lies in describing quantitative differences between the postcolonial varieties of Indian and Sri Lankan English and their historical input variety of British English with regard to the frequencies of the individual meanings of *give* and *take*. Nevertheless, Gilquin's (2008) semantic classifications of *give* and *take* in American English as shown in Tables 1 and 2 will be used as the descriptive apparatus for this study.

The corpus data used in the analysis have been taken from the three ICE corpora ICE-GB, ICE-India and ICE-Sri Lanka. ICE-Sri Lanka is being compiled at the time of writing and, for the present study, a pilot corpus with 115 written texts, i.e. almost 60% of the final version of the written component was used. The same number of texts from the same text categories of ICE-GB and ICE India were chosen as comparable corpora representing the major neighbouring variety in the region (i.e. Indian English) and the historical input variety (i.e. British English). The design of the two ICE [W 115] corpora is shown in Table 3:[1]

Table 3. Design of ICE [W 115]

Text ID	Text category	Finalised	Size (words)
W1B-001 to 004	*Social letters*	4/15	c. 8,000
W1B-016 to 029	*Business letters*	14/15	c. 28,000
W2A-011 to 017	*Informational (learned) social science*	7/10	c. 14,000
W2A-021 to 025	*Informational (learned) natural science*	5/10	c. 10,000
W2A-031	*Informational (learned) technology*	1/10	c. 2,000
W2B-001, 003 to 009	*Informational (popular) humanities*	8/10	c. 16,000
W2B-011 to 014	*Informational (popular) social science*	4/10	c. 8,000
W2B-021	*Informational (popular) natural science*	1/10	c. 2,000

Table 3 (cont.). Design of ICE [W 115]

Text ID	Text category	Finalised	Size (words)
W2B-031 to 032	*Informational (popular) technology*	2/10	c. 4,000
W2C-001 to 020	*Informational (reportage) press/news reports*	20/20	c. 40,000
W2D-001 to 010	*Instructional administrative*	10/10	c. 20,000
W2D-011 to 019	*Instructional skills/hobbies*	9/10	c. 18,000
W2E-001 to 010	*Persuasive (press editorials)*	10/10	c. 20,000
W2F-001 to 020	*Creative (novels/short stories)*	20/20	c. 40,000
Total		**115 texts**	**c. 230,000**

3. Corpus findings and discussion

As already mentioned, Gilquin (2008) undertook an online sentence production experiment in order to test the cognitive salience of the individual meanings of the two verbs *give* and *take*. The experimental data showed, for example, that in 42 per cent of the cases, *give* was used with the sense TO HAND, i.e. the most prototypical meaning of *give*. However, as shown in Figure 1, this is by far not the most frequent meaning of *give* in the corpus data. Findings like these – both for *give* and *take* – lead Gilquin (2008) to conclude that frequency in language use and cognitive saliency do not always converge.

In the present study, the corpus-based aspect of Gilquin's (2008) analysis is extended to the analysis of intervarietal differences in the use of high-frequency polysemous verbs. More specifically, the paper reports on quantitative differences between Sri Lankan, Indian and British English with regard to the frequencies of the individual meanings of the verbs *give* and *take*.

The analysis of the corpus data was undertaken by going through each occurrence of the two verbs and assigning it to one of the semantic categories listed in Tables 1 and 2. The categorizations were checked and corroborated by a native speaker. In the manual categorization of the findings from the three ICE corpora, it turned out to be advisable, however, to add another category in the case of *give*, namely the DONATE/PRESENT category. It was difficult to assign sentences with this particular meaning to any of the other categories. For example, if somebody *gives* a present to somebody else, they may at the same time HAND it to the person and they also PROVIDE the person with the present. But they do more than that: they provide it as a gift, i.e. they DONATE it. Thus, a new category was added – see Table 4.

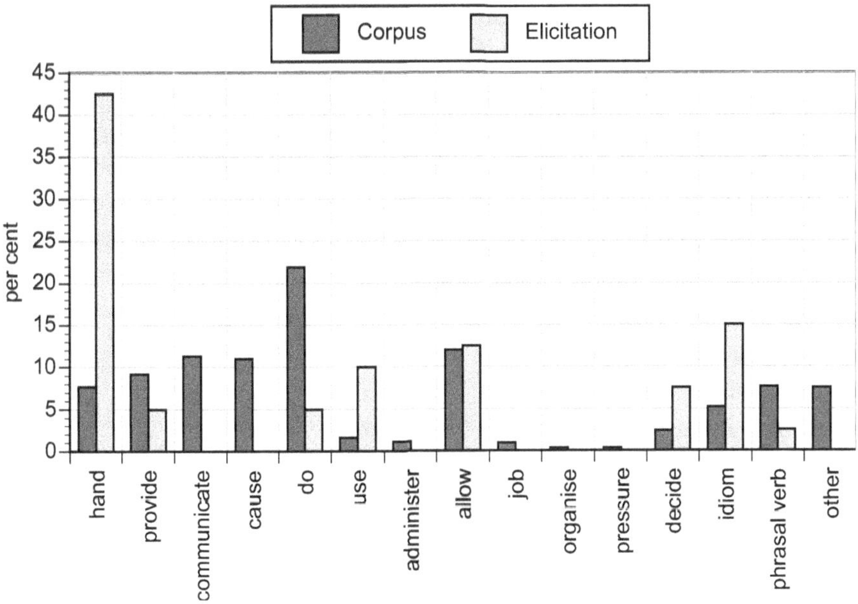

Figure 1. Distribution of the senses of give in corpus and elicitation data (per cent) (Gilquin 2008: 245)

Table 4. Meanings of *give* (extension of Table 1)

	Sense	Example
16	DONATE/PRESENT	*Thank you for the table cloth you* ***gave*** *us for our wedding.*

Comparing the findings of the verb *give* in the three corpora, one can see statistically significant distributional differences between all three varieties. If we focus on individual semantic categories, however, we find that in most cases two of the varieties seem more similar to each other frequency-wise, while the third one stands out. This is the case, for example, in the categories HAND, CAUSE and ALLOW, cf. Table 5. This observation, however, does not follow a distinct pattern; sometimes British English is markedly different from the two ESL varieties, while in other cases, Sri Lankan English or Indian English are closer to British English and diverge from the other ESL variety. These findings thus confirm what has already been described with regard to lexicogrammatical routines such as light-verb constructions across South Asian Englishes (cf. Hoffmann et al. in press), namely that South Asian Englishes are not a homogeneous group of varieties and that in some regards individual South Asian Englishes seem to be more different from neighbouring varieties than from British English.

Table 5. Frequencies of the meanings of *give* in ICE-GB [W 115], ICE-SL [W 115] and ICE-India [W 115]

		Frequencies (per 230,000 words)		
		GB (n=320)	Sri Lanka (n=312)	India (n=326)
1	HAND	8.10	9.27	36.16
2	PROVIDE	76.45	63.34	67.28
3	COMMUNICATE	18.88	20.86	15.96
4	CAUSE	17.99	10.81	18.49
5	DO (DELEXICAL SENSE)	48.58	16.22	51.29
6	USE	2.69	3.08	9.25
7	ADMINISTER	17.09	33.99	14.28
8	ALLOW	42.27	25.48	26.06
9	JOB	5.38	2.30	1.68
10	ORGANIZE	5.38	0.76	1.68
11	NO LONGER RESIST PRESSURE	0.00	0.00	0.00
12	DECIDE	9.89	19.30	5.04
13	IDIOMS	11.68	18.54	10.93
14	PHRASAL VERBS	17.99	15.43	9.25
15	OTHER	0.90	0.76	0.00
16	TO DONATE/TO PRESENT	13.48	0.76	6.72

(ICE-SL vs. ICE-India p <0.01; ICE-SL vs. ICE-GB p <0.01; ICE-GB vs. ICE-India p <0.01, all 1 d.f.)

The distributional findings from Table 5 are visualized in Figure 2. Figure 2 shows the findings from the British corpus as a baseline with the number of occurrences in ICE-GB indicated (in brackets) alongside each of the semantic categories. The divergence of the Sri Lankan English results from British English can be seen in the light grey bars and that of Indian English in the dark grey bars. The figure shows clearly which categories differ and which are similar in their distribution among the varieties. Especially striking are the differences of the meanings HAND (with Indian English diverging greatly from the other two varieties), DO/DELEXICAL SENSE (with Sri Lankan English diverging greatly from British and Indian English), ADMINISTER (again with Sri Lankan English diverging from the other two), and ALLOW (with both ESL varieties diverging equally strongly from the historical input variety). However, note that it is not always the same variety that diverges from the others in the same way. In the case of HAND, a considerable overuse[1] of the meaning can be observed in Indian English, while Sri Lankan and British English frequencies are very similar. Light-verb constructions (DO/DELEXICAL SENSE), however, are rare in Sri Lankan English, while the frequencies of Indian and British English are similarly high. In the case of ADMINISTER, one can see an overuse in Sri Lankan English, while there is a slight underuse in Indian English compared to British English.[2] ALLOW is among the few meaning categories in which the two ESL varieties indeed diverge from the baseline equally.

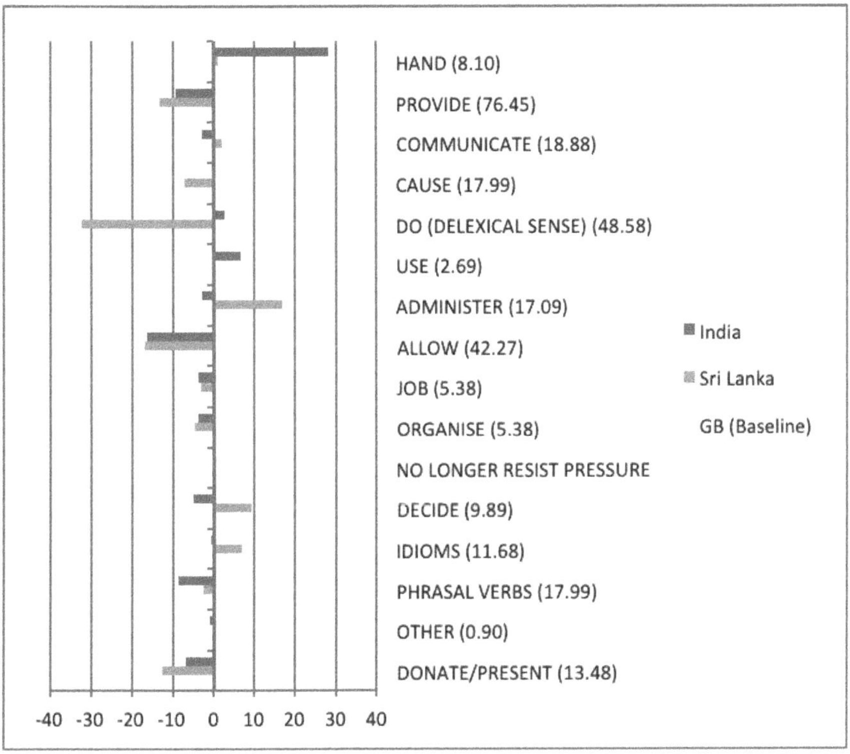

Figure 2. Frequencies of the meanings of *give* in ICE-GB [W 115] (baseline), ICE-SL [W 115] and ICE-India [W 115]

As Table 6 shows, the comparison of the verb *take* shows a statistically significant difference between Sri Lankan and Indian English, whereas on the whole, the two ESL varieties do not differ significantly from British English. When focusing on the individual meanings, one can again find some cases in which two varieties are similar to each other while the third one differs from the two more clearly. However, in the case of *take*, there are various categories in which all three varieties are equally dissimilar to each other (e.g. RECORD and CONSIDER) or all three show similar frequencies (e.g. ASSUME, PHRASAL VERBS).

Figure 3 visualizes the findings from Table 6, again showing the British frequencies as baseline, the divergence of the Sri Lankan data in light grey and the divergence of the Indian data in dark grey bars. Once more one can see a number of categories in which the varieties diverge from each other to a larger or lesser extent. Fairly striking differences can be seen especially in MOVE, which is equally less frequent in the two ESL varieties than in British English, in USE, which shows an overuse in Indian English while it is underused in Sri Lankan English, and the IDIOMS, where one can observe a strong underuse in Sri Lankan English, while Indian English and British English are closer together frequency-wise.

Table 6. Frequencies of the meanings of *take* in ICE-GB [W 115], ICE-SL [W 115] and ICE-India [W 115]

		Frequencies (per 230,000 words)		
		GB (n=429)	Sri Lanka (n=419)	India (n=386)
1	GRAB	16.19	20.08	13.46
2	MOVE	51.27	37.08	37.84
3	BUY	0.00	0.00	0.00
4	INGEST	9.89	9.27	6.72
5	REQUIRE	24.29	16.99	21.02
6	DO (DELEXICAL SENSE)	58.47	57.94	52.97
7	RECORD	7.18	3.84	14.28
8	ENGAGE IN	16.19	11.57	5.04
9	CONSIDER	27.88	21.62	14.28
10	ACCEPT	19.78	6.95	14.28
11	ASSUME	2.69	3.08	2.51
12	EXPERIENCE	5.28	3.08	4.19
13	USE	20.68	27.81	17.64
14	CAPTURE	8.10	5.41	5.04
15	WORK	0.00	0.00	0.00
16	IDIOMS	73.76	50.99	70.63
17	PHRASAL VERBS	41.38	40.94	39.51
18	OTHER	2.69	2.30	5.04

(ICE-SL vs. ICE India $p<0.01$, 1 d.f.; ICE-SL vs. ICE-GB not significant; ICE-GB vs. ICE-India not significant)

Table 7. Topmost frequent categories of *give* in ICE-GB, ICE-SL and ICE-India

	Great Britain (Freq /230,000 w)	Sri Lanka (Freq /230,000 w)	India (Freq /230,000 w)
1	PROVIDE (76.45)	PROVIDE (63.34)	PROVIDE (67.28)
2	DO (DELEXICAL SENSE) (48.58)	ADMINISTER (33.99)	DO (DELEXICAL SENSE) (51.29)
3	ALLOW (42.27)	ALLOW (25.48)	HAND (36.16)
4	COMMUNICATE (18.88)	COMMUNICATE (20.86)	ALLOW (26.06)
5	CAUSE (17.99)	DECIDE (19.30)	CAUSE (18.49)

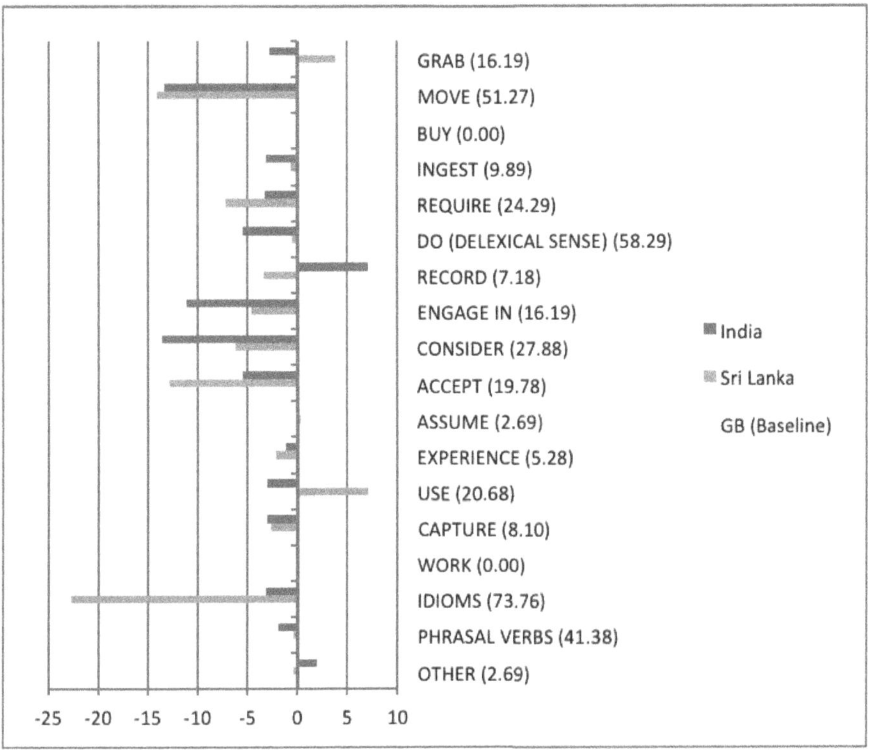

Figure 3. Frequencies of the meanings of *take* in ICE-GB [W 115], ICE-SL [W 115] and ICE-India [W 115]

When focusing on the most frequent categories, one can construct a profile of the topmost frequent meanings in each variety. Table 7 shows the five most frequent semantic categories of *give* in Great Britain, Sri Lanka and India. In all three corpora, PROVIDE is the most frequently used category for *give*. Comparing the other four ranks, however, considerable differences between varieties are found. For example, ADMINISTER is the second-most frequent category in ICE-SL but it does not appear in the top five ranks of the other two varieties.

In the following, the five most frequent categories of the verb *give* in the three varieties will be exemplified by concordances from the three ICE corpora. Examples (1) to (5) are taken from ICE-GB, examples (6) to (10) from ICE-SL and examples (11) to (15) from ICE-India.

(1) or train is far greater than the reality. This booklet *gives* guide-lines to help you travel safely and confidently on public transport. (PROVIDE) (ICE-GB [W 115] W2D1-10.txt)

(2) As he got into a first-class carriage he sketched a mock salute, and *gave* me a great wink. A couple of days later he rang (DO – DELEXICAL SENSE) (ICE-GB [W 115] W2F.txt)

(3) could put a lot of my friends at risk. We have to *give* ourselves a little time to reorganize and get them back to safety (ALLOW) (ICE-GB [W 115] W2F.txt)

(4) with strangers and avoid being overheard. Try not to *give* your name, address or place of employment, or to reveal if you live alone (COMMUNICATE) (ICE-GB [W 115] W2D1-10.txt)

(5) in the mirror, the mascara that she had borrowed from Glenda smeared and *giving* her a comically satanic look. She was past caring (CAUSE) (ICE-GB [W 115] W2F.txt)

(6) knew what I wanted to do with my life. It *gave* me the direction and guidance I was looking for after my (PROVIDE) (ICE-SL [W 115] W2D-011.txt)

(7) Platelets concentrates, fresh frozen plasma and cyoprecipitates should be *given* instead. For neonatal transfusions, it is a (ADMINISTER) (ICE-SL [W 115] W2F-019.txt)

(8) Mudiyanse and the injustice perpetrated. Thus he was *given* permission to build a house on a vacant plot of land. (ALLOW) (ICE-SL [W 115] W2C-019.txt)

(9) not even the military intelligence could fathom why. They *gave* all kinds of excuses. If they are militarily (COMMUNICATE) (ICE-SL [W 115] W2E-002.txt)

(10) and appropriate punishment is *given* if the judgement is made that illegal (DECIDE) (ICE-SL [W 115] W2A-024.txt)

(11) The objective of this group of optional papers is to *give* the student an introduction to Linguistics for the teaching of English (PROVIDE) (ICE-India [W 115] W2D-006.txt)

(12) "Amma, when you go back, *give* this careful thought. Linda is a good woman an (DO – DELEXICAL SENSE) (ICE-India [W 115] W2F-015.txt)

(13) when I first entered the visitors' parlour, Sister Cecilia got up and *gave* me her chair. Preferred to perch uncomfortably (HAND) (ICE-India [W 115] W2F-008.txt)

(14) Even in their present highly sanitised form, the Maoris *gave* a glimpse of their rich culture, its stress on muscular and cerebral (ALLOW) (ICE-India [W 115] W2D-012.txt)

(15) The sub-junior level meet was also being clubbed together to *give* the meet a colourful appearance, the MAAA general secretary, Mr Pralhad (CAUSE) (ICE-India [W 115] W2C-002.txt)

Table 8 shows the most frequent meanings of the verb *take* in the three corpora. As in the case of *give*, substantial differences can be observed, and some categories again feature in only one of the three lists (e.g. the fifth-ranked USE in ICE-SL).

Table 8. Topmost frequent categories of *take* in ICE-GB, ICE-SL and ICE-India

	Great Britain (Freq /230,000 w)	Sri Lanka (Freq /230,000 w)	India (Freq /230,000 w)
1	IDIOMS (73.76)	DO (DELEXICAL SENSE) (57.94)	IDIOMS (70.63)
2	DO (DELEXICAL SENSE) (58.47)	IDIOMS (50.99)	DO (DELEXICAL SENSE) (52.97)
3	MOVE (51.27)	PHRASAL VERBS (40.94)	PHRASAL VERBS (39.51)
4	PHRASAL VERBS (41.38)	MOVE (37.08)	MOVE (37.84)
5	CONSIDER (27.88)	USE (27.81)	REQUIRE (21.02)

Examples (16) to (30) are taken from ICE-GB, ICE-SL and ICE India and exemplify the five most frequent uses of the verb *take*.

(16) Sand distribution is asymmetric, sedimentation *taking* place mainly in a downwind direction. (IDIOMS) (ICE-GB [W115] W2A-023)

(17) at Roland has been studying colour psychology, because the company have *taken* the unusual step of using orange pinpoint LEDs (associated with the front (DO – DELEXICAL SENSE) (ICE-GB [W 115] W2B-013.txt)

(18) name on a list of people who need to do a 4 day First Aid course because you *take* students on field trips. I am unable to arrange a (MOVE) (ICE-GB [W 115] W1B16-29.txt)

(19) example, if you are working one week on, one week off, the average would be *taken* over the fortnightly cycle. If there is no (PHRASAL VERBS) (ICE-GB [W 115] W2D1-10.txt)

(20) energy department were perfunctory, and it is hard to believe they were being *taken* seriously either by those doing the inspecting or those being inspected (CONSIDER) (ICE-GB [W 115] W2C.txt)

(21) cheap and vulgar type; Canada and France are two vibrant democracies that have *taken* such steps. So much for Ranil Wickremesinghe's (DO – DELEXICAL SENSE) (ICE-SL [W 115] W2F-011.txt)

(22) poor man's life with your demands of money, you harassed him because he *took* care of me and now you put on this display For whose (IDIOMS) (ICE-SL [W 115] W2F-002.txt)

(23) Interests and grievances alone do not lead different groups to *take* up positions. Suspicions may play a vital role in (PHRASAL VERBS) (ICE-SL [W 115] W2F-017.txt)

(24) finalised at 11.00pm the previous day. When it had been *taken* to Siri Kotha for the signature of the party General Secretary, N. V. K. K (MOVE) (ICE-SL [W 115] W2A-023.txt)

(25) a person in your caliber. Please do *take* this as an opportunity that you received to correct yourself and it is your (USE) (ICE-SL [W 115] W2C-011.txt)

(26) This change I'm going to narrate now *took* place two weeks after the Great Chase. (IDIOMS) (ICE-India [W 115] W2F-002.txt)

(27) they had got up on time to go to the stables. They *took* a long nap in the afternoon but never shut out the daylight by going under (DO – DELEXICAL SENSE) (ICE-India [W 115] W2F-014.txt)

(28) minority community from the communally virulent valley, which seems to have been *taken* over by the Pakistan-trained subversives. (PHRASAL VERBS) (ICE-India [W 115] W2E-002.txt)

(29) by the sights. She was like a little child who had been *taken* to a big fair. Her son was amused at (MOVE) (ICE-India [W 115] W2F-015.txt)

(30) but as you can see, it's still quite a young tree, the banyan *takes* a long time to grow. Your great-gran (REQUIRE) (ICE-India [W 115] W2F-003.txt)

Generally speaking, the differences that can be noted for *give* and *take* are gradual rather than categorical. In other words, the frequencies of the individual meanings do not differ in any of the categories in such a striking way that one might suggest an entirely different use of the verb in any of the three varieties compared to the others. This corroborates the assumption that the polysemy of the two verbs at hand – and thus, the prototypicality of the meanings listed in Tables 1 and 2 – is culture-independent (or even language-independent), as suggested by Ravin and Leacock (2000). In fact, it is remarkable that virtually all occurrences of the two verbs in the Sri Lankan, Indian and British corpora could be assigned to one of the available categories that were originally designed for a study on American English. The cultures of the three countries differ from the United States as well as from one another in a considerable way. The fact that the categories could nevertheless be applied with almost no exception seems to indicate a certain degree of culture-independence of the prototypical meanings of the two verbs.

The fact that some categories which occurred in Gilquin's (2008) data did not occur at all in any of the three ICE [W 115] corpora is due rather to the limited size of the corpora than to cultural differences. Gilquin not only used written, but also spoken corpora which are expected to contain different, especially more colloquial usages of words, while in the present study only written data from a limited number of text-categories were used.

As some of the semantic categories that Gilquin (2008) introduced were only rarely attested or not attested at all in the ICE [W 115] corpora, in a final step we subsumed all cells with fewer than 5 occurrences per 230,000 words under the category OTHER. The rationale behind this re-categorization is the attempt to distinguish between the fairly frequent and routinized uses of individual meanings of the two verbs on the one hand, as shown in Tables 7 and 8, and the rare and creative uses of other meanings of the verbs on the other.

Table 9 gives the frequencies of the extended category of OTHER for the verb *give* across the three ICE [W 115] corpora.

Table 9. Semantic re-categorization of *give* according to occurrences in ICE-GB [W 115], ICE-SL [W 115] and ICE-India [W 115]: combining low-frequency categories into OTHER

		Frequencies (per 230,000 words)		
		GB (n=320)	Sri Lanka (n=312)	India (n=326)
1	HAND	8.10	9.27	36.16
2	PROVIDE	76.45	63.34	67.28
3	COMMUNICATE	18.88	20.86	15.96
4	CAUSE	17.99	10.81	18.49
5	DO (DELEXICAL SENSE)	48.58	16.22	51.29
6	ADMINISTER	17.09	33.99	14.28
7	ALLOW	42.27	25.48	26.06
8	DECIDE	9.89	19.30	5.04
9	IDIOMS	11.68	18.54	10.93
10	PHRASAL VERBS	17.99	15.43	9.25
11	TO DONATE/TO PRESENT	13.48	0.76	6.72
12	OTHER	14.35	6.90	12.62

The extended category OTHER in Table 9 is interesting because it includes the wide range of individual low-frequency meanings which can be viewed as less routinized in language use than the high-frequency meanings. The category OTHER is clearly strongest in Britain followed by India, with Sri Lanka lagging behind. This could be seen as an indication that semantic widening is a process linked to the evolutionary stage in which a variety of English finds itself. In British English, the frequency of unusual low-frequency meanings of the polysemous verb *give* is higher than in the two ESL varieties. India, however, seems to be closer to British English in this regard. As British English, Indian English and Sri Lankan English refer to different stages of development (with native British English being most advanced and institutionalized, second-language Indian English being endonormatively stabilized and Sri Lankan English still being in the process of becoming nativized), one could argue that the range of meanings of high-frequency verbs increases the more advanced the variety of English is in its development.

In Table 10 one can see that in the category OTHER, it is again Sri Lankan English as the least advanced variety of English that shows fewer instances of *take* with peripheral and low-frequency meanings. The low-frequency meanings of high-frequency polysemous verbs certainly warrant further investigation in future research.

Table 10. Semantic re-categorization of *take* according to occurrences in ICE-GB [W 115], ICE-SL [W 115] and ICE-India [W 115]: combining low-frequency categories into OTHER

		Frequencies (per 230,000 words)		
		GB (n=429)	Sri Lanka (n=419)	India (n=386)
1	GRAB	16.19	20.08	13.46
2	MOVE	51.27	37.08	37.84
3	INGEST	9.89	9.27	6.72
4	REQUIRE	24.29	16.99	21.02
5	DO (DELEXICAL SENSE)	58.47	57.94	52.97
6	RECORD	7.18	3.84	14.28
7	ENGAGE IN	16.19	11.57	5.04
8	CONSIDER	27.88	21.62	14.28
9	ACCEPT	19.78	6.95	14.28
10	USE	20.68	27.81	17.64
11	CAPTURE	8.10	5.41	5.04
12	IDIOMS	73.76	50.99	70.63
13	PHRASAL VERBS	41.38	40.94	39.51
14	OTHER	10.66	5.83	11.74

4. Concluding remarks and avenues for future research

To conclude, the results of this pilot study indicate that there seem to be clear and identifiable quantitative differences in the use of polysemous verbs between different varieties of English, which might demonstrate a so far neglected aspect of structural nativization. Much more research into polysemy across varieties is therefore needed. What needs to be looked at much more closely is the possible reasons and explanations for the findings presented in this paper. Different collocational patterns, different frequencies of light-verb constructions and other factors might be of interest.

As in Gilquin's (2008) corpus analyses, the results of this study need to be complemented with experimental data on the cognitive salience of the various meanings of polysemous words. This might help to address the question of whether there are cognitive differences between, for instance, British English and South Asian English speakers. In general, we do think that the results of the present analysis show promising prospects for further studies of polysemy in New Englishes in general, and polysemy of high-frequency verbs in South Asian Englishes in particular.

Notes

1 At this point it should be noted that the ICE-Sri Lanka project has progressed since the time when this analysis was undertaken. When presented at the ICAME 2009, the corpus included 165 written texts, i.e. more than 80% of the final version of the written component. In the meantime, the written component of ICE-Sri Lanka has been finalised, while work on the spoken component is in progress. On completion, ICE-Sri Lanka will be a unique resource as it represents the first large-scale corpus of present-day acrolectal Sri Lankan English (cf. Mukherjee et al. 2010).

2 The terms *overuse* and *underuse* should not be understood as derogatory or stigmatizing descriptions of language use in *New Englishes*. They should be taken as neutral terms which refer – at a merely descriptive level – to British English as the baseline variety.

References

Geeraerts, D. (1989), 'Prospects and problems of prototype theory', in: D. Geeraerts (ed.) (2006) *Cognitive Linguistics: Basic readings*. Berlin: De Gruyter. 141-165.

Gillard, P. (ed.) (2003), *Cambridge Advanced Learner's Dictionary*. Cambridge: Cambridge University Press.

Gilquin, G. (2008), 'What you think ain't what you get: Highly polysemous verbs in grammar and mind', in: J.-R. Lapaire, G. Desaguiler, J.-B. Guiguard (eds.) *Du Fait Grammatical au Fait Cognitif – From Grammar to Mind: Grammar as Cognition, Volume 2*. Pessac: Presses Universitaires de Bordeaux. 235-255.

Goldberg, A. E. (1995), *Constructions. A Construction Grammar Approach to Argument Structure*. Chicago: The University of Chicago Press.

Hoffmann, S., M. Hundt and J. Mukherjee (in press), 'Indian English – an emerging epicentre? A pilot study on light-verbs in web-derived corpora of South Asian Englishes'. To appear in *Anglia*, 129(3).

Langacker, R. W. (2008), *Cognitive Grammar. A Basic Introduction*. New York: Oxford University Press.

Mukherjee, J. (2008), 'Sri Lankan English: Evolutionary status and epicentral influence from Indian English', in: K. Stierstorfer (ed.) *Anglistentag 2007 Münster: Proceedings*. Trier: WVT. 359-368.

Mukherjee, J., M. Schilk and T. Bernaisch (2010): 'Compiling the Sri Lankan component of ICE: Principles, problems, prospects', *ICAME Journal*, 34: 64-77.

Nihalani, P., R. K. Tongue, P. Hosali and J. Crowther (2004), *Indian and British English: A Handbook of Usage and Pronunciation*. Second edition. Delhi: Oxford University Press.

Ooi, V. B. Y. (2000), 'Asian or Western realities? Collocations in Singaporean-Malaysian English', in: J. M. Kirk (ed.) *Corpora Galore: Analyses and Techniques in Describing English.* Amsterdam: Rodopi. 73-78.

Ravin, Y. and C. Leacock (2000), 'Polysemy: An overview', in: Y. Ravin and C. Leacock (eds.) *Polysemy. Theoretical and Computational Approaches.* Oxford: Oxford University Press. 1-29.

Rosch, E. and C. B. Mervis (1975), 'Family resemblances: Studies in the internal structure of categories', *Cognitive Psychology,* 7: 573-605.

Rundell, M. (ed.) (2002), *Macmillan English Dictionary for Advanced Learners.* Oxford: Macmillan Education.

Schneider, E. W. (2007), *Postcolonial Englishes. Varieties around the World.* Cambridge: Cambridge University Press.

Sinclair, J. (ed.) (2001), *Collins Cobuild English Dictionary for Advanced Learners.* Glasgow: HarperCollins Publishers.

Summers, D. (ed.) (2001), *Longman Dictionary of Contemporary English.* Harlow: Pearson Education.

Wehmeier, S. (ed.) (2000), *Oxford Advanced Learner's Dictionary.* Oxford: Oxford University Press.

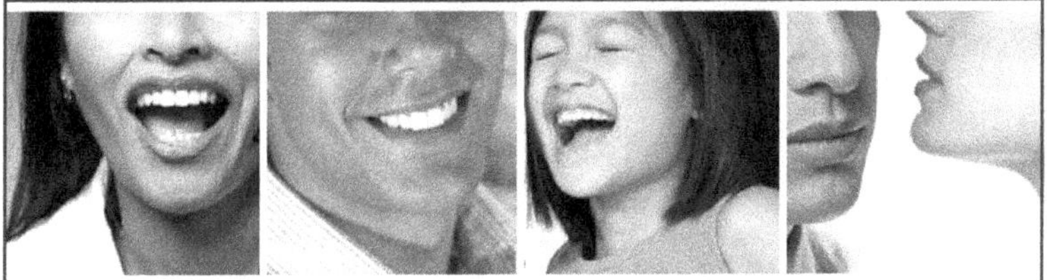

www.ingramcontent.com/pod-product-compliance
Lightning Source LLC
LaVergne TN
LVHW020634300926
849161LV00004B/704